Praise ~~j~~

Engaging Dōgen's Zen

"*Engaging Dōgen's Zen* is a wonderful collection of essays inquiring into the meaning of Dōgen's teaching and practice in the twenty-first century, written by a number of sincere practitioner-scholars engaged in an examination of *Shushōgi* and *Fukanzazengi*. I recommend this book to all Zen practitioners and all people who are interested in Buddhism and spirituality presently and in the future."

—Shohaku Okumura, author of *Realizing Genjōkōan*

"The right foot of mental clarity rests on the left thigh of continuous practice. The left foot of poised engagement rests on the right thigh of tradition. Even while 'just sitting,' Dōgen says we can walk the Way of the buddhas. The remarkable essays in this volume, all personal expressions of thoughtful practice and compassionate engagement, collectively serve as a field guide to that Way, bringing philosophical insight, experience, and discipline to what Dōgen called the 'oneness of body-mind,' the true sense of feeling whole."

—Thomas P. Kasulis, author of *Intimacy or Integrity*

ENGAGING
DŌGEN'S
ZEN

THE PHILOSOPHY
OF PRACTICE
AS AWAKENING

Edited by Tetsuzen Jason M. Wirth,
Shūdō Brian Schroeder, and Kanpū Bret W. Davis

Wisdom Publications
199 Elm Street
Somerville, MA 02144 USA
wisdompubs.org

Library of Congress Cataloging-in-Publication Data

Names: Wirth, Jason M., 1963– editor. | Schroeder, Brian, 1959– editor. | Davis, Bret W., editor.
Title: Engaging Dogen's Zen: the philosophy of practice as awakening / edited by Tetsuzen Jason
M. Wirth, Shūdō Brian Schroeder, Kanpū Bret W. Davis.
Description: Somerville, MA: Wisdom Publications, 2017. | Includes bibliographical references and
index.
Identifiers: LCCN 2016001830 | ISBN 9781614292548 (paperback) | ISBN 161429254X (paperback)
Subjects: LCSH: Dōgen, 1200-1253. | Zen Buddhism. | BISAC: RELIGION / Buddhism / Zen
(see also PHILOSOPHY / Zen). | RELIGION / Philosophy. | RELIGION / Buddhism / Sacred
Writings.
Classification: LCC BQ9449.D657 E55 2017 | DDC 294.3/420427—dc23
LC record available at https://lccn.loc.gov/2016001830

ISBN 978-1-61429-254-8   ebook ISBN 978-1-61429-269-2

20 19 18 17 16
5 4 3 2 1

Cover and interior design by Gopa & Ted2, Inc. Set in Minion Pro 10.7/14.9.

For our friends of the Way at Eishōji Sōtō Zen
training facility, CoZen (A Circle for the Cooperative Study,
Practice, and Teaching of Zen), the Seattle University EcoSangha,
the Idunno Zen Community at the Rochester Institute
of Technology, the Heart of Zen Meditation Group
at Loyola University Maryland, the Rochester Zen Center,
and for all who endeavor to negotiate the unsurpassable Buddha Way.

Contents

A Note on the Text

For the sake of accuracy and consistency, in most cases we have placed macrons over Japanese long vowels (for example, Dōgen rather than Dogen). We have, however, made an exception for persons or institutions who use their Japanese names but do not customarily employ macrons or wish to employ them. In general Japanese names will be written in the Japanese order of family name first, except in cases where authors of works in English have used the Western order; in such cases, the family name will be given in small capital letters (for example, Masao ABE, Shohaku OKUMURA). Chinese names are given in pinyin. The following abbreviations are used to indicate the source language for technical terms, phrases, and proper names: Jp. for Japanese, Ch. for Chinese, Skt. for Sanskrit, and P. for Pali. If no such indication is given, the source language is Japanese.

We have standardized the use of the terms "Buddha Dharma," "Buddha Mind," "Buddha Nature," and "Buddha Way" in the contributors' essays. We have left intact, however, different spellings of these terms as they appear in cited publications.

Any potential proceeds from this book go to Eishōji, a nonprofit Sōtō Zen training facility in Seattle, Washington. See http://nwzencommunity.org/about.html.

The photographic images are by Nathan L. Wirth (http://nlwirth.com/photography). The first photo is titled "Buddha & Rocks," the second "Buddha & Dreams," and the final "Buddha and Moon."

The calligraphy on the dedication page is by Kobayashi Gentoku Rōshi, abbot of Shōkokuji Training Monastery in Kyoto, Japan.

Acknowledgments

The editors would like to express our gratitude to Josh Bartok, Tony Lulek, Ben Gleason, Laura Cunningham, and all of the other hard-working and generous people at Wisdom Publications who helped bring this volume to the light of day. We would also like to thank Nathan Wirth for the use of his beautiful photographs and Kobayashi Rōshi for his teaching and for his CoZen calligraphy. We are especially grateful to Kosho ITAGAKI for his teaching and for inspiring this project. Finally, we would like to thank all of the contributors for their generous, patient, and insightful work on behalf of this volume and on behalf of the Dharma more broadly. May all beings flourish.

Introduction

Tetsuzen Jason M. Wirth

The *Sōtō Kyōkai Shushōgi* (*The Meaning of Practice-Realization in the Sōtō Fellowship*), known more widely simply as *Shushōgi* (*The Meaning of Practice and Verification*), first appeared in 1890, partly in response to the quickly evolving changes and tumult of the Meiji era. After Commodore Matthew Perry arrived in Tokyo Bay in 1853 with his show of military force, the gates to the West, for better or worse, were reopened. By 1868, a Buddhist persecution or *haibutsu kishaku* (abolish Buddhism and discard Śākyamuni) movement had erupted. Moreover, given the rapid ascendency of Western mores—including the reintroduction of Christianity, the rise of the so-called New Religions, the founding of the university system, the increasing disinterest in traditional Japanese culture, the often violent decoupling of Shinto and Buddhism (in favor of the branding and reconfiguring of a state-centered Shinto), and the gathering militarization of the government—Sōtōshū (the Sōtō sect or school of Zen Buddhism) faced grave challenges. As part of the sect's rebuilding process, spurred on by the hard work of influential lay promoters like Ōuchi Seiran (1845–1918), commissioned by a lay organization of over a thousand Sōtō Zen fraternities (the Sōtō Fushūkai), and carefully compiled over a period of three years with both lay and monastic practitioners in mind, *Shushōgi* tersely encapsulated some of the key teachings of Dōgen in thirty-one paragraphs and five sections. *Shushōgi* essentially consists of interwoven passages selected from Dōgen's voluminous magnum opus *Shōbōgenzō* (*The Treasury of the True Dharma Eye*).[1] In 1892, Eiheiji and Sōjiji, the two Sōtō headquarter temples, helped assuage their querulous rivalry by issuing a joint edict in support of *Shushōgi*.[2] The great Zen historian Heinrich Dumoulin, SJ, assessed the accomplishment:

One of the achievements of the Sōtō school during the Meiji period that had broad, positive effects was the publication of *Shushōgi*, a text that presented the main teachings of Sōtō Zen in easily understandable language. Nearly all of the selections contained in the work's five chapters were taken from Dōgen's *Shōbōgenzō*. Although the manuscript was the result of collaborative efforts between Eiheiji and Sōjiji, the bulk of the work was done by lay people, especially Ōuchi Seiran. All those involved took great pains to maintain fidelity to the original teachings of Dōgen. Meditation and enlightenment were not extolled and details of monastic living were omitted in order to focus more clearly on the main elements of Zen Buddhist teaching. Thus *Shushōgi* provided the Sōtō school with an authoritative text of great religious and practical value. Relying as it did on Dōgen's writings, it offered an effective introduction to the thought of the great master, who has been presented to the West as a central figure in Zen.[3]

Some contemporary interpreters are less sanguine about extolling a text that purports to present the pith of Dōgen's writings while omitting even a mention of meditation or the rigors and rituals of monastic life. The intense demands of Dōgen's "oneness of practice-realization"[4] are seemingly replaced with the less demanding practice of "*shūi anjin* (peace of mind attained through the founder's ideas)."[5] Heine notes that "because of the prominence attributed to the abbreviated text by both head temples, Dōgen has generally been known in modern times, not primarily for *Shōbōgenzō*, which throughout history was largely lost, misunderstood, or limited in distribution to a highly specialized faction, but for *Shushōgi*, which is short and readily accessible."[6] Changing Dōgen's emphasis to "repentance (*sange*)," which was also in part intended, Heine tells us, as a "response to the challenge of Christianity," coupled with the text's brevity and accessibility, contributed significantly to the "success and popularity" of the Sōtō school since this period. *Shōbōgenzō*, however, continues to befuddle many Japanese who attempt to read it even in the more accessible versions translated into contemporary Japanese.[7]

Of course, *Shōbōgenzō* has always challenged anyone who would take it seriously, regardless of their culture, be it Zen training, intellectual prowess, or access to classical and/or contemporary East Asian languages. *Shōbōgenzō* is an inexhaustible treasury, rewarding both practice and long, intense study with seemingly endless and radically transformative insights. There is, however, no easy way into it and perhaps the very idea of a primer (if that is what *Shushōgi* is taken to be) is hopelessly naive. This is not to say, however, that *Shushōgi* is without value either for practice or for study. As this volume will attempt to show, seen for what it is, it can still generously reward both endeavors.

In order to appreciate *Shushōgi* more appropriately, it is important to discard entirely the expectation that it is a shortcut to *Shōbōgenzō* or to Dōgen. It is sometimes touted, for example, that *Shushōgi* in some way alludes to all ninety-five fascicles of *Shōbōgenzō*. Heine in his accounting insists that it refers to only twenty-four fascicles,[8] but one does not have to be that specific to see quickly that it would be absurd to characterize *Shushōgi* as the essence of *Shōbōgenzō*. It is highly selective in its focus and its omissions are glaring. It would be scandalous to both serious practitioners and scholars to present *Shushōgi* as the authentic pith of *Shōbōgenzō*, but this does not mean that it does not have real value as both an encapsulation of some aspects of *Shōbōgenzō* and a document worthy of meditation and chanting in its own right.

Clearly *Shushōgi* was a document for a new kind of audience and that is both its strength and its weakness. There is some genuine compassion in trying to open Dōgen to new and wider audiences, and in a way that is pragmatic about the limited accessibility of *Shōbōgenzō*. Zen can sometimes come across as elitist and practicable only for monks. Even then, only a small portion of monks have ever had serious exposure to the whole *Shōbōgenzō*. In contemporary Japan, Sōtō Zen is most often associated with the funeral business (the Sōtō school once reported that 80 percent of laypeople visit Sōtō temples only for matters related to the funeral ceremony, while less than 20 percent do so for reasons related to practice).[9] Funerals may be a good source of revenue for a temple, but it is hard to imagine that Dōgen would have championed this kind of focus. The overwhelming majority of Zen students in Japan are the first-born sons of temple heads, training not always necessarily to open the true Dharma eye but rather mainly to inherit their father's temple. This is another marked contrast with Dōgen who sternly insisted in the *Shōbōgenzō* fascicle "Butsudō [The Buddha Way]" that those who speak of Zen as a school or sect (*shū*) are devils—"those who groundlessly refer to themselves in this way are demons who violate the Buddha Way, enemies who are not welcomed by buddhas and ancestors."[10] No school, no culture, no language, no gender, no sutra, and no artwork has a monopoly on the Dharma. *Shushōgi*, however, has the clear imprint of lay practitioners both in terms of the composition of its compilers and its intended audience. It represents an attempt to share rather than hoard the Dharma eye.

It is nonetheless easy to suspect immediately that the document bears the marks of the historical and political conditions of its production, including what for some are the worrisome aspects of the weight of nineteenth-century Sōtō politics. No doubt this is to some extent true and it is fair to ask questions like: Does the emphasis on *sange metsuzai* (repentance in terms of purifying bad karma)[11] represent more of an attempt to compete with Christianity than to present the gist of Dōgen's own thought and practice?[12] Does this emphasis on *sange metsuzai* enervate the radical social critique of the many inequalities in the dust of the everyday *sahāloka* (world of suffering) by sequestering equality into an absolute dimension, as the Critical Buddhists contend? Are we equal only in our Buddha Nature[13] such that other kinds of more quotidian inequalities are tolerated?[14] Is there a pernicious and perhaps even insuperable gap between what Heine calls "Dōgen Zen" and "the thought of Dōgen himself"?[15]

It is certainly not the intention of this volume to reinforce or otherwise promulgate these or any other distortions, and it is important to mark these concerns as pitfalls for an appreciation in both study and practice of *Shushōgi*. It is, for all of its flaws, not a bad idea, with honesty and sincerity, to engage all of the Zen tradition, with all of its high points and low points, with hermeneutic savvy. "No historical figure, or text that he or she creates, is an island. Dōgen stands in a dynamic, reciprocal relationship with Dōgen Zen. . . . Dōgen and Dōgen Zen are entangled in an ongoing process of creative misunderstanding and creative hermeneutics."[16] All contemporary practitioners and scholars cannot fully extricate themselves from Dōgen Zen and this is, in some wonderful ways, part of the beauty and challenge of contemporary practice. What is this Kamakura master, largely neglected even in his own country until the twentieth century, to contemporary practitioners of Dōgen Zen? The very taking up of the Way and of Dōgen's Way is to continue to shape the life and practices and awakenings of Dōgen Zen in the English-speaking world, which is still in its infancy as it continues to awaken the possibilities of new soils of practice and new circumstances under which to practice.

It is with this hermeneutic savvy that this volume attempts to awaken what is valuable for both thinking and practice in *Shushōgi*, and as such, this is a question of continuing to translate Dōgen for a contemporary audience and continuing to negotiate the contours of Dōgen Zen. How does one do this? An important clue is already found in Dōgen's own writings. How did he update and "translate" the Chan heritage for thirteenth-century Japan, a land that he regarded as bereft of awakening? What are Dōgen's own reading practices? How did he understand the practice of reading and studying, both in themselves and as they pertained to practice?

Our aim with this volume is to provide a helpful introduction and companion to Sōtō practice—and other Zen and other Buddha Dharma practices more broadly—by providing a critical edition of *Shushōgi* that is also practice oriented. Although we appreciate the value of *Shushōgi* for both practice and thinking, we do not assume that it in all ways faithfully presents the fullness of Dōgen's practice and wisdom.

As we have already seen, an obvious example of the gulf between *Shushōgi* and Dōgen's own writings is the utter lack of any mention of zazen. It would be absurd to equate the great teacher of *shikantaza* (just sitting) with a document that does not even mention zazen. As we already see in the early fascicle "Bendōwa," although there are many "gates" to the Buddha Dharma, Dōgen insisted that zazen was the *shōmon* or front gate, the entrance into all of the other ways. If one wants to go into the kitchen, one should use the kitchen door, not bang one's head against the outside wall.

The great master Śākyamuni authentically transmitted this splendid method of attaining the way, and all buddha tathāgatas of the past, future, and present attain the way by practicing zazen. For this reason it has been transmitted as the front gate. Furthermore, all ancestors in India and China attained the way by practicing zazen. Thus, I now teach this front gate to human beings and devas.[17]

This is not to say that this volume makes the same demand on its readers. We concur with Taigen Dan Leighton when in his essay in this volume he invites us to enter into dialogue with Dōgen's contemporaries like "Myō-e, Shinran, and Nichiren, as well as the medieval Japanese Tendai and Esoteric traditions." The same could be said for all other Buddhist traditions, indeed, the vertical depths of all religious traditions. We have also noticed with excitement and gratitude that the dialogue has been especially fruitful with many of the indigenous traditions of the Americas.

Nonetheless, Dōgen Zen enters into this rich and cherished ongoing dialogue through the front gate of zazen, a gate whose practice cultivates the equanimity, respect, compassion, and genuine curiosity that animates such dialogical encounters, and so it is especially worrisome that no mention of this gate occurs in *Shushōgi*. To remedy this glaring lacuna, Kanpū Bret W. Davis has provided a close and careful reading, prepared with an eye to scholarship and philosophy but one that especially serves the needs of practice, of Dōgen's seminal work on the front gate, *Fukanzazengi* (*Universally Recommended Instructions for Zazen*). In this programmatic text Dōgen introduced to Japan the Zen practice that he learned in China from Tiantong Rujing[18] of the Caodong school.[19]

Also conspicuously missing from *Shushōgi* is any serious discussion of *dokusan* and kōan training. For that we recommend *The True Dharma Eye: Zen Master Dōgen's Three Hundred Kōans.*[20]

Our aim is to provide a series of critical reflections on *Shushōgi* and an extended commentary on *Fukanzazengi* that would be helpful to those who are cultivating a Zen practice (Sōtō or otherwise), other forms of Buddha Dharma practice, or even non-Buddhist spiritual practice. We have divided *Shushōgi* into thirteen sections and linked each of these sections to the fascicles in *Shōbōgenzō* from which they are drawn,[21] and we have invited thirteen scholar-practitioners to provide commentaries that aim to speak to contemporary practice needs while at the same time being intellectually stimulating. The volume opens with a series of introductory essays regarding various facets of *Shushōgi* and Dōgen more generally.

It is important to emphasize that this volume is not intended merely as a set of formal scholarly essays. Part of the experiment of this volume was to gather together scholars who also have a serious commitment to practice and authors who are primarily—but not exclusively—known for their practice, including Tenshin Charles Fletcher Rōshi, who is the abbot of Yokoji Zen Mountain Center in southern California, and the Rev. Kōshō ITAGAKI of the Eishōji Sōtō Zen training facility in Seattle, who was the chief inspiration for this project and first urged the editors to pursue it.

Most of the authors, however, are academics who also have a serious commitment to Zen practice. This includes not only the editors of this volume, but also thinkers and practitioners like Taigen Dan Leighton, who is an author of many books on Dōgen and translations of Dōgen and who also leads the Ancient Dragon Zen Gate in Chicago, and David Loy, a philosopher and practitioner who lectures and gives workshops and Zen training sessions and retreats all over the world. This double commitment also holds in some fashion or another for almost all of those whose wonderful commentaries shed light on *Shushōgi*.

Some of the authors (Jien Erin McCarthy and Mark Unno), as well as all of the editors, are also members of a newly formed practice-scholarship group called CoZen,[22] which is explicitly dedicated to this double commitment and who work in various ways so that practice illuminates scholarship and scholarship illuminates practice. As is this volume, it is dedicated to overcoming the duality of study and practice; it emerges from the space of the nonduality of study and practice. Practice deepens study and study deepens practice. CoZen wants to avoid scholarship for the sake of mere scholarship, as if the accumulation of intellectual capital about the Dharma is ipso facto worthy of human living and striving. It also wants to avoid practice without philosophical understanding and critical reflection, for these too can and should be—and have often, since the time of Śākyamuni and certainly in the person of Dōgen, in fact been—aspects of a holistic practice of the Buddha Dharma.

One sometimes finds in Zen practice an unconvincing dualism between practice and study. While it is true that Zen practice is explicitly not the same thing as developing an intellectual appreciation of Zen ideas—zazen, not the library, is the front gate—it does not follow, at least not for Dōgen, that practice should be anti-intellectual or that there is not an important place for serious study. Zen practice takes us beneath and beyond thinking, but it is from here that thinking returns to itself, awakened. As Kanpū Bret W. Davis articulates in his commentary on *Fukanzazengi*:

> Nonthinking is not simply not-thinking, understood as either the suppression of thought or a contentless object of thought; nor does it exclude either not-thinking or thinking. Nonthinking is not opposed to thinking. It is the ultimate "where-from" and "where-in" of thinking; it is the open field of awareness that encompasses and engenders thinking. This is a crucial point that needs to be emphasized, since Zen is often mistaken— by misguided proponents as well as mistaken opponents—as entailing and even promoting an anti-intellectualism.

The front gate to Dōgen's writings is not through lopsided discursive athleticism and scholarly diligence. As the title itself indicates, *Shōbōgenzō* seeks to open the true Dharma eye. The title of Dōgen's magnum opus also alludes to the Buddha's first transmission. Holding up a flower, the Buddha blinked and Mahākāśyapa smiled. The Buddha responded, "I possess the true Dharma eye, the marvelous mind of nirvana, the true form of the formless, the subtle Dharma gate that does not rest on words or letters but is a special transmission outside of the scriptures. This I entrust to Mahākāśyapa."[23] The transmission beyond words and letters emphasizes that the Dharma is not transmitted as information or a doctrine. It is transmitted, as Dōgen insisted, only buddha-to-buddha[24] and it therefore requires the ongoing, ever evolving, and often surprising non-separation of practice and awakening or realization.

Nonetheless, in "Bukkyō [Buddha Sutras]," Dōgen defends the importance of the three vehicles and twelve divisions of the teaching and in essence defends the entire Buddha Dharma canon. As Kanpū Bret W. Davis tells us in his *Fukanzazengi* commentary in this volume, Dōgen's conception of the monastery called for a Study Hall[25] where each monk had a desk to study traditional Buddha Dharma texts.[26] Yet how does one communicate the true Dharma eye when it exceeds the range of discursivity and demonstration? In "Bendōwa [On the Endeavor of the Way]," Dōgen boldly warns, "in studying sutras you should not expend thoughts in the vain hope that they will be helpful for attaining realization."[27] The academic thought of realization realizes nothing. Of course, it is immediately important to insist that by "transmission outside of sutras," Dōgen does not mean that one should not read sutras and refuse to engage in the practice of study; indeed *Shōbōgenzō* is full of critical accounts of those who study poorly. In "Keisei Sanshoku [Valley Sounds, Mountains Colors]" and other fascicles, Dōgen recounts the story of the diligent monk-student Xiangyan who was challenged by Guishan: "You are bright and knowledgeable. Say something about yourself before your parents were born, but don't use words learned from the commentaries."[28] Xiangyan took to his books working overtime to find something in them that allowed him to say something outside of them. "Deeply ashamed, he burned his books and said, 'A painting of a rice cake does not satisfy hunger. I will be just a cooking monk, not expecting to understand buddha dharma in this lifetime.'"[29] Xiangyan's folly would be an example of what Dōgen strikingly dubs "bondage to Buddha," namely, "being bound by the view that our perception and cognition of enlightenment is actually enlightenment."[30] Brain Zen, that is, confusing ideas about Zen with Zen experience, is not the practice of what Dōgen repeatedly called "the oneness of practice-realization."[31]

In "Hokke Ten Hokke [Dharma Blossoms Turning Dharma Blossoms]," itself an allusion to the *Hokke Kyō* (*Lotus Sutra*), we learn of the interaction between the Sixth Patriarch, Huineng, and the monk Fada, who had chanted the *Lotus Sutra* three thousand times. "Even if you chanted the sutra ten thousand times, if you don't understand the meaning of it, you won't even know your own errors."[32] Dōgen warns that "you can see from Fada's case that those who vainly count letters, as numerous as pebbles and sands [of the Ganges], cannot understand."[33] In the "Shin Fukatoku [Ungraspable Mind, first version]," we learn of the monk Deshan who called himself Diamond King Chou because there was no part of the *Diamond Sutra* that he had not mastered. However, when asked about the ungraspable mind of the past, present, and future by an old woman with rice cakes—with which of these minds will you satisfy your hunger?—he could not answer. "How regrettable," Dōgen bemoans, "the king of commentators, who wrote commentaries on hundreds of scrolls, a lecturer for decades, was so easily defeated by a humble old woman with a single question."[34] Clearly studying does not mean being able to reproduce intellectual arguments or cite from memory important passages from the authoritative texts. Dōgen wrote a beautiful fascicle called the "Sansui Kyō [Mountains and Waters Sutra]," according to which the sutra is the living great earth itself.

In "Kankin [Reading a Sutra]" Dōgen is quite clear on what it means to study a sutra: "To read a sutra is to take up and assemble all Buddha ancestors, turn them into an eyeball, and read it."[35] Indeed, those who "expound discourses of teaching outside the Way for the sake of seeking fame cannot practice the Buddha sutras"[36] for sutras do not require mere diligence and scholarly acumen because they are practice, or better still, the oneness of practice and realization. "A sutra is a sutra of the entire self. We say this because you yourself are the self of all buddha ancestors, and the self of all sutras."[37] To read is to pluck out the Dharma eye and make it yours—to awaken to the Buddha Nature that you share with all beings on and as the great earth. We asked our writers to pluck out the Dharma eye and make it their own and this is also what we ask of the readers of this volume.

This is the spirit—a study of *Shushōgi* and *Fukanzazengi* that is also a study of the entire self—that animates this volume. In studying the essays and revisiting what remains precious in *Shushōgi* and *Fukanzazengi*, that is, in letting them breathe just as we learn to breathe in zazen, one also learns to forget the self, and in our daily care for our teaching and writing and service and practice, our Dōgen Zen touches with great and compassionate creativity Dōgen and Śākyamuni, as well as all of our sisters and brothers, indeed, the great earth itself.

PART I

GENERAL ESSAYS

1 Reflections on Dōgen's Practice and Philosophy

KŌSHŌ ITAGAKI[1]

INTRODUCTION

Shushōgi (*The Meaning of Practice and Verification*) is a document compiled in 1890 primarily for the aid of lay practitioners by selecting some key passages from Dōgen's *Shōbōgenzō* (*Treasury of the True Dharma Eye*), the primary source for the teachings of the Sōtō school of Zen Buddhism. The compilation of *Shushōgi* was intended to act as an introduction to the four themes of Mahāyāna Buddhist teachings: "eradicating our iniquities (bad karma) through the practice of repentance,"[2] "accepting the precepts and entering the ranks of the buddhas and patriarchs,"[3] "making the vow to benefit all beings,"[4] and "showing our gratitude to the buddhas and patriarchs through the wholehearted practice of Buddhism."[5]

These four themes, called the "Four Main Principles" (*Yondai Kōryō*), along with their introduction, have been at the heart of Sōtō teachings since 1941. However, possibly because these teachings were meant for lay followers, the practices taught in *Shushōgi* have not included the one practice, *shikantaza* (wholehearted engagement in zazen meditation), which was absolutely central to the founder of the Sōtō school, Eihei Dōgen. From the time of the original assembly of *Shushōgi*, the principal criticism that *Shushōgi* does not faithfully transmit the essence of Dōgen's teachings has persisted. For these reasons, the *Sacred Teachings of Dōgen Zenji* (*Dōgen Zenji Seikun*) (1924), edited by Dr. Nukariya Kaiten, has a fundamentally different emphasis than that of the current *Shushōgi*.

Moreover, the teachings of Keizan Jōkin Zenji (1268–1325), the second founding father of Sōtō Zen,[6] are entirely absent in the current *Shushōgi*. In addition to the latter, Kikuchi Daisen Rōshi has compiled the *Addenda to the Sōtō Zen Fellowship[7] Shushōgi* (*Sōtō Kyōkai Shushōgi-zoku*),[8] which is based on Keizan Zenji's seminal work, *Denkōroku* (*The Transmission of the Light*). There is also a second work drawn from Keizan, namely, the *Denkō Sokun* (*The Teachings of the Transmission of the Lamp Patriarch*), compiled by Shōkō Mitsuo. From these works we can see that *Shushōgi* is far from a complete exposition of the teachings of the Sōtō sect. Possibly because it lacks any discussion of zazen, few Zen practitioners in the West bother to read it. Indeed, few even know of its existence. Nevertheless, *Shushōgi* is significant because it can still act as an introduction to some—but not all—of the important teachings found in Dōgen's *Shōbōgenzō*.

Accordingly, we here at Eishōji in Seattle have decided to assemble critical editions of *Shushōgi* in the context of the teachings of the Sōtō school. First of all, we planned to conduct an examination of the English version of the current *Shushōgi* included in the *Sōtō School Scriptures for Daily Services and Practices* published by the Sōtō Head Office. This plan has come to fruition in the present volume. In the future, we hope to expand upon this work by also taking into account the role of Keizan by examining the *Addenda to the Sōtō Zen Fellowship Shushōgi* compiled by Kikuchi Daisen Rōshi. Finally, we would like to produce a new *Shushōgi* that speaks more directly to the needs of contemporary practitioners in the West both without ceding anything essential to New Age practices of Buddhism and while avoiding the restrictions imposed by the historical and political exigencies of the Sōtō school during the Meiji era.

This final aspiration, namely, to create a new *Shushōgi* for a new time and a new context, will be a difficult task. This is because the Sōtō Fellowship has traditionally held a common evaluation of the worth, meaning, significance, and functioning of *Shushōgi* for roughly a century. Although *Shushōgi* is largely unknown in the West, it has almost universal acceptance by the Sōtō Fellowship of Japanese followers. Despite this, it has all too easily rigidified through time. Even though scholars have made small changes in the text, it remains basically the same as the original version. There seems to be little room for flexibility in this context. Moreover, the traditional and most basic economic foundation of Japanese Sōtō temples remains the highly profitable funeral business. Also, since the Edo period (1603–1867), temples remain in the family and are handed down through the generations from father to first-born son.[9] This temple system became the established order and was not easily changed. This temple plan and the community of Sōtō temples has and continues to have a large influence on the prevailing Sōtō fraternity, increasing its rigidity so that any flexibility it might once have had has basically evaporated.

Contemporary Japanese Buddhist Institutions

Two special features of contemporary Japanese Buddhist institutions are "funeral Buddhism" and "temple inheritance." The former was established during the Edo period[10] as a new charge for village temples, namely, to verify that the people in the local village were not Christians.[11] The custom of temple funerals arose from this requirement. Previously, funerals were held under the direction of the village headman. This was because temple funerals were traditionally held only for monks or nuns—there was no tradition of lay funerals. The ceremonies used for monk funerals consequently had to be adapted to create a new lay funeral ceremony.

Having undertaken *jukai* (the acceptance of the Mahāyāna precepts) was a prerequisite for receiving a temple funeral. This would not have been a problem for monks or nuns, all of whom were required to accept the precepts as a matter of course, but it posed a problem for laypeople, most of whom had rarely even considered accepting them. For those who had not taken them when alive, it became necessary to take them after death, and this became a new part of the funeral, thus further distorting established monastic ceremonies.

Another effect of the formation of temple funerals for the laity was that the temples became surrounded by or connected to the temple graveyard. It was not easy to move to another village or area when one's ancestors were buried in the village temple graveyard. Another byproduct of this system was to strengthen the economic foundation of the temples by providing them with a new source of income (collecting fees for the performance of lay funerals), and this became a factor in providing for the stability of the village temple, which in turn further entrenched the *danka* (parishioner household) system.

After the Edo period ended, the Meiji era (1868–1912) explicitly legalized the marriage of Buddhist priests. The "funeral courtesy donations" multiplied temple incomes and stabilized their economic foundations. Temple priesthood became a professional occupation. Although the temples were not officially private property, they were managed and operated within the family[12] and passed down through familial lines.

The priesthood for most all Buddhist denominations (not just Sōtō) had essentially become a profession, and priests made their living based on specialized skills, such as the knowledge of the necessary procedures for conducting funerals and other rituals. In so doing, they deviated from the long-established work of monks and priests to teach the Four Sufferings—birth, old age, sickness, and death—and the Four Noble Truths—suffering,[13] its origin, its cessation, and the path to its cessation. They had transformed the original role of the monks and priests into something utterly foreign.

From the time of the establishment of the Sōtō tradition as a sect, it has had two *honzan* (headquarter) temples, Eiheiji and Sōjiji. This bifurcation has been the root and soil from which sectarian Sōtō Zen has grown. Would Dōgen have imagined that the tradition of his teachings would become the vulgarized Buddhism of the present, where the admonitions of his Chinese Caodong teacher, Zen master Tiantong Rujing[14]— to always pursue the universal teachings of Buddhism, and to stay away from centers of political power—have been almost utterly forgotten? Is it not the case that Eiheiji and Sōjiji, and even Rinzai Zen, have strayed so far from their origins that they have become exemplars of the very kinds of Buddhism that Dōgen had so strongly criticized?

Zen in the United States

Japanese Buddhism was introduced in the United States over a century ago. However, the Zen Buddhism that was transmitted at that time was directed to Japanese ethnic communities who had emigrated but still maintained the relationship of the temple to the household (*danka*) and hence upheld the old Japanese *danka* system. The duties of the missionaries were first to conduct funerals and other services for their parishioners, and second to teach their children Japanese culture. All of the various denominations of Buddhism shared in common these same basic functions. Every temple had an attached Japanese language school. Therefore, each temple had its master(s) of ceremonies and services and its Japanese language instructor(s). Since the resident priests had been appointed precisely to fill these functions, efforts to bring Zen to America were, for the most part, limited to the communities of Japanese immigrants.

Suzuki Daisetsu (1870–1966), known in the West most commonly as D. T. Suzuki, was among the first to introduce genuine Zen philosophy—rather than transplant the *danka* system, which had little to do with Zen or the Buddha—to the United States and the West more broadly through his many writings and his famous lectures at Columbia University and elsewhere. Moreover, Beat movement writers like Allen Ginsberg (1926–1997) and Jack Kerouac (1922–1969), or expositors of Asian wisdom like Alan Watts (1915–1973), happily embraced his writings and soon Zen became a fixture of the "baby-boomer" generation.

It seems to me that one of the reasons that American culture was able to skew Zen teachings was because they were not all that well understood by many of their early American advocates. The authentic tenets of Zen Buddhism were distorted in some important ways as they shifted from their original Japanese context. It may be that human thought, whether Western or Asian, shares the same broad spectrum of characteristics. But when formed through the filter of Japanese culture, ideas and emphases often substantially differ from the way they are understood in other cultures. Dōgen's thought, which passed through the particular filter of Japanese culture, is impossible for Westerners to comprehend and make their own just through a cursory reading or lecture.

Moreover, since the introduction of Zen philosophy to the West by people like D. T. Suzuki, the word "Zen" has become associated with exotic mysticism. Also, quite a few people think of zazen as one type of meditation among many with a religious tint, or as some kind of especially penetrating form of yoga. Knowing something about this "mystical Zen" has become a popular way to make a person appear as having a respectable pastime that is superior to the trivial pursuits of others.

Some people view Zen as a useful way to improve and rectify their life-style, and consequently some Zen centers have become a kind of New Age self-help center. These centers focus on isolated aspects of Dōgen's teachings without being able to appreciate them as a whole. They put together marketable self-improvement training programs, sell them as a commodity to those who have this kind of conception of Zen, and make a handy profit. There have even been cases where, after a few weeks of training, a person, having made a suitable "offering" of an always hefty sum, can receive the *shishō* or certificate of Dharma transmission. Such incidents could not be further from a true understanding of the teachings of Zen master Dōgen.

This is not always the case, but such occurrences are prevalent enough that we should ask ourselves if it is not time to rethink and clarify the original teachings of Zen and Dōgen. We need not reject "Beat Zen," or New Age eclectic Zen, or Zen as a sophisticated intellectual pursuit, such as they are. But I think that it is essential that we reexamine the teachings of Dōgen and make sure that we are not diluting them through the filter of cultural preferences. It therefore follows that we should examine the basis of currently held interpretations of the essentials of Dōgen's teachings and confirm or disconfirm their validity.

Contributors

The contributors to this project are monks and priests, academics, and those who work in the community, but few of them started out as students of Buddhism. A number were students of Continental philosophy having other areas of interest. Nonetheless, it is through such paths that many of them appreciatively came upon Zen master Dōgen. Although not all of them read Japanese, many of them are practitioners who have tried, using all of their abilities and leaving no stones unturned, to look deeply into the marrow of the ultimate truths of Sōtō Zen. In the end, no particular language or culture owns or has a monopoly on the truth of Zen.

Many students today who study such important texts as Dōgen's *Shōbōgenzō* and Keizan's *Denkōroku* have come to understand them through various translations. Some might argue that the texts can only be appreciated in their native language—and all of the texts in this volume have been carefully edited to make sure that translations were not a hindrance—but we have found that the fresh eyes of those who take practice seriously and who, working with Japanese readers, explore the translations also have a genuine access to the truth of Zen experience as well as the real meaning of the original texts.

It would be very fortunate if readers were easily able to gather the wide range of viewpoints presented in these translations to help them grasp the fundamental essence of Sōtō Zen. Furthermore, if the authors and editors who labored on this project can help Zen practitioners and those who are trying to deepen their lives to appreciate better the teachings of Sōtō Zen and make these teachings part of their lives, then the goals of this project will have been attained.

BRIEF COMMENTS ON SIX BIG TOPICS

Following are my views on six themes to help the reader better understand Mahāyāna Buddhism and Sōtō Zen, with a view to deepening their understanding of *Shushōgi*.

1. Religion

If we understand the word "religion" exclusively in the context of Judaism, Islam, Christianity, and Hinduism, then Zen is not a religion. This is because in Zen there is nothing corresponding to the God of Judaism, Christianity, and Islam, or the polytheism of Hinduism. The etymology of "religion," from the Latin term *religare*, means to bind fast, to connect tightly, because one is attempting to connect oneself to God. If this is what is meant by religion, then we cannot call Mahāyāna Buddhism a "religion." For some other sects of Buddhism, Śākyamuni Buddha might be the object of worship, but this is absolutely not the case for Zen. Although Mahāyāna Buddhism includes traditions that require faith in certain doctrines, there is nothing corresponding to the belief of forming or returning to a relationship with any God or gods.

If we were to acknowledge any particular kind of faith embraced by Zen, it would not be a faith in God or the Buddha, but rather a faith in the very act of living. For Sōtō Zen in particular, the object of faith is simply life itself—life embraced right here and now, in this very moment.

It would be difficult for Jews, Christians, and Muslims, practitioners of indigenous religions, and Hindus to reconcile their practice with a form of Buddhism that does not require reverence of new deities. This would only produce conflict. Zen, however, does not ask this of those who engage in Zen practice. If someone from another religion appreciates the fundamentals of Sōtō Zen, there is nothing in this path that demands that they have to first give up their religion. Any imam, Christian priest, rabbi, shaman, or Brahman priest could also become a Zen practitioner. There would be nothing strange about this at all.

Some time ago, I had the opportunity to partake in Bernie Glassman's Bearing Witness Retreat at Auschwitz-Birkenau Concentration Camp. Jews, Christians, Muslims, Zen practitioners, and others of various traditions all gathered together at the camp. Each morning members of the various traditions would offer their respective services, all of which were open to members of all faiths and practices. I had the impression that people were partaking in these different traditions out of genuine curiosity and respect. Even those who had come from the Middle East, where many such traditions are in conflict, were able to rise above traditional animosities and embrace a common purpose.

Prior to this experience, I would never have thought that such communion was possible. How did this happen? Perhaps it is a result of the contribution from the teaching and practice of Sōtō Zen that is free of the belief in any kind of God or Supreme Being. I could see how Zen, which concentrates on the act of living itself, could help provide some of the glue that allowed everyone to live together in harmony. Even now I clearly remember this experience. It was a turning point in my thinking—as though the scales fell from my eyes as they did for Saul on his way to Damascus.[15]

2. *Mahāyāna Buddhism*

The most basic intent of Buddhism is to liberate beings from suffering. Buddhism uses the metaphor of a river with a near shore and a far shore: the near shore symbolizes the realm of suffering, and the far shore, the realm of no suffering. At issue is the problem of how to cross the river. In Theravāda Buddhism, only monks and nuns who have attained enlightenment through specialized training can attain the far shore of nirvana. Laypersons, on the other hand, can only attain liberation in their next life by embracing the Three Treasures (Buddha, Dharma, Sangha), keeping the Five Precepts (not killing living creatures, not taking what is not given, abstaining from misconduct in sexual matters, abstaining from false speech, and abstaining from intoxicants), making offerings to the monks and nuns, supporting the local temple, and building up merit (good karma).

Mahāyāna Buddhism arose as a critical response to the Theravāda teaching that not all beings can be saved. The *Heart Sutra*,[16] the pith of Mahāyāna wisdom teaching, is a reproof of the Theravāda position. Śariputra represents the Theravāda and the Bodhisattva Avalokiteśvara[17] the Mahāyāna. The Bodhisattva refutes many basic Theravāda teachings and teaches the emptiness[18] of all things. From the start, Mahāyāna insists that the intention of Buddhism is to help every being reach the far shore and to relieve suffering. Every being without exception can cross the river of suffering and reach the far shore. The Buddha Dharma is like the pilot of the boat that brings all beings to the other shore, showing us that all things in heaven and earth have Buddha Nature and are expressions of *dharmadhātu* and the great Buddha sea.

Mahāyāna Buddhism is comprised of many sects. They all agree that everyone can cross the river of suffering, but they differ as to the manner in which this should be accomplished. I think that these differences can easily be explained by using the analogy of a floodgate in the middle of the river. Pure Land Buddhism teaches that Amida Buddha will help all beings as they endeavor to pass through this floodgate. If one relies on the *nembutsu* ("mindfulness of the Buddha") through chanting the phrase *Namu Amida Butsu*, Amida Buddha will categorically and without fail intervene to bring you to the far shore. The *Lotus Sutra* branch of Buddhism, associated with Nichiren, teaches that if you adhere to its namesake text, you will reach the far shore.

Zen, however, teaches that you can cross the river through your "own power"[19] in contrast with Shinran and the True Pure Land school's emphasis on "other power."[20] It teaches us "not to rely on words and letters"[21] nor to be chained to the sutras.[22] Rather, it teaches us to listen directly to the echoes of our own hearts and minds and to awaken to the direct truth.[23]

3. What Does Sōtō Zen Emphasize?

Some Zen teachings seem to imply that there is something like a gate in the river of suffering through which one must pass to reach the far shore—one could think of it as something like a "water gate" or "river gate"[24] a kind of "door" in the river. By accruing and applying the fruits of practice, anyone can get the knack of passing through them, and can easily reach the other shore—that is, attain nirvana. This is one way of understanding why some teachers typically use kōans (although there are other ways in which they can be used skillfully).

The emphasis is different in Sōtō Zen because there is no need to get such a "knack" or acquire this kind of skill. We need only to detect the reality and nature of one's own life. Why? This is because, from the beginning, we are all in the gate and it has always been open. There is no need for the knack of passing through the gate or opening it. If we can only "see our original face,"[25] we are entirely free to cross from this side to the other side. In a sense, we are the gate itself. Only we, ourselves, can make this confirmation. No one else can do this for us. It is like trying to find your glasses while you are already wearing them. Only by throwing one's whole self into zazen—Dōgen's *shikantaza*—can we resolve our lives into their proper form, and in so doing, truly confirm our own nature.

4. Dōgen's Copernican Revolution

I think that there is no problem with saying that enlightenment, *satori*, is something like acquiring a skill or a knack (in the positive sense), but some threads of Zen have taught that we practice zazen in order to attain enlightenment. In other words, one attains enlightenment after practice. First comes practice and then comes enlightenment. By contrast, in Sōtō Zen, one does not practice zazen in order to attain enlightenment— instead it is because one is already enlightened that one can practice. This is Sōtō Zen's most characteristic component. Dōgen's teaching as to the true nature of practice was so radically innovative that it effectively comprised a kind of Copernican Revolution. It was like putting all your effort into accomplishing something very important and then discovering that you already had it. In other words, if you practice with the intention of attaining enlightenment, Dōgen confirms that you already are enlightened.

Practice[26] is not therefore some esoteric and mysterious kind of training focusing on transrational kōans; it is something altogether different. Instead of putting all your effort into trying to get something you do not now have, the teachings of Dōgen lead entirely in the opposite direction. What you need to be doing with practice is confirming your enlightenment.

When Dōgen was studying and practicing at Hieizan,[27] he learned that "from the beginning, we all have Buddha Nature—this primordial nature is pure and clean." However, when Dōgen asked his Tendai teachers why we had to practice if we already had Buddha Nature, they had no good answers. Resolving to find an answer to his question, Dōgen left Hieizan and went to the Rinzai temple, Kenninji, in Kyoto, which had been recently established by Eisai, the first ordained Zen master in Japan. He became a disciple of Eisai's disciple Myōzen,[28] but he still could not find a satisfactory answer.

So he and Myōzen found a way to travel to China. There he visited a variety of Buddhist temples and personally experienced Buddhist training under a number of teachers. Finally, when he was about to give up and return to Japan, he found his true master, Rujing, at the Jingde[29] temple, and under his instruction, he was able to realize the "throwing and casting off of body and mind."[30] He realized that he had "always been enlightened" and returned to Japan. All of us, right now, just as we are, are already in the realm of our ultimate destination. He realized that there is nothing greater, nothing smaller. Dōgen, unlike earlier monks who traveled to and studied in China, returned to Japan transporting neither Buddhist statues nor scriptures—he brought only what he had realized, the truth of the Buddha Dharma. We call this "returning with empty hands."[31] The essence of the Buddha Dharma with which Dōgen returned home is: "From the beginning, your eyes are horizontal and your nose is perpendicular." Dōgen only brought back that everywhere, nothing is hidden—not any special esoteric teaching or secret.

5. All Beings—Buddha Nature

Among the teachings of Mahāyāna Buddhism we can find the doctrine "All beings—Buddha Nature."[32] Depending how you read these four kanji characters, the meaning is very different. What is the relationship between "All being(s)" and "Buddha Nature"? There are two readings. One is: "All beings have Buddha Nature." The other is: "All being is Buddha Nature." Dōgen illuminates the second—"All being is Buddha Nature." If we take the first reading as saying "All beings" have "Buddha Nature," Buddha Nature is then something you have within you. If that is so, we should search for this thing called Buddha Nature within us, and polish it in order to get rid of the dust. If, on the other hand, we read the passage as saying "All being is Buddha Nature," the meaning is very different. This is one of Dōgen's most fundamental teachings.

"All being" means everything. "All being" does not point to any one being in particular. It simply means "All," the whole of being, with no exceptions—"the universe just as it is." The universe includes all kinds of objects or entities. The planet earth is one such entity. The earth includes innumerable kinds of entities, including the natural world of mountains, rivers, and living beings, including human beings, animals, as well as plants, and so on. All of these entities seem like separate beings, but they are all components of the earth, and the earth itself is a component of the universe. Dōgen called the universe the "great earth," meaning not the planet earth but all that is without exception. The universe, the great earth, is "all being." It is Buddha Nature.

Among particular beings, there are differences, which are the distinctive characteristic of the former, namely, singularity. Nothing in all of being is superior or inferior. For the sake of convenience, people make distinctions and value judgments, but these can only apply in the context of individual situations. They do not pertain to reality itself, where there is neither good nor bad, neither greater nor lesser, neither superior nor inferior. All existence is complete just as it is. In Mahāyāna Buddhism, this teaching is expressed as: "Equality is distinction. Distinction is equality."[33] Distinction means difference, and is not merely the label of a doctrine. Everything is for that time, and existence at that time is everything; relative distinctions are not absolute.

6. The Constituents of Giving Are All Equally Empty

The Path of the Six Perfections[34] is essential for any Mahāyāna Buddhist. They include: giving, morality, forbearance, effort, meditation, and wisdom.[35] Although the word "giving" implies the everyday simple notion of giving—such as giving to charity—in the context of the Six Perfections, it means something different. "Giving" here is a composite of three constituents. The easiest way of explaining this is through the teaching: "The constituents of 'giving' are all equally empty."

There are three elements to giving—the giver, the receiver, and the gift. To be a giver, there must be a receiver: to be a receiver, there must be a giver. And, without a giver and a receiver, there can be no gift. If any of these elements are missing, the others cannot be. This is the teaching: "The constituents of giving are all equally empty." No constituent has a higher or lower value than any of the others. When you notice this, you realize that they all are interconnected. None is higher, none lower; none is superior, none inferior—there is no real distinction among them. As we investigate this matter, we realize that throughout the universe nothing is superior and nothing is inferior; all are interrelated, and all are empty of inherent value or inherent distinction. It may seem that in our everyday reality, each individual thing has distinct essential properties and value. Even among such distinctions, however, all things[36] are interconnected and interrelated. When you fully realize this—that there are no fences or conflicts of values in giving—you see that there is no reason for preference, and no reason for discrimination. We realize that in giving, "the constituents of giving are all equally empty."

Translated by Dainen David Putney

2 Updating Dōgen: *Shushōgi* and Today

TAIGEN DAN LEIGHTON

Eihei Dōgen was a teacher in the first half of the thirteenth century in Japan. He brought back his understanding of Chan/Zen literature and teaching from China and founded what is called the Sōtō Zen school of Japanese Buddhism. Now Dōgen's translated writings are making a major contribution to the current introduction of Buddhism, and not solely Zen, from Asia to the West (Europe and the Americas). But for most of the time since Dōgen lived, his writings were studied only by small numbers of Sōtō clerics. Only occasional minor spurts of increased involvement with Dōgen's writings occurred within the Sōtō sect, usually as a response to outside influences such as the Ōbaku school arriving from China in the early seventeenth century, or governmental edicts such as in the early Tokugawa or Meiji periods. Dōgen remained a cherished founding figure throughout Sōtō history, but his writings were not usually a significant part of that. This is probably somewhat due to the challenging quality of Dōgen's writings, with his complex, poetic wordplay, even aside from the now archaic language Dōgen used, perhaps comparable to Chaucer's language for modern English. But in the 1920s a Japanese philosopher brought Dōgen's writings to popular attention in Japan, beyond the Sōtō school. Watsuji Tetsurō (1889–1960) celebrated Dōgen as a traditional, worthy Japanese philosopher to counter the domination then of imported Western philosophy. This led to modern interest in Dōgen, both in Japan and eventually the West.

Shushōgi (*The Meaning of Practice and Verification*) was compiled as a distillation of Dōgen's writing in 1890 by a group led by Sōtō lay practitioner and scholar Ōuchi Seiran. They wanted a condensed text derived from Dōgen for lay parishioners at that time to chant. *Shushōgi* has been an important part of Japanese Sōtō liturgy ever since. *Shushōgi* has sections from many of Dōgen's fine teachings, and may well still serve as a highly useful introduction to Dōgen, as the commentaries in this book will demonstrate. But *Shushōgi* emphasized particular aspects of Dōgen's teachings that were deemed most appropriate and applicable for a late nineteenth-century Japanese lay audience. These include emphases on karma, ethics, and repentance that were especially important in Dōgen's later teachings.

Dōgen's writings are all based on teachings given to specific students. From 1233 to 1243 he taught general audiences at his temple in the outskirts of the capital of Kyoto; from 1243 until his death in 1253, he primarily taught monk disciples at his temple, Eiheiji, established in the remote mountains far north of the capital. He was not promulgating theoretical philosophical doctrines outside the context of practical religious teachings for the students he addressed. I do not believe that Dōgen ever changed his basic Dharma perspectives, although certainly at different phases of his career he shifted emphasis somewhat based on his form of teaching and his particular audience. Later teachings in his *Eihei Kōroku*[1] clarify that Dōgen never shifted away from the critical importance of zazen practice and its universal application, although this was emphasized more in his earlier teachings. But in the late nineteenth-century updating of Dōgen in *Shushōgi*, zazen is not even mentioned. This is especially striking for modern Western students, many first attracted to Dōgen exactly for his meditation practice and teachings.

Dōgen's complete writings are immense and wide-ranging, at least as large a corpus of writings as from any eminent teacher in the long history of Zen. But *Shushōgi* reflects the ongoing need to update and reinterpret these medieval Japanese teachings for new generations. This need for updating is certainly true as well for the current Western interest in Zen, and Dōgen. But it seems unlikely that we will see a condensed distillation of Dōgen's writings like *Shushōgi* for a modern audience.

Updating of Dōgen occurs today through the many diverse translations of his works that continue to appear. For liturgical purposes, modern Sōtō temples in the West chant translations of some of his early works, especially "Genjōkōan [Actualizing the Fundamental Point],"

Fukanzazengi [Universally Recommended Instructions for Zazen], and the "Jijūyū Zammai [Self-Fulfillment Samādhi]" section of "Bendōwa [On the Endeavor of the Way]," all also chanted in Japanese Sōtō liturgy along with *Shushōgi*. This selection of early Dōgen texts for chanting reflects the modern Western Sōtō emphasis on zazen practice. Very few Western Zen centers chant *Shushōgi*, although it is used occasionally as material for teaching in a small number of centers. Significantly, along with translations, many informed Western commentaries on Dōgen's writings are now appearing that help interpret his teachings for modern practitioners and readers of Dōgen. This volume presents more such constructive reflections by able commentators.

Dōgen's writings are richly evocative and profound, full of good spiritual nourishment, and can provide relevant support for modern spiritual practice. In the inevitable process of updating Dōgen for our time, we should not be afraid to gather what is helpful now, as did *Shushōgi* compilers. Dōgen faced a significant gulf in Buddhist cultures when he introduced Chinese Chan to medieval Japan. Ōuchi Seiran and *Shushōgi* compilers faced a wider chasm between thirteenth-century medieval monks and late nineteenth-century Japanese laypeople, exposed to influences from the West. But neither of these gaps compare to the much deeper cultural abyss between Buddhist Asia and Dōgen on one side and the modern West on the other. To truly engage Dōgen we need to find analogues from which to interpret him in our modern Western cultural matrix. Current Dōgen interpretations have invoked Western psychology and poetry to discuss Dōgen's teachings about mind and his poetic writings. Western understandings of Dōgen will benefit from scrutiny of our own spiritual biases, and study of the indigenous, native traditions of our lands.

As a Dōgen scholar, but also as an authorized Dharma successor in a lineage descended from Dōgen, and thus as one deeply grateful and even devoted to his writings, I have no hesitation in saying that I do not necessarily agree with everything Dōgen ever said. Perhaps what he felt important to say in the context of Kamakura period Japanese Buddhism may not be relevant today. For example, sometimes Dōgen harshly criticized other Buddhist schools and teachers, much less those "outside the

Way," that is, non-Buddhists. Such attitudes were common for teachers establishing new movements in medieval times. And one may discern and value the insightful concerns about practice and teaching that Dōgen was expressing in these critical comments. But in our current age, deep religious pluralism where we actually appreciate as well as tolerate at least some perspectives of other spiritual traditions may be necessary to the very survival of our species. We need to listen and learn from others. Narrow-minded fundamentalism of all stripes, including from secular traditions such as consumerism, has engendered violence and hatred in our world.

Taking a fundamentalist approach to Dōgen Zen would dishonor Dōgen's teaching. For example, an erroneous attitude that he taught zazen only and disdained all other teachings and practices, contrary to *Shushōgi* excerpts, would not reflect the true range of his teaching. For Westerners not steeped in the cultural grounding of East Asian Buddhism as Dōgen's students were, we might actually understand Dōgen better and enhance our own modern practice of Dōgen Zen through study of some of his worthy contemporaries. Fascinating and provocative Japanese Buddhist figures of Dōgen's time, such as Myō-e, Shinran, and Nichiren, as well as the medieval Japanese Tendai and Esoteric traditions and subtle aesthetics and culture, all offer helpful contexts for understanding Dōgen and more fully appreciating his insights and uniqueness. A flexible approach to Dōgen's work and background can help us more effectively interpret and update our own understanding and expression of his teaching. In this context, *Shushōgi* is a valuable document for seeing a somewhat modern Japanese reading of Dōgen.

3 Dōgen and Śākyamuni

TENSHIN CHARLES FLETCHER

Everyone at a deep level wants to return home, to be at home. To be at home in one's own skin anytime, anywhere. The Way of the buddhas is just this. Master Dōgen, in his fascicle "Henzan [All-Inclusive Study]," writes:

> Master Gensha taught the assembly, "Śākyamuni and I practiced together." A monk came up and asked, "I wonder, who did you two practice with?" The master said, "With the third son of Zhe on a fishing boat."

This is an interesting exchange that shows the essential appreciation of practice. Gensha's father was a fisherman and Gensha was the third son. There are plenty of people to practice with or under, yet essentially each one of us stands in the same place as the buddhas.

In the process of practice it is realized that we are all in the same boat. Śākyamuni illuminated the human condition and laid out a great way to end suffering. This same way was confirmed and expressed through Dōgen, who acknowledged the efforts of the founder on many occasions. Yet one cannot rest on the efforts of the past and the examples set by these old ones. If the religion, way of life, or philosophy is to be genuine and effective, it needs to be lived and to reach the folks of this and each generation. It shouldn't be a cultural or historical preservation society.

So Śākyamuni and I practiced together and it is true that Śākyamuni is this whole world of our sense sphere and beyond. He had the same basic ingredients as this "I" of today, with similar impulses and conditioning. To put it another way, we talk of the Tathāgata Buddha, or the one who has attained thusness since beginningless time. Each one of us has attained thusness, yet if it is not recognized and practiced, we are a long way from home.

Dōgen essentially reiterates this over and over. The title of his major work—*Shōbōgenzō* (*The Treasury of the True Dharma Eye*)—is a reflection of this. Attributed to the transmission story of Śākyamuni to Mahākāśyapa, it confirms the experience that our lives are the great treasury of experience, truth, and reality. That has always been apparent to those who live it and is our birthright today. Generally it is not appreciated, as it is not practiced, used, and lived. Even in the comments on the precepts—for example, the precept "Do not talk of the shortcomings of others"—Dōgen says, "Within the Buddha Dharma it is the same Way, the same Dharma, the same realization, the same practice." This is a hard statement to realize, let alone to put into practice. It is obvious that Dōgen had this appreciation and lived it. Like it or not, we all practice together as this world, as it always has been, since beginningless time through Śākyamuni down to today. Yet each one of us has our own place and unique attributes.

Śākyamuni and I practiced together. It is the same way today as 800 or 2,500 years ago, transcendent of culture, yet equally apparent in our culture today.

Teachers repeat the value of what is often overlooked. It is our role to show people over and over what they already have yet don't appreciate. Both Śākyamuni and Dōgen emphasize zazen. Why? Because zazen works. There is no reason why it should. Yet if you sit still, you begin to notice things like habitual thinking, views that do not jive with life, and just maybe an intrinsic rightness that has been overlooked. The process is not linear and is not goal oriented in that, quite often, the deeper realizations come in from the side and are not what we were necessarily looking for.

Just sitting meditation (*shikantaza*), emphasized by Dōgen, criticized by many, is the practice/realization actualized by all the awakened ones. At this so-called stage, it is not a method per se, yet Śākyamuni's "I" is revealed as whatever is going on. There is no limit to what is practiced/realized, as *shikantaza* is living in itself.

I had a conversation on practice with a couple of Rinzai masters regarding *shikantaza*. They both said, "*Shikantaza* is the hardest kōan." Why? Because there is no passing and no one to approve.

Dōgen talks of an encounter with a *tenzo* (cook), where the old *tenzo* was working in the hot sun drying mushrooms. Dōgen asked, "Why don't you get someone younger to do the work for you?" He replied, "If not me, who? If not now, when?" Words echoing down through the years! Even in business it is appreciated. Without this, practice would be for others to do. Yet it would do little to ease basic human angst. In the attempting, a lot is learned—as much from mistakes as from success. If this place or this one is to thrive, I will do my damnedest to make sure it does. Echoes of Śākyamuni under the Bodhi tree, where he vowed not to get up until he resolved his life question!

Both Dōgen and Śākyamuni were first and foremost practitioners and only secondarily teachers, realizing that by setting an example, the lesson is both a lot deeper and a little more accessible. One obvious fact of this kind of teaching is that you get to know the teacher intimately, seeing them in all kinds of moods, energy levels, and seeing how they deal with the arising of all kinds of challenges, no matter their state of mind. Working intimately, one sees the attributes and the shadow. It is encouraging that teachers are not perfect, and whatever perfection we project has to be practiced by this one in the same training context. So, Śākyamuni and I practice together, a living being echoed through generations. Returning home. Cultivating one's own garden, sharing one's own food. Raising children to appreciate their own lives.

4 Practice-Realization: Dōgen Zen and Original Awakening

SHŪDŌ BRIAN SCHROEDER

The Way is originally perfect and all-pervading.
How could it be contingent on practice and realization? . . .
What need is there for special effort?
—*Dōgen*, Fukanzazengi

ON DOCTRINES AND TRUTH

Philosophical and religious doctrines or teachings rarely have simple and straightforward singular meanings but rather usually contain multivalent and complex nuanced formulations susceptible to a wide range of interpretive possibilities. The parameters of plausible interpretation are set by the way the doctrine itself is formulated as well as by the entire field of doctrines within which a particular doctrine is located. As the constellation of the doctrinal field changes, so do the parameters within which any doctrine in that field can be interpreted. Doctrines have no meaning outside of the interpretive contexts in which they are embedded just as ideas have no reality independent of the minds that think them.

With regard to Zen practice, doctrines are also useful and can be a skillful means[1] for understanding the Buddha Dharma[2] inasmuch as they can assist a deepening of practice. They can also, however, be damaging in proportion to the extent that they limit or even undo the positive results of practice by restricting our understanding of self and existence in general to the dogmatism of a purely conceptual or intellectual standpoint—in other words, to a partial and thus narrow experience.[3] We cannot escape the fact that we can only see something from a certain viewpoint. As some Zen texts remind us, the eye cannot see itself. Awareness of this epistemological predicament, however, can have the salutary effect of freeing us from the self-righteousness that comes from the belief that we are in the privileged possession of "the truth."

With respect to the work of Eihei Dōgen Zenji, it is important to keep in mind that there is no single way to interpret and understand his teachings. In typical Zen fashion, Dōgen's language oscillates between the philosophical and the poetic, between what seems immediately clear and obvious and what is hidden and obscure. Although he is considered a fully awakened master in Zen circles, his writings also demonstrate a developmental aspect, as he himself came into greater realization of the Buddha Dharma and what it means to be an awakened being. This is in part exhibited in the longstanding debate about whether Buddha Nature[4] is always present or that which we come into realization of through practice, and whether this awakening is immediate or gradual. Dōgen's standpoint on this matter is ambiguous and necessarily so. Allowing this ambiguity to stand is integral to not only understanding Dōgen's Zen mind but also for coming to a fuller sense of the Buddha's teaching of non-ego or no-self,[5] or what the Kyoto school philosopher Nishitani Keiji terms a "*self* that is not a self."[6]

HISTORICAL BACKGROUND OF ORIGINAL AWAKENING

The meanings of original awakening[7] and acquired awakening,[8] and their relation to one another, have long been a concern of Mahāyāna Buddhism, although the roots of this issue extend back to the earliest days of Buddhism, as the notion of acquired awakening is present in the teaching of the historical Buddha, Śākyamuni. The concept of original awakening, however, is a later development, although its proponents claim that it has always been present in the Buddha's teaching, since original awakening is eternal, without beginning or end in time.

Original awakening[9] is the teaching that all beings (and if one follows the teaching of Eihei Dōgen this includes nonsentient beings) are somehow already awakened or enlightened—that is, already Buddha Nature. In fact, many scholars see original awakening and Buddha Nature as practically synonymous. The idea of original awakening appears in the early history of Indian Mahāyāna writings, and particularly in two prominent texts, the *Tathāgatagarbha Sūtra* and the *Mahāparinirvāna Sūtra*.[10] The notion of original awakening first appears juxtaposed to the notion of acquired awakening in another classic Mahāyāna text, *The Awakening of Faith in the Mahāyāna*, which is attributed to Aśvaghoṣa. The original Sanskrit version of this work is lost but it was translated into Chinese in the mid-sixth century (although many scholars now think that is was composed in Chinese) and shaped significantly the development of Buddhism in China and Japan.

Some scholars argue that the concept of *hongaku* (original awakening) was simply an extension of the older Sanskrit term *tathāgatagarbha* (womb or seed of the Buddha), even though the term *hongaku* has no Sanskrit equivalent. *Tathāgatagarbha* is an interesting concept with an ambivalent meaning: on the one hand there is the aspect of womb, which implies both something that is and is not, and what is also actual and potential, in the sense of being the empty space in which growth occurs; and on the other hand, there is the aspect of seed or germ, that which takes root and grows.[11] So the concept of *tathāgatagarbha* resonates equally with the two fundamental Buddhist notions of reality: emptiness[12] and suchness or phenomenality.[13] The *Tathāgatagarbha Sūtra* taught that inherent in all sentient or conscious beings is the kernel or core of awakened existence, and this is precisely what needs to be realized, what we need to awaken to, namely, our original Buddha Nature.

The *tathāgatagarbha* doctrine can perhaps be best explained as arising out of a need to affirm the positive role of language in the face of its radical critique found in the *Prajñāpāramitā Sūtras* and the Madhyamaka treatises. Thus the development of the *tathāgatagarbha* doctrine cannot simply be understood as the intrusion of indigenous thought; it was also a response to a perceived inadequacy within Buddhist doctrine.

ORIGINAL AWAKENING AND KARMA

The teaching of original awakening or Buddha Nature is what perhaps most distinguishes the *tathāgatagarbha* tradition from the Madhaymaka standpoint of the great philosopher and Dharma ancestor Nāgārjuna, who most advanced the concept of emptiness and posited the fundamental

nondifference between samsara (the cycle of birth and rebirth) and nirvana (the extinguishing of the cycle of birth and rebirth).[14] The connection between these latter two terms can be confusing and often leads to
the naive assertion that nirvana is simply samsara and vice-versa. These
concepts are not, however, identical in meaning; they designate certain
aspects of existence or the Dharma when viewed from different perspectives. Samsara is definitely negative in connotation, insofar as the endless cycle or round of existence is precisely from what we want freedom
(nirvana) because this is where karma can be generated in such a way
that we become attached to it. Attachment to karma is what binds us
to the runaround of samsara. The Sanskrit term *karma* literally means
action, deed, or work, but it also connotes the object or intention of an
action. Attachment to karma means clinging to or even identifying with
the consequences of our actions, both physical and mental, so that the
action does not stand on its own, thereby gathering together not only the
doer and the action, but also other beings that are affected by the action.
Only when karma is simply allowed to be, which is possible only from
the standpoint of non-ego, is the Buddha Dharma, which permeates and
interrelates all existence, fully manifest. The self that understands karma
primarily in relation to itself is a self that is bound in the delusion of
ignorance,[15] and therefore unable to realize its fundamental awakened
existence. Distinguishing between samsara and nirvana does not, however, negate their fundamental unity if we understand that to mean an
intimate, absolute interrelation. Nāgārjuna's great insight into the relation between nirvana and samsara was a watershed moment in the history of Buddhist thought. It ultimately paved the way for the negation
or overcoming of the absolute opposition of such conceptual pairings as
emptiness and phenomenality, enlightenment and delusion, being and
nonbeing, and life and death, and enabled these terms to be affirmed in
their similar interrelated unity. Thus was the Buddha's core teaching of
dependent origination[16] deepened philosophically on the metaphysical,
ontological, and epistemological levels.

　　To return to the notion of karma: this is something we cannot avoid;
everything generates karma. That is why from a Zen perspective, as
Dōgen writes in *Fukanzazengi* (*Universally Recommended Instructions*

for Zazen), we should "not think 'good' or 'bad.'"[17] To see it otherwise is to essentialize karma, that is, reduce it to a fixed status or understand it as fundamentally unchanging in its expression (as take, for example, the proverbial "once a bad egg always a bad egg"). Likewise, to essentialize karma is also to do the same to the self, since the self and its actions are a unity. Turning either karma or the self into any form of "essence" necessarily results in positing a dualism on the metaphysical (for example, soul/body), ontological (agent/action), and epistemological (knower/known) levels. From a Buddhist standpoint, such dualisms are conceptual formations. It is perhaps more accurate to say that karma is a problem only if one construes karma as something that obstructs the realization of nirvana. The fact is, karma simply is. Karma literally means action or deed. It is generated on multiple registers—the physical and the psychological, both individually and collectively, with effects that can occur immediately and/or well into the future. Integral to awakening is overcoming ignorance, seeing reality, as Dōgen underscores in the very title to his collected writings, *Shōbōgenzō*, with the "true Dharma eye." Understanding that we are not bound by karma, that we are free to redirect its flow or movement and thereby alter the constellation of causal relations, is a major aspect of the awakened mind.

Dōgen's primary concern in *Fukanzazengi* concerns the unity of practice and realization/awakening.[18] The position of original awakening arguably expresses this unity by expanding the notice of practice beyond that of mere religious discipline to include the much broader range of everyday activity, of karma. This point is expressed in the Mahāyāna position that the *Dharmakāya* (the reality or truth embodiment of the Buddha) is not something purely noumenal or "out there" (the *paranirvāna* of earlier Buddhism), but is rather the body itself—in other words, the totality of phenomenal existence.

ORIGINAL AWAKENING AND THE CRITIQUE OF CRITICAL BUDDHISM

Since the time of the celebrated sixth Chinese ancestor Dajian Huineng,[19] Zen has often tended toward the position of sudden awakening[20] as the expression of realizing Buddha Nature. Yet the Zen of Dōgen often seems to emphasize a gradual path to awakening to one's true nature and a rejection of sudden awakening. On closer inspection, however, such distinctions fall away. As Dōgen writes in another context: "although not one, not different; although not different, not the same; although not the same, not many."[21] In the present case, original awakening is inseparable from the process of acquired awakening, which is precisely why all past, present, and future buddhas and bodhisattvas continue to practice even though they are already awakened as fully realized beings.

The development of the doctrine or teaching of original awakening, or inherent enlightenment, marks a profound shift in the history of Buddhist thought. The concept of *hongaku* came to full prominence during the Kamakura period of Japanese history (1185–1333) and is associated largely with the Tendai sect of Buddhism, although it also significantly impacted the development of the Nichiren, Pure Land, and Zen schools of Buddhism. Though a prevalent teaching in Japanese Buddhism, it has been a matter of debate for over a thousand years and has received renewed attention recently through the critique of "Critical Buddhism."[22] The primary philosophers identified with this movement—Hakamaya Noriaki and Matsumoto Shirō, both associated with the Sōtō-based Komazawa University—claim that the notion of original awakening is non-Buddhist and basically ignores what they consider to be the original or pure teaching of the Buddha, namely, the doctrines of non-ego, dependent origination, and emptiness. Moreover, they argue that the concept of original awakening has exercised a pernicious effect on Japanese culture and politics, since in the past many appealed to this viewpoint to justify imperialistic actions and consequently exonerate themselves from the deleterious effects of those actions.

Critical Buddhism has been instrumental for introducing into contemporary discourse the problematic aspect of the notions of Buddha Nature and original awakening. Perhaps the principal concern they raise is whether there is a pure or original or true Buddhism that we can somehow get back to. Our scholarship certainly does not provide us with such access. The writings that do exist were only written down centuries after the Buddha taught. When we become fixated on the idea of what the true path is, on the original intention and meaning of the Dharma, then we risk falling into the very thing that both Śākyamuni and Nāgārjuna constantly criticized and warned us about, namely, substantializing and essentializing the Dharma. The contribution of Critical Buddhism is that it provides us once again with the opportunity to reflect, on the one hand, on what it means to be originally awakened and, on the other, how we come to that realization.

With respect to Dōgen's thinking, Hee-Jin Kim captures well the tension of the matter of *hongaku*: "Dōgen was born into and imbibed the *hongaku* tradition and, throughout his life, struggled to negotiate his way *within* it, and well as *beyond* it. Instead of idealizing it, or abandoning it, or replacing it with another notion, Dōgen endeavored to see through it more clearly and penetratingly, by way of his religious method."[23] The danger of Critical Buddhism, Kim notes, in its attempt to recover an original Buddhism and weed out what it thought to be either nonauthentic or inessential in Chan/Zen, is "'throwing out the baby with the bathwater' with respect to the *hongaku* tradition as a whole."[24] Having come out of the Tendai tradition, Dōgen was well aware of both the strengths and weaknesses of the *hongaku* standpoint, and the development of his own thinking reflects a continual engagement with that standpoint, all the while neither fully accepting nor rejecting it. Dōgen Zen, despite its long association with Sōtōshu, manifests a more nuanced and critical view of original awakening and how it informs and shapes the related notion of Buddha Nature and *tathāgatagarbha*.

Dōgen and the Nature of Awakening

When Dōgen left Japan for China as a dissatisfied Tendai monk at the age of twenty-three to find the authentic Buddha Dharma, he was consumed by a single question: How is it that if we are already originally awakened, the buddhas, bodhisattvas, and great ancestors continued to practice some path toward awakening? What is the need to do so if one has attained enlightenment? What Dōgen comes to realize is what he writes in his first treatise, *Fukanzazengi*:

Nonthinking. This is the essential art of zazen. The zazen I speak of is not meditation practice. It is simply the dharma gate of joyful ease, the practice-realization of totally culminated enlightenment. It is the kōan realized; traps and snares can never reach it.[25]

The phrase "practice-realization" is hyphenated here in its English translation in order to emphasize the fundamental connection between the two terms. Practice and realization are, from Dōgen's perspective, one and the same. The buddhas and bodhisattvas continue to practice because they are realized, awakened beings. Zazen is not a means to an end; neither is it a method, practice, or path we take up in order to reach some desired end or goal. The early *Shōbōgenzō* fascicle "Bendōwa [On the Endeavor of the Way]" clearly addresses this point in its contention that practice is an intention-free process; in other words, awakening is not something to be sought for and acquired through zazen. This is not to say that zazen cannot further our advance toward realization. This is certainly not what Dōgen claims either, but he does maintain that what it means to awaken is to recognize that this is possible only through commitment to the practice, based on the conviction that this practice will blossom. This is the heart of the teaching in *Shushōgi* (*The Meaning of Practice and Verification*).

Awakening requires a firm reliance on practice, the meaning of which is to see with the "true Dharma eye" the Buddha Nature of all things, and thus our own true nature. This is accomplished by turning the Dharma eye inward. In his famous *Zazenwasan* (*Chant in Praise of Zazen*), the Rinzai master Hakuin Ekaku reiterates this insight:

And when we turn inward and prove our True-nature—that True-self is no self, our own Self is no-self—we go beyond ego and past clever words. Then the gate to the oneness of cause and effect is thrown open.[26]

In realizing our true nature—that is, our original, inherent awakening— karma relinquishes its stifling hold on us and we can therefore "see," to again quote Hakuin, that "this earth where we stand is the pure lotus land, and this very body—the body of Buddha."[27] Dōgen is the master who perhaps teaches us most about both the ultimacy and universal range of practice:

> Depending on our practice, the practice of the buddhas is manifested, and the great way of the buddhas penetrates everywhere. Therefore, the practice of a single day is the seed of the buddhas, the practice of the buddhas.[28]

Now, the concept of original awakening was not accepted wholeheartedly by Dōgen, who often displayed ambivalence toward it and to its equally difficult correlate of Buddha Nature. There are passages in *Shōbōgenzō* that suggest he is closed to this notion, and yet in other places he appears to be amenable to it, as for example in his extension of the concept of Buddha Nature to include nonsentient beings such as mountains, rivers, and animals. One may rightly argue that in making this move he is actually affirming that originally all beings and objects are Buddha Nature, that is, originally awakened. And yet, he is critical of the concept of original awakening because it is through the process of zazen that we move toward a deeper understanding or realization of who we truly are. One possible way of explaining this would be to draw a distinction between original awakening and final awakening.

A danger with the concept of original awakening, and this is what Critical Buddhism draws our attention to, is that it results in a view that leads many to think that whatever we do is practice-realization, or even everything that exists is buddha (that is, enlightened and perfect), including unethical actions and other defilements of the Dharma. This is a dangerous consequence of uncritically accepting the formulaic doctrine that samsara is nirvana. Dōgen was shocked when he encountered this attitude among some of the so-called masters in the monasteries during his sojourn in China, which he associated with the often lax, degenerate practices and views they espoused—for example, the lack of unified practice structure, not shaving the head, types of robes (or not), secular dietary habits, etc. In other words, an abandonment of strict practices followed a prevalent idea circulating at the time that if everything is already in an awakened state then even the most ordinary or even profane actions can be considered enlightened acts, and any kind of disciplined practice is unnecessary. Dōgen utterly refused this viewpoint, and it was not until he encountered the way of Tiantong Rujing's[29] Caodong Chan,[30] with its emphasis on zazen, that he realized the authentic practice of the buddhas.

Zazen Practice and Awakening

Master Rujing's practice was very simple. It was what Dōgen termed *shikantaza* ("just sitting"), a breathing rather than a thinking practice. As Dōgen writes in *Fukanzazengi*, "zazen is the kōan realized." This set his Zen apart from the Buddhist practice of his contemporaries, and even the Zen of Linji[31] and Eisai, which focused more on kōan meditation, but also emphasized what is commonly referred to as sudden awakening.

Rinzai Zen uses the kōan during zazen as a means to achieve *kenshō*, that is, seeing into one's nature. In Sōtō Zen one generally does not encounter the terms kōan and *kenshō*, but it is not that Dōgen dismissed them out of hand. Indeed, there is a place for the kōan in his thinking, as Dōgen himself collected a number of them together during his travels in China, but their usage during zazen was never institutionalized as part of Sōtō practice. And it was not until the eighteenth century when Hakuin all but rescued Rinzai from collapsing that kōan practice was revivified by rigorously standardizing and institutionalizing it as a form of meditation.

How does this relate to the question of original awakening? The debate now occurring in response to Critical Buddhism, which is forcing many to reexamine the presuppositions of Sōtō Zen, leads us also to reconsider the difference between sudden and gradual awakening. Of concern is that these debates are not so much sharpening our critical reflection about Zen and Buddhism as they are rather driving wedges into the greater sangha, which are resulting in exacerbating the differences between traditions rather than seeking that which is common. If we take a look at Dōgen's practice what we find in his emphasis on *shikantaza* is actually a full embrace of the notion of original awakening. "The zazen I speak of is not meditation practice [or 'learned meditation']," he writes. So what is it then? It is the moment when we begin to recognize that all things are indeed interdependently arising, that all beings and dharmas are interconnected. This is not to be construed in terms of a gradual approach to realize original awakening. This is why fully awakened beings continually practice. It is not because they still need to get from point A to B; that spatial-temporal difference in getting from one point to another is cut through by the nonspatial dimension of original awakening. The intersection of space and time is where we are at any given moment. This intersection is our identity, tenuous as it may be, and, according to Abe Masao, the point at which the question of origin is located.[32] In addressing the relation between original and acquired awakening, Abe also used the image of an intersection to explain the relation between original and acquired awakening: Imagine acquired awakening, he said, as a horizontal plane, wherein we are moving toward some end or aim, and original awakening as a vertical plane. The horizontal plane is space and time. The movement of the vertical plane is the breaking through of the nonspatial and the nontemporal.[33]

Original awakening is unchanging; it is the eternal aspect of existence, what the thirteenth- to fourteenth-century German Rhineland mystic Meister Eckhart refers to as the "eternal now." In other words, this is what we at any point in our respective spatial-temporal journeys are able to come to realize. What we gain in various methods that may be construed as gradual or acquired awakening is simply the realization of the original nature. The buddhas continually practice because they, like we, are spatial-temporal beings. To be cognizant of the eternal, unchanging aspect of Buddha Nature at any given moment is the hallmark of authentic realization. Sometimes, if we are fortunate enough, it just happens here or there, but through the continual practice of zazen Dōgen thought that we would always be coming up against the intersecting moment of original and acquired awakening. This moment is where true realization is found, nowhere else.

Recasting the vexation of his earlier years regarding the continual need for practice after awakening, in "Bendowā" Dōgen writes:

While it is clear that those who have not yet realized buddha-dharma should practice zazen and attain realization, for those who have already understood the buddha's correct teaching, what should they expect from zazen?[34]

The answer is nothing. By letting go of the desire that expectation should or will result in a certain gain or result, one experiences the freedom or releasement (what Eckhart termed *Gelassenheit*) from samsara that is nirvana. In Dōgen's terms, practice is the same thing as realization. As long as the Buddha Dharma is practiced wondrously,[35] with whole-hearted effort and right mind, we realize our original nature. It is neither a conceptual knowing nor some mystical transformative moment. It is simply realizing that within our practice is our commitment, our resolve, our faith, our action, and this is what leads us to realize, as Dōgen did, that drawing hard-and-fast distinctions between original and acquired awakening only serves to fragment the community rather than lead to a broader, more inclusive notion of sangha.

ON ESSENTIALIZING PRACTICE-REALIZATION

The intersection of the horizontal and vertical is a moving through space in time. In the *Shōbōgenzō* fascicle of the same name, Dōgen refers to this as *uji* (translated variously as "time-being" or "being-time"), which is a fundamental concept for understanding what he means by Buddha Nature. *Uji* is process; but because it is simultaneously the intersection of space and time as the "now," it stands outside process. This movement on the horizontal space-time continuum of acquired awakening is confused at times with gradual awakening. Dōgen never taught, however, that we move from a state of nonawakening to a fuller awakening or a complete awakening. That is the wrong way to view "the meaning of practice." If we see zazen in that way then we begin to essentialize the meaning of zazen—that is, force it to conform to a preset trajectory of signification—in the very way that the Critical Buddhists claim those who embrace the notion of Buddha Nature are essentializing a concept of the self, and therefore do not realize the emptiness of the ego. But if in an effort to avoid this essentializing we then employ the concept of sudden awakening, we run the risk of divorcing realization from practice. Dōgen understands that these moments of sudden realization can and do occur, but they are cultivated through the process of zazen.

Dōgen placed great emphasis on process and developed extensive and firm guidelines about how to do nearly every daily activity in the monastic setting, which he held was the ideal place to cultivate practice-realization of the Buddha Dharma. But Dōgen did not think that by adhering to all these regulations one would necessarily reach full awakening; rather, by following these guidelines one keeps the mind focused constantly on the moment. By keeping the mind centered and attentive to all the minute details about how to eat, drink, wash, use the toilet, sit, breathe, sleep, etc., the mind is focused on the meaning of practice, and the moment-to-moment activity of the nonthinking mind serves as the verification of this meaning. To repeat, this is why awakened beings continue to practice. Being fully in the moment is the sudden realization of original awakening. This may admittedly be a nonstandard interpretation of what sudden awakening is usually understood to mean, but it is one that harmonizes with Dōgen's insistence on the gradual process of continually learning how to be fully in the moment as the meaning of practice-realization.

Sudden realization is not a once-and-for-all event, because these moments constantly have to be realized. Rather, as interpreted here, sudden awakening is what Dōgen identifies in *Fukanzazengi* as "non-thinking"[36]—the moment when one does something not out of mere habit but by becoming one with the action. This is the moment of awakening in which, as Dōgen famously states, "mind and body drop away." Whether it is sitting still, focusing on the breath, laying out *ōryōki* bowls, or wiping your behind, being fully in the moment is what is cultivated in practice. When that occurs, this is a moment of sudden realization, but at the same a moment that is reached paradoxically by a gradual process of awakening. We should not delude ourselves into thinking that our awakening is actual in any final sense, or even able to be fully actualized. That would be to essentialize awakening, to turn what is fundamentally a process into a final state of being. The Buddha's great realization about dependent origination is that there is no Absolute, no Ātman-Brahman, no final rest or resolution. Existence is a process of interrelated events. Buddha Nature or *Dao* is the name of this process. Realizing this and fully embracing and accepting it is awakening.

AWAKENING AND PARADOX

The pervasiveness of Buddha Nature is realized in original awakening when seen in relation to practice. Thus is the unity of Buddha Nature and mind made manifest. Buddha Nature is not, however, something we possess, aspire to, attain, or can even know; rather, it is that which gives us a ground, even if that ground is groundless in its unknowability. Buddha Nature is perhaps the most paradoxical standpoint of Buddhism. On the one hand, Buddha Nature is that which is, as stated above, unchanging and eternal. There are no degrees or types of Buddha Nature; it neither increases nor decreases, nor does it come in and out of existence. Yet, on the other hand, in the fascicle titled "Busshō [Buddha Nature]," Dōgen writes, citing the teaching of Huineng, "impermanence is itself buddha nature"[37]—in other words, Buddha Nature is ever-changing. Furthermore, in the same fascicle, a conversation is related between the fourth Chinese ancestor, Dayi Daoxin,[38] and the fifth ancestor, Daman Hongren,[39] about having no Buddha Nature. The paradox, Dōgen writes, is about "Buddha Nature that is empty, and Buddha Nature that is existence."[40] It is, at least in part, a matter of conception, of realizing the true nature of "mind."

There is no Buddha Nature in the sense of a knowable essence or ground, and yet Buddha Nature is the name of the absolute standpoint. To arrive at this realization is to arrive at the standpoint of emptiness, which, according to Dōgen, can only be fully realized through the practice-realization of zazen. This is what "actualizes the fundamental standpoint" that allows for the releasement of attachment that enables us to "see" the Buddha Nature of all existences.

Original awakening, Buddha Nature, is that which is grounded in what is paradoxically groundless, that is, emptiness. The paradoxical statement "form is emptiness, emptiness is form" is the central doctrine of the *Heart Sutra*, which permeates all Buddhist teaching. When the mind is able to grasp the meaning of this statement without reducing it to a rational formulation there is a relinquishing of desire to comprehend and thereby possess or take hold of the doctrine or teaching. That is the moment when dependent origination becomes manifest and the authentic nature of the "self" as non-ego is "seen" by the "true Dharma eye."

As Dōgen Zenji, perhaps better than anyone else, demonstrates in his writing, Buddha Nature can be grasped by the mind and elucidated in language, but at the same time cannot be fully actualized except through practice-realization. Philosophizing or thinking about the Buddha Dharma is a form of practice, which is precisely why Dōgen was so attentive to his writing and teaching. Yet, paradoxically, from the standpoint of his Zen, such activity is fundamentally empty—in other words, Buddha Nature, or original awakening, can only be actualized in, through, and as practice. Thus Dōgen states in *Fukanzazengi*:

> Therefore, put aside the intellectual practice of investigating words and chasing phrases, and learn to take the backward step that turns the light and shines it inward. Body and mind of themselves will drop away, and your original face will manifest.

This "face" is the nonrational, nondiscursive mind that is able to somehow grasp paradox while at the same time letting it be, not trying to explain it. This is the moment of the horizontal and vertical intersection, the moment of the sudden realization of what has always been originally there. This is what is acquired through the persistent and gradual process of zazen, a process that Dōgen understood as practice-realization, absolutely embodied here and now when fully in the moment of *shikantaza*. This is the realization of the closing thought of *Shushōgi*—that "mind itself is buddha."

5 Walking with Mountains, or What *Shōbōgenzō* and Dōgen Mean to Me

GLEN A. MAZIS

I realize I have been lingering with the thoughts and feelings of my childhood and adolescence; they never left me and always made Buddhism the compelling gate and path for me. Dōgen's *Shōbōgenzō* is a refuge for my sanity and an inspiration for my aliveness. I feel Buddhism is unparalleled as a religious and philosophical articulation of the centrality of the body in achieving human fulfillment and liberation from needless suffering. It also has the clearest understanding of how human embodiment is intermeshed with the whole of existence in its myriad concrete beings, each of which is precious. We can only draw upon the resources of vitality, compassion, and intrinsic value of these beings by moving from the ego's clouding of embodiment's mirror of perception, feeling, and intuition. The intrinsic value of these beings as singularly existing, partaking in the excellence of being manifest among the ten thousand things, is shared with all other beings in the play of appearing that needs no doing, no improving, and no achieving, but just is. The ego adds these demands to the world about it as the way it sees the ten thousand things. They become objects at its disposal or opposition in the clouding of the mirror of perception. When we wipe away these distortions then we can be open to discovering the formlessness of the world. We can then take sustenance from all living beings and practice for ourselves the true formlessness of existence. Both as a philosopher and as a person, this was the only way or path that made sense to my mind and felt right to my heart.

In this statement of my practice and its relationship to Dōgen's *Shōbōgenzō*, I would like to share a few of Master Dōgen's formulations from *Shōbōgenzō* about embodiment, perception, and emptiness that touch me deeply. They are a guide for me about expressing the body's relations with the world and the myriad things. Part of the sadness I often feel is how contemporary American culture sees itself as increasingly embodied by fetishizing the body as a possession to be made more appealing or more powerful or efficiently functioning, rather than seeing the body as our way into experiencing our interconnection and interdependence with all other beings. Contemporary American culture turns to finding fulfillment in the body's relations with the world as still separate from that world and using the body as a vehicle of desires. From Dōgen's perspective, American culture is only increasingly deluded about what human embodiment is, because of its holding on to the body as an object of possession and identification, instead of as one's enmeshment in a larger whole. I experience our American culture's supposed celebration of the body as a plunge into deeper levels of suffering for those I care about who are my family, friends, community, and country, and I believe it stymies so many in our quest for spiritual liberation and even for some sort of philosophical clarity. These mistaken ideas about the body can be witnessed within our culture emerging in the problems of compulsive material consumption; an epidemic of obesity, spreading addictions to alienated sex, drugs, alcohol, the internet, frenzied entertainment, and other distracting activity; child abuse, elder abuse, animal abuse, and so on—in a long and saddening list of social ills that testify to clouded perception arising from mistreated and misunderstood embodiment.

In the *Shōbōgenzō* fascicle "Bendōwa [A Talk about Pursuing the Truth],"[1] which introduces the aim of the succeeding inquiries, Dōgen states:

> At this time, everything in the Universe in ten directions—soil, earth, grass, and trees; fences, walls, tiles, and pebbles—perform the Buddha's work. . . . The grass, trees, soil, earth reached by this guiding influence all radiate great brightness, and their preaching of the deep and fine dharma is without end. Grass, trees, fences and walls become able to preach for all souls, [both] common people and saints, and conversely

all souls, [both] common people and saints, preach for grass,
trees, fences and walls.[2]

In other words, the Dharma is taught by all things, because we are embodied beings, and they can speak with us directly through our senses and
bodies made of the same coming together of things. Yet this Dharma
teaching or radiation of Buddha Nature is not recognized by us in our
clouded state of body-mind, because we see grass, trees, soil, fences, and
walls as "objects." Our culture insists on the idea articulated by Descartes
that objects are beings we experience as resistant to us since they are self-
subsistent beings encountered by a self-subsistent, perceiving self. Then we
believe that objects are different from us and distant from us and can only
be grasped through categories. This imposition of categories onto our perceptions begins the relentless progression of dependent coorigination. This
form of apprehending the world as distant and adversarial feeds the desire
to incorporate the world into our being as it simultaneously dissipates our
felt apprehension of interdependence with the world. When we practice
zazen, we see more clearly this tragic falling away from who we are in our
dominant culture's advertisements and endless projects to master and gain,
and in how it leads us to consume always more to achieve status, while in
doing so we relinquish the ongoing nourishment of the world. This freely
given nourishment of senses that are cleared from grasping Dōgen calls the
"flowering in the air" or the "walking of mountains." They beckon to us.

The myriad things can only appear to us as they are in their formlessness and emptiness, or lack of self-subsistence, if we clear the mirror
of our embodiment. Then the experience of the world becomes transformed: "The world of consciousness, and the [world] of consciousness
of objects, lack nothing—they are already furnished with the concrete
form of real experience. The standard state of real experience, when activated, allows no idle moment. Zazen, even if it is only one human being
sitting for one moment, thus enters into mystical cooperation with all
dharmas and completely penetrates all times."[3] Practicing zazen, aligning
the body with the breath that is the wind of this cooperation, this interdependence, the Dharma resounds. Both these passages also allude to
the way in which embodiment is not "our" embodiment; in other words

there is no "the body" "possessed" by a human being—there is only a moment in the circulation of continual arisings of grass, trees, fences, and walls that moves within and through human embodiment as an activated experience of cleared perception, feeling, and consciousness.

These ideas are amplified in Dōgen's considerations of the *Heart Sutra* in the next fascicle of the *Shōbōgenzō*. For me, these ideas are the heart of my practice and the sense I have gained over the decades of coming into a different relationship to the world around me through zazen and these teachings. I feel so touched and given a gift of aliveness and wonder by the things around me: of course, each leaf, flower, tree, and hill, but also the color of the wall over there, its wood grain moving in a wonderful rhythm; even the sound of the car, which also hurts but in other ways helps our world, is a kind of song that I am privileged beyond my understanding to be able to hear. Of course, I also nudge my environment so that it cooperates generously to offer me even more of its gifts: as I write this piece, I have a gurgling, splashing waterfall fountain next to me and another a few feet away from me in a pond, and their song is indescribably delicious and energizing, as well as whispering within the steady flow of energy a relaxing calm that hopefully is woven into my words.

In the *Shōbōgenzō* fascicle "Maka Hannya Haramitsu [Mahā-Prajñā-pāramitā]," Dōgen gives an amplification of the wisdom of the *Heart Sutra*, at times quoting passages and at times expressing its sense in his own words. It seems important to me that he starts by quoting the first line of the sutra, but interjects a phrase of his own into the midst of the otherwise intact line as he writes, "When Bodhisattva Avalokiteśvara practices the profound *prajñāpāramitā*, the whole body reflects that the five aggregates are totally empty." Nishijima and Cross point out in their comments upon the text that this insertion of "the whole body" into the first line as the reflection of the emptiness of the five aggregates—that is matter, feeling, thinking, enacting, and consciousness—should be noted, especially since the five aggregates usually do refer to the body-mind, and Dōgen seems to be adding special emphasis to this notion of the whole body as being emptiness. When this wisdom is realized, he again quotes the sutra, "matter is just the immaterial and the immaterial is just matter," but he adds to these lines declaring that "matter is matter, the immaterial is the immaterial." By doing this, Dōgen tries to have us see that it is not the case that self-subsistent materiality is self-subsistent immateriality and vice versa. He is pointing to not some sort of mystical coincidence of opposite substances, but rather that both are empty—interdependent and inseparable—that is to say, foundationless, if one were to attempt to take them as states of being. What this means to me is that matter is matter in the sense that we know grass, trees, soil, fences, and walls as material beings, but their being material is foundationless, is interdependent and inseparable from the immaterial; and similarly, the immaterial is immaterial as we experience it in love, compassion, knowledge, in the realms of meaning that partake of no tangible matter, and yet this, too, is foundationless in the sense of interdependence and inseparability with the material. The material is the other side or the lining of the immaterial, and the immaterial is the other side or lining of the material.

These passages have guided me as a philosopher, teacher, and as a human being. I do not think ideas are separate from the things around us, nor is love, nor is freedom, nor is beauty, and to me that means always finding ways to make a material expression of all spiritual or intellectual ideas. It means that, as a friend, I must find a material expression of my care, or as a husband, it is most important in the ten thousand daily material acts of kindness and care that my love for my wife be expressed, not just in abstract feelings or thoughts or even just words. It means my students must show me an idea in a concrete action, like how they treat their children or parents differently if they are talking about the concept of respect or care or the categorical imperative or whatever idea or ideal they learn in a philosophy class. It is here, too, that I have always found a resonance in my regard for the thought of Merleau-Ponty when he writes "the invisible is not the contradictory of the visible: the visible itself has an invisible framework, and the in-visible is the secret counterpart of the visible, it appears only within it . . . it is in the line of the visible."[4] The invisible, such as this person's love or compassion showing in their shining face, is the lining, the other side of the visible yet only through and within the visible—not as other, not as another kind of substance, for neither is substantial. What we see of their visible eyes, of the lines of the cheeks and lips of their smile, of the open-hearted gesture of the

arms and shoulders, chest and hands, is also the invisible gleam of compassion, the light of their love, and the lines of concern and care. It is in
this looking around me with clearer eyes that I have brought my regard
for the teaching of Dōgen and Merleau-Ponty together.

Yet it is in my practice, the Buddha Way, and teachings like those of
Dōgen's that I find a path to try to enact and realize this kind of vision
that I also admire in the thought of Merleau-Ponty. Dōgen and Buddhism provide a concrete practice. For this to be realized as shining forth
in its truth, however, one must let drop the dualistic grasping mind. This
can only happen when the ego is freed from propping up its own identity
through seeing the world as self-subsistent beings and events that it needs
to incorporate into its own being. I suppose that is why the sutra that has
always meant the most to me is the *Heart Sutra*, and I feel grateful to
Dōgen for his commentary on it in *Shōbōgenzō*. The sutra tells us that the
five aggregates are "no matter, no feeling, [no] thinking, [no] enaction,
[n]or consciousness" as strivings of an agency upon or toward a world.
In this "nonattainment" of "unequaled equilibrium," there is no subject
to achieve anything, and the body that is no body as an object returns to
the open world. Dōgen's commentary on what this means cites a poem
and likens this "whole body" to a "mouth, hanging in space; / not asking
if the wind is east, west, south, or north"—a mouth that chatters for all
others equally, like the sound of a bell in the wind, which is wisdom, *prajñā*. The whole body "embodies" or brings forth the wisdom manifest as
all beings, which emerges from space as a nondiscursive communication
between beings and within each being; that is the ultimate wisdom. Our
"whole body" as suspended in the wind, in the currents of the air, and as
mouth, giving voice to all that the world continuously says to us, but of
no more self-importance than the lilting tones of the wind-chime singing
in the wind—this is a sense of my body that I can feel when I settle into
zazen.

In the fascicle "Genjōkōan [The Realized Universe]" Dōgen states:
"When we use the whole body-and-mind to look at forms, and when we
use the whole body-and-mind to listen to sounds even though we are
sensing them directly—it is not like the mirror's reflection of an image,
and not like the water and the moon. While we are experiencing on one

side, we are blind on the other side."[5] To look at the world as form—as having self-sufficiency, an independent identity—means that we only see one side, despite our believing we are being embodied and "sensing them directly." This kind of perception means that we limit ourselves; we bind ourselves to "experiencing one side," and we have lost sight of, are "blind" to, "the other side." We have, in our grasping need for identity, clung to form, and in doing so, a sense of self on the one side of the world as the observer has become self-enclosed, has again entered into dependent co-origination, which will leave us with a body of lack, of desires, for what it has lost sight of is its intrinsic Buddha Nature. This is not the body of embodiment as the whole body, but it is rather the body of delusion that is really a kind of disembodiment despite its apparent indulgence in the bodily; for what appears to this body are mere ghosts, even if our media culture holds these ghosts before us as the "good life" of fancy possessions and power over others. To let go, to be taken into the world, to come to ourselves from the ten thousand things around us has been my inspiration and the gift of practice for me. In looking around at our culture, it would seem to be an unending pressure and frustration to have to constantly and vainly attempt to produce ourselves and to burnish this sense of self, when instead we could cultivate hearkening to the way the world of all places and times calls us to join it. We can be the cosmos and not feel isolated and insignificant.

Dōgen contrasts this sort of perceiving the world with embracing the Dharma in which this-sidedness of self-perceiving is gone. He says: "To learn the Buddha's truth is to learn ourselves. To learn ourselves is to forget ourselves."[6] Taking in the world allows us to forget our identities as the self who has achieved this or that, owns this or that. It is not that we can't feel delighted by painting a beautiful painting, or in my case, teaching an exciting class, but it is to not get caught in taking it "seriously," which means "one-sidedly," since "I" did nothing. It was the students, the traditions of the university, the sky above, Socrates of thousands of years ago, the great-grandmothers of my students, the author of the book we are studying, the sun outside the windows, and myriad other beings that all worked for countless eons in being present in the experienced excitement of the class. We learn that to be what we are means to no longer be the one side of perceiving the world as self, but rather dropping into an encompassing, a being taken up into a walking of the world, in which there is no longer the unidirectionality of one as the source agent. As Dōgen continues, "To forget ourselves is to be experienced by the myriad dharmas. To be experienced by the myriad dharmas is to let our own body-and-mind, and the body-and-mind of the external world, fall away."[7] In other words, our realization of the dharmas comes from our openness to the dharmas speaking to us. Letting the alienating forms fall away from the world's appearance is to let the world act upon us. It is a clearing of the mirror of consciousness that clouds our views. That is to say, "our seeing" is not our seeing, but the seeing of the world's myriad beings, and "our body" is not our body, but the whole body of ourselves, the world, the myriad beings, all times and places. For me, Dōgen expresses not only the Dharma but its felt sense, as well as my philosopher's need to sketch out some sort of image of a deeper understanding in the silence that underlies words.

As someone who loves poetry, and finds it more of a pointer than most discursive language to what we experience "outside the boxes" of our categorizations, I appreciate Dōgen's own poetry, and his citation of poems, as in the fascicle "Shoaku Makusa [Refrain from Unwholesome Action]," when he quotes a poem to point to this larger body of which we are a current: "The Buddha's true dharma-body / Is just like space. / It manifests its form according to things / Like the moon [reflected] in water."[8] The whole body attuned to the Dharma is one in which manifests what the deluded mind experiences as other to itself, or what traditional Western philosophy calls "the object," but here the Dharma-body is not "my" body or "your" body, or "the" body, but fills space, is at one with space, visions forth the ten thousand things in manifestation with no distance to be overcome, like the unity of the moon shining on the surface of the water; the Dharma-body comes forth from within the very skin and flow of what it is.

The most meaningful passages for me in the *Shōbōgenzō* are in the fascicle "Sansui Kyō [Mountains and Waters Sutra]." Here, Dōgen explores the body and its liberated perception that has transcended the limitations of clinging to form, to dualism, and to ego-centered agency in articulating the walking of the mountains and our walking with them, and the ways of the waters walking as mountains and moving in all directions.

I will only explore briefly what it means to me when Dōgen declares: "The walking of mountains must be like the walking of human beings; therefore, even though it does not look like human walking do not doubt the walking of the mountains."[9] In our dominant culture, we believe that there is a problem in saying that the mountains walk, since we identify walking as a human activity of an agency of a certain form employing other forms, or in other words, working through causalities of identifiable relations among beings framed as mere objects and only objects. Certainly my students at college would look askance at a declaration of mountains walking. Yet, in this way, not only do we misunderstand the walking of mountains but we also misunderstand the ways in which we, humans, walk—a contention with which Dōgen agrees when he states: "If we doubt the walking of the mountains, we also do not yet know our own walking. It is not that we do not have our own walking, but we do not yet know and have not yet clarified our own walking. When we know our own walking, then we will surely also know the walking of the Blue Mountains."[10] Dōgen is pointing to the fact that there is no "the body" as an object that walks, at least not in its fullest meaning. We objectify ourselves and lose the depth of existence on this planet. We cut out so many levels of our connectedness with other beings, and the felt meaning we can enjoy, when caught up with other beings. There are other senses of "being moved" in our felt existence and in the perception of the world than the mere change of physical location. So, for example, I can be moved by a passage, and this changes who I am. I can be moved into other understandings and ways of existence through chanting the *Heart Sutra* or practicing zazen. So, it is the case that whenever I read these lines of Dōgen, I am walking with him and then have the felt realization that I have been walking with him and with the mountains all my life and even before my singular life. This sense can easily be lost in the bustle of everyday life. Yet I have experienced what Dōgen claims: that it may be hard at times to know our own walking as the walking of the myriad beings who are with us and within us and for whom we walk. Sometimes when we clear our spirit and our perception, we can feel how we have been walking with the Blue Mountains for all time and how the Blue Mountains have themselves been walking for all time and always will be walking.

But we must let drop our egoistically shaped and clung-to, objectified body. If we fail to let this objectified body drop, then we would miss out on the simplest of perceptions, like the fact that I soar in the sky with the birds overhead in looking at them, or that I hover with that bright green hummingbird that has whizzed by as I write this passage, or that I reside in the yellow black-eyed Susan blossoms who have been waving at me and thinking with me each day I write this essay. The hummingbirds, the black-eyed Susans, the lavender butterfly bushes, the trickling water in the fountain, among the myriad other beings, joined all my teachers and my family and friends in writing this essay, for which I am grateful.

Dōgen's evocation of mountains walking makes me envision the many paintings of mountains, and in these paintings, artists have articulated the walking of mountains that many of us do not notice. This thought, too, is a reference back to the beginning of my path. When I was a little boy, over my bed there hung a painting by Paul Cézanne, who spent many decades, especially his last decade, repeatedly painting Mont Sainte-Victoire in Southern France. The painting I grew up with had a mountain in the background and a body of water in front of it. I could feel them move, but I might have lost that feeling as I grew older and became engaged in the adult life of responsibilities and tasks without my Buddhist practice. Cézanne experienced some of what Dōgen expresses, as he said that he felt the mountain was painting itself through him. Whenever he painted a landscape, he would sit before it silently for hours of meditation, until he felt he had taken in the "motif" of what was trying to be expressed by the mountain or the field or the stones or the house. For Cezanne, "motif" could not be defined in words or ideas, but only by his paintbrush tracing out the expressive movements he experienced flowing through him from everything about him. If, as Dōgen says, human embodiment is like the mouth that hangs in space, then our expressions, such as a painting, do indeed preach the sermons offered by the earth, soil, grass, pebbles, and tiles to which we hearken as a body returning to them and through them to ourselves, having been moved or transformed.

My favorite Western philosopher, Maurice Merleau-Ponty, says something similar when he says, "He who sees cannot possess the visible unless he is possessed by it, unless he is of it, unless . . . he is one of the visibles, capable, by a singular reversal, of seeing them—he who is one of them."[11] For Merleau-Ponty, as for Dōgen, this "reversal"—that we are not seers without seeing through the seeing of all the myriad beings around us—may be better expressed by dispensing with any language that might be taken as either reification of ourselves and the world as objects or as referring to substances. Merleau-Ponty expresses this by saying our vision is not ours but rather "It is Visibility sometimes wandering and sometimes reassembled."[12] I think he means to indicate the foundationlessness of this seeing of the world by the world that is our seeing. This movement of things and humans through and within each other, as the way that the mountain paints itself through the painter or how we are walking with mountains, leaves the whole body not as "the body" confronting the world but as Dōgen puts it in the *Shōbōgenzō* fascicle "Busshō [Buddha Nature]": "If we seek the state of a body manifesting itself we should picture the roundness of the moon, and when we picture the roundness of the moon we should indeed picture the roundness of the moon because a body manifesting itself is the roundness of the moon."[13] The roundness of the moon, the waving of yellow black-eyed Susans, and the flitting of green hummingbirds are the body manifesting itself. We and the myriad beings are through and within each other and exist by becoming manifest in this moving, shining forth.

It is this sort of movement experienced in his silent meditation that may be expressed by certain artists like Cézanne. This kind of movement of things and humans through and within each other, as the way that the mountain paints itself through the painter or how walking with mountains only happens when we find the whole body not as "the body" confronting the world but as the *Heart Sutra* speaks: "in the state of emptiness, there is no matter, feeling, thinking, enaction or consciousness. There are no eyes, ears, nose, tongue, body, mind . . . there is no sphere of the eyes, nor any other elemental spheres."[14] There are only interdependent beings moving in and through each other, "flowering in the air" within the senses that are the manifestations of being round or yellow or shining brightly in the dark, and "walking with mountains" as manifesting the life of time everywhere, right here and now with us in stride with our steps. I can only use Dōgen's words and turn them around slightly in front of us to keep looking at their facets, because for me they express something that is preached by every leaf, every branch, every bird, every drop of water in the setting in which I am writing this.

However, my first reading and rereading of Dōgen's *Shōbōgenzō* was a section excerpted by Philip Kapleau where Dōgen writes about "Being-Time." It is time that takes me to my practice and permeates its sense for me. Finding ways to enter and affirm time is also the biggest challenge to my practice and my spiritual equanimity. Each time I sit in zazen, I experience what Dōgen has expressed about time. In the *Shōbōgenzō* fascicle "Uji [Being-Time]," Dōgen states that "because real existence is only this exact moment, all moments of Existence-time are the whole of time; and all Existent things and all Existent phenomena are Time. The whole of Existence, the whole Universe, exists in individual moments of Time."[15] It used to be that this sense was experienced by me in zazen—I was breathing and the Buddha was breathing and all those who had ever done zazen and were to do zazen were all breathing together, and the breath came not just from around and above and below but from the furthest reaches of space/time. Yet now I feel this more often at other times, too. I can fleetingly know in my *hara* the walking of all things, and yet since the fleeting is always there, even when I seem to have lost it, the walking always walks within. In the walking of the mountain, once perceived through the clearer human embodiment, there is the coexistence of the ancients, the times of flood and eruption, the paths of the myriad beings still resounding in the padding of those who move on its gentle slope now. This is some of what Dōgen's expression of the ongoing stride of the Blue Mountains means to me. When I can dwell in this stride and sense of all time now and in all things, then I can drop my harried loss of center in the bustle of postmodern life, then I can lessen my fright about loss and the death of those I love, and go beyond my lapses in affirming our existence.

Dōgen, having actualized the whole body of realization, can experience the mountain in its full showing of interdependence, and this has been my hope for our culture, for those I love, and for myself: to catch sight of this walking. Also like Dōgen, I know I have to learn to acknowledge, accept, and affirm that it will not be seen by all:

It is because the mountains are walking that they are constant. The walking of the Blue Mountains is swifter than the wind, but human beings in the mountains do not sense it or know it. Being in the mountains describes the opening of flowers in the [real] world. People out of the mountains never sense it and never know it—people have no eyes to see the mountains, do not sense, do not know, do not see, and do not hear this concrete fact.[16]

To be embodied means to be able to see the walking of the Blue Mountains at all different speeds and with differing rhythms, and to see beings opening like flowers, myriad other beings, all blossoming, walking, opening, and even flowing. Dōgen discusses how those who insist on enumerating properties of the mountains are startled to hear it said that the mountains flow, but this is the gift of human embodiment to take up and enter the flow, which is neither within nor without, neither merely visible nor invisible. To be a body, I have come to believe in my existence, is to be open to a depth of sense that wonder can sound but never fathom. This gift of embodiment leads Dōgen to conclude, "The Blue Mountains are already beyond the sentient and beyond the insentient. The self is already beyond the sentient and beyond the insentient. We cannot doubt the present walking of the Blue Mountains."[17] As long as I am given the gift of breath, I will vow to walk with the mountains and deepen my faith in the constancy of their walking, even if, in my inconstant practice at times I lose this clarity and openness of vision. Dōgen remains a teacher who inspires me, who I know is always walking on the path of insight, if I allow myself to go with him. The hills across the river face me each day and call me to their walk.

Gasshō.

PART II

SHUSHŌGI—TEXT AND COMMENTARY

Shushōgi
(*The Meaning of Practice and Verification*)

This translation of *Shushōgi* is taken from the *Soto School Scriptures for Daily Services and Practice*, ed. and trans. Carl Bielefeldt and T. Griffith Foulk, with Rev. Taigen Leighton and Rev. Shohaku OKUMURA (Tokyo: Sotoshu Shumucho and the Soto Zen Text Project, 2001).

As explained in the introduction to this volume, aside from the first sentence of paragraph ten, which derives from the *Avataṃsaka Sūtra*, *Shushōgi* consists of passages woven together from various fascicles of Dōgen's *Shōbōgenzō*. Prior to each commentary, we have indicated the fascicles from which the passages derive. Fascicle numbers provided are taken from the most readily available complete translation of *Shōbōgenzō*: Dogen, *Treasury of the True Dharma Eye: Master Dogen's Shobo Genzo*, ed. Kazuaki Tanahashi (Boston and London: Shambhala, 2010). Note that the numbering varies somewhat in other editions. With some modifications made for the sake of literal accuracy, we have borrowed translations of fascicle titles from the Tanahashi edition. We have also included transliterations of the original Japanese titles to assist the reader in identifying these fascicles in other editions.

GENERAL INTRODUCTION

1. The most important issue of all for Buddhists is the thorough clarification of the meaning of birth and death. If the buddha is within birth and death, there is no birth and death. Simply understand that birth and death are in themselves nirvana; there is no birth and death to be hated nor nirvana to be desired. Then, for the first time, we will

be freed from birth and death. To master this problem is of supreme importance.

2. It is difficult to be born as a human being; it is rare to encounter the buddha-dharma. Now, thanks to our good deeds in the past, not only have we been born as humans, we have also encountered the buddha-dharma. Within the realm of birth and death, this good birth is the best; let us not waste our precious human lives, irresponsibly abandoning them to the winds of impermanence.

3. Impermanence is unreliable; we know not on what roadside grasses the dew of our transient life will fall. Our bodies are not our own; our lives shift with the passing days and cannot be stopped for even an instant. Once rosy-cheeked youth has gone, we cannot find even its traces. Careful reflection shows that most things, once gone by, will never be encountered again. In the face of impermanence, there is no help from kings, statesmen, relatives, servants, spouses, children, or wealth. We must enter the realm of death alone, accompanied only by our good and bad karma.

4. Avoid associating with deluded people in this world who are ignorant of the truth of causality and karmic retribution, who are heedless of past, present and future, and cannot distinguish good from evil. The principle of causality is obvious and impersonal; for inevitably those who do evil fall, and those who do good rise. If there were no causality, the buddhas would not have appeared in this world, nor would Bodhidharma have come from the west.

5. The karmic consequences of good and evil occur at three different times. The first is retribution experienced in our present life; the second is retribution experienced in the life following this one; and the third is retribution experienced in subsequent lives. In practicing the way of the buddhas and ancestors, from the start we should study and clarify the principle of karmic retribution in these three times. Otherwise, we will often make mistakes and fall into false views. Not only will we fall into false views, we will fall into evil births and undergo long periods of suffering.

6. Understand that in this birth we have only one life, not two or three. How regrettable it is if, falling into false views, we are subject to the consequences of evil deeds. Because we think that it is not evil even as we do evil, and falsely imagine that there will be no consequences of evil, there is no way for us to avoid those consequences.

REPENTING AND ELIMINATING BAD KARMA

7. The buddhas and ancestors, because of their limitless sympathy, have opened the vast gates of compassion in order to lead all beings to awakening. Among humans and devas, who would not enter? Although karmic retribution for evil acts must come in one of the three times, repentance lessens the effects, or eliminates the bad karma and brings about purification.

8. Therefore, we should repent before buddha in all sincerity. The power of the merit that results from repenting in this way before buddha saves and purifies us. This merit encourages the growth of unobstructed faith and effort. When faith appears it transforms both self and other, and its benefits extend to beings both sentient and insentient.

9. The gist of repentance is expressed as follows: "Although we have accumulated much bad karma in the past, producing causes and conditions that obstruct our practice of the way, may the buddhas and ancestors who have attained the way of the buddha take pity on us, liberate us from our karmic entanglements, and remove obstructions to our study of the way. May their merit fill up and hold sway over the inexhaustible dharma realm, so that they share with us their compassion." Buddhas and ancestors were once like us; in the future we shall be like them.

10. "All my past and harmful karma, born from beginningless greed, hate, and delusion, through body, speech, and mind, I now fully avow." If we repent in this way, we will certainly receive the mysterious guidance of the buddhas and ancestors. Keeping this in mind and acting

in the appropriate manner, we should openly confess before the buddha. The power of this confession will cut the roots of our bad karma.

Receiving Precepts and Joining the Ranks

11. Next, we should pay profound respects to the three treasures of buddha, dharma, and sangha. We should vow to make offerings and pay respects to the three treasures even in future lives and bodies. This reverent veneration of buddha, dharma, and sangha is what the buddhas and ancestors in both India and China correctly transmitted.

12. Beings of meager fortune and scant virtue are unable even to hear the name of the three treasures; how much less can they take refuge in them. Do not, being compelled by fear, vainly take refuge in mountain spirits or ghosts, or in the shrines of non-Buddhists. Those kinds of refuges do not liberate from sufferings. Quickly taking refuge in the three treasures of buddha, dharma, and sangha will not only bring release from suffering, it will lead to the realization of enlightenment.

13. In taking refuge in the three treasures, we should have pure faith. Whether during the Tathāgata's lifetime or after, we place our palms together in gasshō, bow our heads, and recite: "We take refuge in buddha, we take refuge in dharma, we take refuge in sangha." We take refuge in the buddha because he is the great teacher. We take refuge in the dharma because it is good medicine. We take refuge in the sangha because it is an excellent friend. It is only by taking refuge in the three treasures that we become disciples of the buddha. Whatever precepts we receive, they are always taken after the three refuges. Therefore it is in dependence on the three refuges that we gain the precepts.

14. The merit of taking refuge in the buddha, dharma, and sangha is always fulfilled when there is a spiritual communication of supplication and response. When there is a spiritual communication of supplication and response, devas, humans, hell dwellers, hungry ghosts, and animals all take refuge. Those who have taken refuge, in life after life, time after time, existence after existence, place after place, will

steadily advance, surely accumulate merit, and attain unsurpassed, complete, perfect enlightenment. We should realize that the merit of the threefold refuge is the most honored, the highest, the most profound, and inconceivable. The World-Honored One himself has already borne witness to this, and living beings should believe in it.

15. Next we should receive the three sets of pure precepts: the precepts of restraining behavior, the precepts of doing good, and the precepts of benefiting living beings. We should then accept the ten grave prohibitions. First, do not kill; second, do not steal; third, do not engage in improper sexual conduct; fourth, do not lie; fifth, do not deal in intoxicants; sixth, do not criticize others; seventh, do not praise self and slander others; eighth, do not be stingy with the dharma or property; ninth, do not give way to anger; and tenth, do not disparage the three treasures. The buddhas all receive and uphold these three refuges, three sets of pure precepts, and ten grave prohibitions.

16. Those who receive the precepts verify the unsurpassed, complete, perfect enlightenment verified by all the buddhas of the three times, the fruit of buddhahood, adamantine and indestructible. Is there any wise person who would not gladly seek this goal? The World-Honored One has clearly shown to all living beings that when they receive the buddha's precepts, they join the ranks of the buddhas, the rank equal to the great awakening; truly they are the children of the buddhas.

17. The buddhas always dwell in this, giving no thought to its various aspects; beings long function in this, the aspects never revealed in their various thoughts. At this time, the land, grasses and trees, fences and walls, tiles and pebbles, all things in the dharma realm of the ten directions, perform the work of the buddhas. Therefore, the beings who enjoy the benefits of wind and water thus produced are all mysteriously aided by the wondrous and inconceivable transformative power of the buddha, and manifest a personal awakening. This is the merit of nonintention, the merit of nonartifice. This is arousing the thought of enlightenment.

MAKING THE VOW TO BENEFIT BEINGS

18. To arouse the thought of enlightenment is to vow to save all beings before saving ourselves. Whether lay person or monk, whether a deva or a human, whether suffering or at ease, we should quickly form the intention of first saving others before saving ourselves.

19. Though of humble appearance, one who has formed this intention is already the teacher of all living beings. Even a girl of seven is a teacher to the fourfold assembly, a compassionate father to living beings. Do not make an issue of male and female. This is a most wondrous principle of the way of the buddha.

20. After arousing the thought of enlightenment, even though we cycle through the six destinies and four modes of birth, the circumstances of this cycling themselves are all the practice of the vow of enlightenment. Therefore, although until now we may have vainly idled away our time, we should quickly make the vow before the present life has passed. Even if we have acquired a full measure of merit, sufficient to become a buddha, we turn it over, dedicating it to living beings that they may become buddhas and attain the way. There are some who practice for countless kalpas, saving living beings first without themselves becoming buddhas; they only save beings and benefit beings.

21. There are four kinds of wisdom that benefit living beings: giving, kind speech, beneficial deeds, and cooperation. These are the practices of the vow of the bodhisattva. "Giving" means not to covet. In principle, although nothing is truly one's own, this does not prevent us from giving. Do not disdain even a small offering; its giving will surely bear fruit. Therefore, we should give even a line or a verse of the dharma, sowing good seeds for this life and other lives. We should give even a penny or a single blade of grass of resources, establishing good roots for this world and other worlds. The dharma is a resource, and resources are the dharma. Without coveting reward or thanks from others, we simply share our strength with them. Providing ferries and building bridges are also the perfection of giving. Earning a living and producing goods are fundamentally nothing other than giving.

22. "Kind speech" means, when meeting living beings, to think kindly of them and offer them affectionate words. To speak with a feeling of tenderness toward living beings, as if they were one's own infant, is what is meant by kind speech. We should praise the virtuous and pity the virtueless. Kind speech is fundamental to mollifying one's enemies and fostering harmony among one's friends. Hearing kind speech to one's face brightens one's countenance and pleases one's heart. Hearing kind speech indirectly leaves a deep impression. We should realize that kind speech has the power to move the heavens.

23. "Beneficial deeds" means to devise good ways of benefiting living beings, whether noble or humble. Those who encountered the trapped tortoise and the injured bird simply performed beneficial deeds for them, without seeking their reward or thanks. The foolish believe that their own interests will suffer if they put the benefits of others first. This is not the case. Beneficial deeds are one, universally benefiting self and others.

24. "Cooperation" means not to differentiate; to make no distinction between self and others. It is, for example, like the human Tathāgata who was the same as other human beings. There is a way of understanding such that we identify others with ourselves and then identify ourselves with others. At such times self and other are without boundaries. The ocean does not reject any water; this is cooperation. It is because of this that water collects and becomes an ocean.

25. In sum, we should calmly reflect on the fact that the practice of the vow of arousing the thought of enlightenment has such principles; we should not be too hasty here. In working to save others, we should venerate and respect the merit that allows all living beings to receive guidance.

PRACTICING BUDDHISM AND REPAYING BLESSINGS

26. Arousing the thought of enlightenment is mainly something that human beings in this world should do. Should we not rejoice that

we have had the opportunity to be born in this land of the Buddha Shakyamuni and to have encountered him?

27. We should calmly consider that if this was a time when the true dharma had not yet spread in the world, we would not be able to encounter it, even if we vowed to sacrifice our very lives for it. We who have at present encountered the true dharma should make such a vow. Do we not know that the buddha said, "When you meet a teacher who expounds supreme enlightenment, do not consider his family background, do not regard his appearance, do not dislike his faults, and do not think about his conduct. Simply, out of respect for wisdom, bow to him three times daily, honor him, and do not cause him any grief."

28. That we are now able to see the buddha and hear the dharma is due to the blessings that have come to us through the practice of every one of the buddhas and ancestors. If the buddhas and ancestors had not directly transmitted the dharma, how could it have reached us today? We should be grateful for the blessings of even a single phrase; we should be grateful for the blessings of even a single dharma. How much more should we be grateful for the great blessings of the treasury of the eye of the true dharma, the supreme great dharma. The injured bird did not forget its blessings, but showed its thanks with the rings of three ministries. The trapped tortoise did not forget its blessings, but showed its thanks with the seal of Yubu. If even animals repay their blessings, how could humans ignore them?

29. Our expression of gratitude should not consist in any other practices; the true path of such expression lies solely in our daily practice of Buddhism. This means that we practice without neglecting our lives day to day and without being absorbed in ourselves.

30. Time flies faster than an arrow, and life is more transient than the dew. With what skillful means or devices can we retrieve even a single day that has passed? A hundred years lived to no purpose are days and months to be regretted. It is to be but a pitiful bag of bones. Even if we live in abandon, as slaves to the senses for the days and months

of a hundred years, if we take up practice for a single day therein, it is not only the practice of this life of a hundred years, but also salvation in the hundred years of another life. The life of this day is a life that should be esteemed, a bag of bones that should be honored. We should love and respect our bodies and minds, which undertake this practice. Depending on our practice, the practice of the buddhas is manifested, and the great way of the buddhas penetrates everywhere. Therefore, the practice of a single day is the seed of the buddhas, the practice of the buddhas.

31. These buddhas are the Buddha Shakyamuni. The Buddha Shakyamuni is "mind itself is buddha." When buddhas of the past, present, and future together fulfill buddhahood, they always become the Buddha Shakyamuni. This is "mind itself is buddha." We should carefully investigate who is meant when we say "mind itself is buddha." This is how we repay the blessings of the Buddha.

General Introduction

6 *Shushōgi* Paragraph 1

TETSU'UN DAVID LOY

The most important issue of all for Buddhists is the thorough
clarification of the meaning of birth and death.
—*From fascicle 11: "Shoaku Makusa [Refrain from
Unwholesome Action]"*

If the buddha is within birth and death, there is no birth and death.
Simply understand that birth and death are in themselves nirvana;
there is no birth and death to be hated nor nirvana to be desired.
Then, for the first time, we will be freed from birth and death.
—*From fascicle 93: "Shōji [Birth and Death]"*

To master this problem is of supreme importance.
—*From fascicle 18: "Hokke Ten Hokke [Dharma Blossoms
Turning Dharma Blossoms]"*

According to the Pāli Canon, Śākyamuni Buddha declared that all he
had to teach was *dukkha,* or "suffering," and how to end it. Whether we
understand Buddhism as a religion, philosophy, psychotherapy, or spiritual path, it begins and ends with suffering in the broadest sense: not only
physical and emotional pain but frustration, dissatisfaction, a basic disease that keeps festering. That life seems to be one damn problem after
another is not accidental: apparently it is the nature of our unawakened
minds to be bothered about something.

Health and wealth may hold some anxieties at bay—for a while—but
there is one fundamental and inescapable type of *dukkha* that haunts all of
us, consciously and/or unconsciously. To be human is to be self-aware, to
know that one is alive—and also to know that one will not always be alive.

Accordingly, *Shushōgi* begins by zeroing in on the essential question: "The most important issue of all for Buddhists is the thorough clarification of the meaning of birth and death." This passage from the *Shōbōgenzō* fascicle "Shoaku Makusa [Refrain from Unwholesome Action]" is hardly the only place in Dōgen's writings where he emphasizes that birth and death is the fundamental problem. The fascicle "Shōji [Birth and Death]" is indeed wholly devoted to addressing this great issue. Here is another translation of the concise and profound statement from that text that is reproduced in the opening paragraph of *Shushōgi*:

> Just understand that birth-and-death is itself nirvana. There is nothing such as birth and death to be avoided; there is nothing such as nirvana to be sought. Only when you realize this are you free from birth and death.

The paradox is breathtaking: a most precise presentation of the Buddhist perspective on life and death, and also the sharpest challenge to our usual way of understanding the relationship between life and death.

Traditional Christianity addresses our fear of death by postulating a soul that does not perish with the body. The Buddhist denial of a soul or self—nonself[1]—does not allow for that particular possibility, but for many Buddhists the duality between samsara (this world of birth-and-death, where there is suffering, craving, and delusion) and nirvana (without birth-and-death, where there is no suffering, etc.) serves the same function. Dōgen's assertion that birth-and-death is itself nirvana is a shocking refutation of such dualities. We are reminded of Nagarjuna's famous declaration in the first "Nirvāna" chapter (25.19–20) of his *Mūlamadhyamakakārikā,* the most important work of Buddhist philosophy:

> There is no specifiable difference whatsoever between nirvāna and the everyday world; there is no specifiable difference whatever between the everyday world and nirvāna.

> The sphere (*koti*) of nirvāna is the sphere of the everyday world. There is not even the subtlest difference between the two.

Understanding the everyday world (samsara) as the place where beings are born and die means that there are two problematic dualisms: our usual, commonsense duality between life and death (often translated as "birth and death"), and the Buddhist duality between this world (where birth and death occur) and nirvana. Dōgen deconstructs both dualities: when we realize the nonduality between birth-and-death and nirvana, we are also freed from the duality between birth and death. What is he pointing at?

Both dualisms are instances of a more general problem with dualistic thinking—good examples of how we "bind ourselves without a rope," to use the Zen metaphor. We often distinguish between polarities because we want one (for example, wealth) and not the other (poverty), but we cannot have either pole without the opposite pole because the meaning of each depends upon (denying) the other. If it is important for me to live a pure life, for example, I must be preoccupied with impurity: discriminating all situations and my responses to them into pure and impure. That is why "the only true purity is to live in a way which transcends purity and impurity," as Chan (Zen) Master Hui-hai put it.

The same problem applies to the dualism between life and death. Replacing the concepts purity-and-impurity with life-and-death implies living in a way that transcends life and death. As before, we discriminate between life and death in order to embrace one and avoid the other, and our tragedy lies in the paradox that these two opposites are also interdependent: there is no life without death and—what we are more likely to overlook—there is no death without life. The real problem is not death but the duality of life-and-death.

> At issue are the boundaries of the self as a symbolized entity, and for that issue the end and the beginning are of a piece. There is a clear sense of the relationship between awareness of death and a delineated self. The second is impossible without the first. Even prior to the disturbing syllogism, "If death exists, then I will die," there is an earlier one: "Since 'I' was born and will die, 'I' must exist."[2]

"Why was I born if it wasn't forever?" cried Ionesco. The Buddhist answer is that I cannot die because I was never born. If we can realize that there is no delineated ego-self that is alive now, then the problem of life and death is resolved. Nonself is thus a middle way between the two delusions of eternalism (there is a self that survives death) and annihilationism (there is a self that is destroyed at death). Buddhism resolves the problem of life and death by deconstructing it. This is not a clever intellectual argument that claims to solve the problem logically while leaving our anguish as deep as before. The evaporation of this dualistic way of thinking reveals what is prior to it. There are many Buddhist names for this prior, but it is significant that one of the most common is the unborn.

In the oldest Buddhist texts, the sutras of the Pāli Canon, two of the best-known accounts of nirvana[3] refer to "the unborn," which is proclaimed as the solution to birth-and-death. Similar claims are common in Mahāyāna scriptures and commentaries. The most important term in Mahāyāna philosophy is *śūnyatā*. The adjectives commonly used to explain *śūnyatā* are: unborn, uncreated, and unproduced. The laconic *Heart Sutra* explains that all things are *śūnya* because they are "not created, not annihilated, not impure and not pure, not increasing and not decreasing." Nāgārjuna echoes this in the prefatory verse to his *Mūlamadhyamakakārikā*, which uses negations to describe the true nature of things: they do not die and they are not born, they do not cease to be and they are not eternal . . .

Much later, Cheng-tao Ke of Yung-chia, a disciple of the sixth Chan (Zen) patriarch in Tang China, proclaimed: "Since I abruptly realized the unborn, I have had no reason for joy or sorrow at any honor or disgrace." The Unborn was also the central teaching of the seventeenth-century Japanese master Bankei: "When you dwell in the Unborn itself, you're dwelling at the very wellhead of Buddhas and patriarchs." The Unborn is the Buddha Mind, and this Buddha Mind is beyond living and dying.

Such a claim is possible only if our everyday, taken-for-granted dualism between life and death is not something in the world but a way of thinking projected onto the world, one of the conceptual structures with which we organize and understand our world—including ourselves. The way to resolve the suffering that accompanies this way of thinking is to realize the sense in which it is delusive. Since our minds have created this dualism, they should be able to uncreate or deconstruct it.

All this provides the context we need to understand the cryptic remarks of Dōgen on birth and death. Since his comments at the beginning of *Shushōgi* are so elliptical, it is helpful to bring in what he writes in the three main *Shōbōgenzō* fascicles that also address this issue. His most extensive remarks are in "Shōji [Birth and Death]," which includes not only the statement quoted earlier, but many other provocative assertions:

> If you search for a buddha outside birth and death, it will be like trying to go to the southern country of Yue with your spear heading towards the north, or like trying to see the Big Dipper while you are facing south; you will cause yourself to remain all the more in birth and death and lose the way of emancipation. . . .
>
> It is a mistake to suppose that birth turns into death. Birth is a phase that is an entire period of itself, with its own past and future. For this reason, in buddha dharma birth is understood as no-birth. Death is a phase that is an entire period of itself, with its own past and future. For this reason, death is understood as no-death.
>
> In birth there is nothing but birth and in death there is nothing but death. Accordingly, when birth comes, face and actualize birth, and when death comes, face and actualize death. Do not avoid them or desire them.[4]

From "Shinjin Gakudō [Body-and-Mind Study of the Way]":

> Not abandoning birth, you see death. Not abandoning death, you see birth. Birth does not hinder death. Death does not hinder birth. . . . Death is not the opposite of birth; birth is not the opposite of death.[5]

The following passage, from "Genjōkōan [Actualizing the Fundamental Point]," relates birth-and-death to time:

Firewood becomes ash, and it does not become firewood again. Yet, do not suppose that the ash is future and the firewood past. You should understand that firewood abides in the phenomenal expression of firewood, which fully includes past and future and is independent of before and after. Ash abides in its condition as ash, which fully includes before and after. Just as firewood does not become firewood again after it is ash, you do not return to birth after death.

This being so, it is an established way in buddha dharma to deny that birth turns into death. Accordingly, birth is understood as beyond birth. It is an unshakeable teaching in the Buddha's discourse that death does not turn into birth. Accordingly, death is understood as beyond death.

Birth is a condition complete in this moment. Death is a condition complete this moment. They are like winter and spring. You do not call winter the beginning of spring, nor summer the end of spring.[6]

What is Dōgen saying in these passages?

Enlightenment is not other than birth-and-death. Dōgen does not offer the consolation of some heavenly pure realm or any other immaterial dimension that transcends this world. We cannot escape birth and death, yet there is liberation in or rather as birth-and-death if we realize something about them.

Birth and death are not opposites. Birth is nothing but birth, death is nothing but death. Face and actualize them, says Dōgen: "Do not avoid them or desire them." Do not grasp at one and try to evade the other. Instead of repressing the problem of life and death, Dōgen's solution is a complete affirmation of both terms, an acceptance that is very different from our usual way of resigning ourselves to them. To deny that life and death are opposites is another way to point out the problem with dualistic thinking. The mutual dependence of those supposed opposites means I live my life paralyzed by dread of death, and I resist my death clinging to the supposed life that is being torn from my grasp. When life and death are not experienced as opposites they will not "hinder" each other in this way.

Then birth is no-birth, death is no-death. We come to the essential point: the way to transcend birth and death is to "forget yourself" in birth and death, to let go of the usual sense of a separate self that is *doing* the birthing or dying, and instead completely become the birthing and dying. When at the time for dying there is nothing but dying—tada, "just that!"—neither avoiding nor seeking it—then death is experienced as no-death. The same holds true for birth, of course, and birth as no-birth is perhaps easier to understand, because a "newborn" (an ironic term in this context) has no sense of being a discrete being (subject) that is enduring a process (predicate) that is distinguishable from itself (its own self). For that infant, birth is no-birth because there is no sense-of-self that is being born. But if no "I" is ever born then there is only the act of birthing, and if there is only the act of birthing then there is really no birth, because the concept of birth presumes that there is some being that is born. Instead, the act of birth-in-itself and (in exactly the same way) the act of death-in-itself are each "an expression complete in the moment" when not experienced in relation to the other or anything else.

To help us understand this, we can relate what Dōgen is saying about no-birth/no-death to his concept of *uji,* or "being-time." *Uji* is a term that Dōgen uses to describe the nonduality between things and their temporality: "time itself is being . . . and all being is time." Objects themselves are not in time, because time is not an objective "container." Rather, time manifests as the temporal processes we identify as objects. "The time we call spring blossoms directly as an existence called flowers. The flowers, in turn, express the time called spring. This is not existence within time; existence itself is time." If, however, everything is temporal—if, in other words, the world is composed not of things but of processes—there is an extraordinary paradox: if there is only time, there is no time. Like everything else, I am not in time because I am time. What I do and what happens to me are not events that occur in time; they are the forms that my being-time takes, when my activities are no longer situated within a clock-time understood as a container external to me. And to be time is to be free from time: if I am time, I cannot be trapped by time. Without time as an objective container, "I" live in what is sometimes called the eternal present. This is another aspect of, or another way to understand, birth as no-birth and death as no-death. I live in (or as) the "eternal now" whenever I nondually become what I am doing—whether it is birthing, dying, or anything else.

No-birth and no-death are particular examples of the more general process Dōgen famously describes in the "Genjōkōan [Actualizing the Fundamental Point]" fascicle: "To study the Buddha Way is to study the self. To study the self is to forget the self. To forget the self is to be actualized by myriad things." I am actualized by myriad things when there is no subject-predicate distinction between a discrete "I" that does something, no sense of a self that is separate from the world it is "in."

This actualization is not something to be grasped conceptually, because it is not something that the (sense of) self can do. That is why meditation is so important. In contemporary terms, the self is an impermanent and insecure psychological construct composed of mostly-habitual ways of thinking, feeling, acting and reacting, remembering and intending, and so forth. These mental processes still continue during meditation, yet because the mind does not respond to them—because it "lets them go"—the sense of a separate self is thereby deconstructed. The anxious self, which is usually preoccupied with trying to make itself more real, lets go and becomes no-thing. In terms of life-versus-death, the ego-self forecloses on its greatest anxiety by letting-go and dying right now. Die before you die, so that when you come to die you will not have to die, as a Sufi saying puts it. To "forget" myself in this way is to awaken to my true nature: I am not inside my head, looking at a world outside me; rather, "I" am one of the many ways in which the cosmos expresses itself, one of the myriad forms of *śūnyatā*, "emptiness," that cannot die because it was never born.

7 *Shushōgi* Paragraphs 2–4

DREW LEDER

It is difficult to be born as a human being; it is rare
to encounter the buddha dharma.
—*From fascicle 89: "Kie Buppōsō (or Kie Sambō)*
[Taking Refuge in Buddha, Dharma, and Sangha]"

Now, thanks to our good deeds in the past, not only
have we been born as humans, we have also encountered
the buddha dharma.
—*From fascicle 87: "Shukke Kudoku*
[The Virtue of Home Leaving]"

Within the realm of birth and death, this good birth
is the best. . . .
—*From fascicle 13: "Kesa Kudoku*
[The Power of the Kesa]"

Let us not waste our precious human lives, irresponsibly
abandoning them to the winds of impermanence.
—*From fascicle 87: "Shukke Kudoku*
[The Virtue of Home Leaving]"

Impermanence is unreliable; we know not on what roadside
grasses the dew of our transient life will fall.
—*From fascicle 5: "Jū'undō Shiki [Rules for the*
Hall of Thick Clouds]"

Our bodies are not our own; our lives shift with the passing
days and cannot be stopped for even an instant. Once rosy-
cheeked youth has gone, we cannot find even its traces.
Careful reflection shows that most things, once gone by,
will never be encountered again.
—*From fascicle 30: "Immo [Thusness]"*

In the face of impermanence, there is no help from kings,
statesmen, relatives, servants, spouses, children, or wealth.
We must enter the realm of death alone, accompanied
only by our good and bad karma.
—*From fascicle 87: "Shukke Kudoku [The Virtue of Home Leaving]"*

Avoid associating with deluded people in this world who
are ignorant of the truth of causality and karmic retribution,
who are heedless of past, present and future, and cannot
distinguish good from evil.
—*From fascicle 85: "Sanji no Gō [Karma in the Three Periods]"*

The principle of causality is obvious and impersonal;
for inevitably those who do evil fall, and those who do
good rise. If there were no causality, the buddhas would
not have appeared in this world, nor would Bodhidharma
have come from the west.
—*From fascicle 90: "Shinjin Inga [Profound Belief in Cause and Effect]"*

During the feast of Passover observant Jews recite the multitude of blessings received from God. After each one, all present call out "*Dayeinu!*"—
"It would have been enough!" It would have been enough to receive
manna from Heaven; but God also provided the grace of the Sabbath;
this too would have been enough, but God further gifted the books of the
Torah. And so on. The *Dayeinu* recitation reminds each person to have
an attitude of gratitude, and to utilize the blessings of God and tradition
to the utmost.

Here, Dōgen presents something like a Buddhist *Dayeinu*. Not only were we born, but born as humans (*Dayeinu*), and even more so, as humans who have encountered the Buddha's teachings (*Dayeinu!*). Our all-too-ordinary lives, filled with boredom, repetition, and disappointment, bear within them latent possibilities waiting to be seized upon with passion and commitment. "Wake up!" this passage shouts. It rings like an alarm clock.

Yet the Buddhist *Dayeinu* is not identical to the Jewish. Here there is no singular God who has bestowed these blessings (though buddhas and ancestors wait eagerly in the wings to help). And whereas *Dayeinu* emphasizes "the enoughness" of blessings received, Dōgen reminds us of the not-enoughness of our "good birth." In and of itself it does us no good. We may need to come back to suffer over and over again, unless we grab our opportunities.

Each day, they surround us. We awaken to a misty-warm spring morning. What a day!—if we but look around. We have a conversation with a friend, a spouse, a student. What a possibility for love!—if we but are open-hearted. We sit down to count our breaths. What a possibility for awakening!—if we but pay full attention. The "good birth" is not simply a historical fact, but presents itself at every moment to which we are fully present.

But this is no easy matter. As Thoreau writes, "The millions are awake enough for physical labor; but only one in a million is awake enough for effective intellectual exertion, only one in a hundred millions to a poetic or divine life. To be awake is to be alive. I have never yet met a man who was quite awake. How could I have looked him in the face?"[1] Of course, Dōgen believes we can look the Awakened One in the face (we have encountered the Buddha Dharma)—and therefore in the mirror.

So now is the time for the "good birth"—right now. It cannot have happened years ago, or occur years in the future. This moment is momentous. What else could be? As such, it must not be wasted. "Every moment and every event of every man's life on earth plants something in his soul." So writes Thomas Merton in a Catholic idiom. "For just as the wind carries thousands of winged seeds, so each moment brings with it germs of spiritual vitality that come to rest imperceptibly in the minds and wills of men. Most of these unnumbered seeds perish and are lost, because men are not prepared to receive them: for such seeds as these cannot spring up anywhere except in the good soil of freedom, spontaneity and love."[2] Therefore, as the text of the general introduction to *Shushōgi* continues:

> Let us not waste our precious human lives, irresponsibly abandoning them to the winds of impermanence.[3]

> Impermanence is unreliable; we know not on what roadside grasses the dew of our transient life will fall. Our bodies are not our own; our lives shift with the passing days and cannot be stopped for even an instant. Once rosy-cheeked youth has gone, we cannot find even its traces. Careful reflection shows that most things, once gone by, will never be encountered again. In the face of impermanence, there is no help from kings, statesmen, relatives, servants, spouses, children, or wealth. We must enter the realm of death alone, accompanied only by our good and bad karma.[4]

Now Dōgen is getting downright depressing. True, the fact of our fortunate birth, and the richness of each moment, presents us with incalculable opportunities—but these will shortly be snatched away. That which is born is ever dying. Rosy-cheeked youth? Think back to its fast friendships, wide-open dreams, travel adventures, amorous lusts. How quickly the dew of a transient life fades away, turning into the dust of memory, until "we cannot find even its traces." Or look to our future. This the Buddha did when he saw for the first time a sick man, an old man, and a corpse, and understood they were all himself—features of coming attractions. Entropy, the physicists tell us, lead all cosmic structures to break down. Unfortunately, that includes "me."

Who is this Dōgen, we might ask—a manic-depressive? He was just speaking of our incredible good fortune to be born human and to have encountered the Buddha Dharma, but now he says bleakly "you are dust, and to dust you shall return."[5] Which is it?

But, of course, both. Only through perceiving the two-sidedness of our existential situation can we be motivated to action. We must view this life—this moment—as incalculably precious. We must also realize how profoundly imperiled we are—how swiftly this opportunity will go down the drain. To ignore either is to fall into ignorance. Forget the singular good fortune of our birth, and life can seem but a dull and meaningless descent to the grave. Forget the truth of our death, and we fall into complacency. We must ever remember both. Impermanence enjoins that we act, and act now. It is now or never.

And no one will act for us. "In the face of impermanence, there is no help from kings, statesmen, relatives, servants, spouses, children, or wealth." It is not that we are existentially alone. Dōgen will say much of the blessings and support provided by buddhas, ancestors, and the spiritual sangha. We take refuge in that which is greater than self. Yet at the same time self-effort is crucial. We must rectify our own karma. No one will rescue us while we sit passively, absolved from taking responsibility.

In *The Way of Man According to the Teaching of Hasidism*, Martin Buber discusses the scene in Genesis where Adam hides, ashamed, and God calls out, "Where art thou?" It is not that God does not know. "This question," Buber writes, "is designed to awaken man and destroy his system of hideouts; it is to show man to what pass he has come and to awake in him the great will to get out of it. . . . Whatever success and enjoyment he may attain, and whatever deeds he may do, his life will remain way-less, so long as he does not face the Voice."[6] *Shushōgi*, too, is a voice bent on destroying our system of hideouts. It asks: "Where art thou?" It enjoins that we claim our way, make of our life a path that will lead us home. As the text continues:

> Avoid associating with deluded people in this world who are ignorant of the truth of causality and karmic retribution, who are heedless of past, present and future, and cannot distinguish good from evil. The principle of causality is obvious and impersonal; for inevitably those who do evil fall, and those who do good rise. If there were no causality, the buddhas would not have appeared in this world, nor would Bodhidharma have come from the west. The karmic consequences of good and

evil occur at three different times. The first is retribution experienced in our present life; the second is retribution experienced in the life following this one; and the third is retribution
experienced in subsequent lives. In practicing the way of the
buddhas and ancestors, from the start we should study and
clarify the principle of karmic retribution in these three times.
Otherwise, we will often make mistakes and fall into false
views. Not only will we fall into false views, we will fall into
evil births and undergo long periods of suffering.

Understand that in this birth we have only one life, not two or
three. How regrettable it is if, falling into false views, we are
subject to the consequences of evil deeds. Because we think
that it is not evil even as we do evil, and falsely imagine that
there will be no consequences of evil, there is no way for us to
avoid those consequences.[7]

If we want to make of our life a path that leads somewhere worthy, and if
we wish to think and act in a skillful and efficacious way, we must understand universal laws. To physically negotiate a hazardous world we must
know something of the laws of physics—force, gravity, momentum. We
had better know to get out of the way of an oncoming truck or that will be
the end of our way, at least in this particular lifetime. If we are engineers
constructing a bridge, we had better understand stresses, torque, and the
like, or risk seeing it collapse.

Similarly, Dōgen suggests we had better understand the workings of
karmic causality lest our life, and future lives, risk collapse. As Newton's
third law of physics states that every action provokes an equal and opposite reaction, so "inevitably those who do evil fall, and those who do good
rise."

This statement of lawfulness, stability, and predictability counterbal-
ances the previous discussion of the "winds of impermanence," and the
"dew of our transient life." Windy and dewy though the universe be, it
also has a rock-solid moral structure assuring causal karmic retributions
that will extend into the indefinite future.

If we do not understand this we manifest a third type of ignorance. Just as we must not ignore the precious opportunity of our birth; nor its fleeting, imperiled nature; so we also must not ignore the limitless consequences for good or ill of the actions we take at each moment. These three modes of awareness (the positive counterpart to the three modes of ignorance) operate synergistically to remind us of the infinite import of our choices. *Shushōgi* unremittingly ups the ante.

We need not accept all the Buddhist teachings on strict karmic causality and rebirth to feel the impact of such messages. Nor must we experience them as threat. They represent an invitation to live intentionally, moment to moment, with care and compassion for self and others. Imagine, for example, that a friend comes to you, irritable and despairing. In such a state she is probably not at her best—she may be impatient, even rude, as she blurts out her troubles. There, right now, you have before you a choice. You can listen, breathe, see deeply beneath the rude behavior to the pain that provoked it. You can treat your friend with compassion and seek a maximally helpful response. Thus you "get out of yourself" even though that self feels a bit offended, and distracted by other tasks. Conversely, you may fail to rise to the occasion. You may only half listen, glancing at your watch. You may even take offense at your friend's manner and withdraw into silence or walk off in a huff. But Dōgen has reminded us (1) that we are human, and know something of the Buddha Dharma; (2) that all is impermanent, and this moment will not come again; and yet (3) the consequences of this moment will last into the indefinite future. You will leave the conversation with an inner feeling of well-being, or of sullen guilt and irritation, that will affect your further day, and in some small way your character. Your relation with your friend will be enriched, with a strengthening of trust and care—or will be bruised, perhaps badly. Trust is not easily repaired. That person may not come again with her problems, or you to her. Karmic echoes resonate down a long hallway of time.

Hearing all this, we may shudder to reflect on our many ignorances, on the damage done. Yet *Shushōgi* will continue next with a piece of good news. Damage need not be irrevocable. Impermanence allows us ever to move forward. Moral causality assures the possibility of solid repair.

We can repent, eliminate, and purify bad karma. To be unaware of the possibility of repentance—and thus to fall into despair at our weak character and past failings—is a last form of ignorance from which we must awaken. Buber writes that God's question, "Where are thou?" can take a demonic form if it continues, "'From where you have got to, there is no way out.' This is the wrong kind of heart-searching, which does not prompt man to turn, and put him on the way, but, by representing turning as hopeless, drives him to a point where it appears to have become entirely impossible and man can go on living only by demonic pride, the pride of perversity."[8] Happily, Dōgen will now show us that "from where we have got to" there is indeed a way out.

8 *Shushōgi* Paragraphs 5–6

STEVEN DeCAROLI

The karmic consequences of good and evil occur at three different times. The first is retribution experienced in our present life; the second is retribution experienced in the life following this one; and the third is retribution experienced in subsequent lives. In practicing the way of the buddhas and ancestors, from the start we should study and clarify the principle of karmic retribution in these three times. Otherwise, we will often make mistakes and fall into false views. Not only will we fall into false views, we will fall into evil births and undergo long periods of suffering.

Understand that in this birth we have only one life, not two or three. How regrettable it is if, falling into false views, we are subject to the consequences of evil deeds. Because we think that it is not evil even as we do evil, and falsely imagine that there will be no consequences of evil, there is no way for us to avoid those consequences.
—*From fascicle 85: "Sanji no Gō [Karma in the Three Periods]"*

The darkness of ignorance is inseparable from nirvana. —*Dōgen*

One way to approach the early sections of *Shushōgi* is to see them as an attempt to draw together two concepts: karma[1] and repentance.[2] Section two of *Shushōgi* emphasizes repentance—the notion that negative karma can be eliminated through acts of contrition—which may appear to some to be a strikingly non-Buddhist idea. While the stress on repentance may in part reflect exposure to Christianity, given the growing presence of Christian ideas in Meiji Japan when *Shushōgi* was compiled, we must not conclude from this that the connotation of the term is the same. In fact, the question of what precisely *Shushōgi* means by repentance is one of the central questions of the text; but in order to appreciate the role repentance plays in *Shushōgi*, it is necessary to consider how Dōgen understands the concept of karma, which is the central theme of paragraphs five and six.

The discussion of karma in *Shushōgi* draws heavily from Dōgen's commentary on causality in the "Shinjin Inga [Profound Belief in Cause and Effect]" fascicle of *Shōbōgenzō*. At the heart of this fascicle is the Wild Fox kōan which tells the story of a former abbot who, after having taught his monks that those who are enlightened are no longer subject to cause and effect, is transformed into a fox for a duration of five hundred lifetimes. One day, seeking assistance in shaking off his wild fox's attitude of mind, the old abbot asked Hyakujō, "Is even someone who does the Great Practice subject to cause and effect?" Without hesitation Hyakujō answered, "Such a one is not blind to causality." Upon hearing this reply the old man was awakened and released from his fox body.

What is the relationship between karma and enlightenment? This is the central dilemma of the kōan. If the realization that accompanies enlightenment entails an awareness of pervasive emptiness, then it is plausible to suppose that karma too must be empty. This, of course, is the answer given by the old abbot who assumes that enlightenment is a release from cause and effect. But in his commentary on the fox kōan, Dōgen vigorously denies the emptiness of karma and makes it quite clear that no one escapes causation. "Be very clear about this," Dōgen writes, "no matter whether it is secular people or monastics who are arguing against the existence of cause and effect, they will be off the Path," for they falsely believe there is no difference between "not being subject to" and "not being blind to."

Like the old abbot, those who assume that enlightenment is a release from karma, and that causation is ultimately empty, fall prey to a powerful error of which they remain unaware. In believing they have achieved insight into the emptiness of things, they miss what is right in front of them—the dualism embedded in this frame of mind between a world conditioned by causation and a world unconditioned by causation, between samsara and nirvana. Those who assume that freedom means escape from causal conditioning immediately divide the world in two, and this dualism, far from offering release from karma, constitutes its source. There is a double ignorance at work here making such views particularly difficult to uproot once they take hold. It is for this reason that Dōgen, in *Shōbōgenzō*, identifies these individuals as being "most in the dark" and that *Shushōgi* expands on why such views are so resistant to corrective guidance: "Because we think that it is not evil even as we do evil, and falsely imagine that there will be no consequences of evil, there is no way for us to avoid those consequences."

The firmness of Dōgen's admonishment underscores the centrality of causation to the tradition of mindfulness. Unfortunately, however, the meaning of karma has often been misconstrued, especially in the West where it is used colloquially as a synonym for fate or providential justice. Within the Buddhist context, karma, which literally means volitional action or deed, has nothing to do with either reward or punishment, but is rather an expression of the ego. Dōgen tells us, "the principle of causality is obvious and impersonal," yet in our habitual state of awareness karmic causality appears to be quite the opposite: both obscure and personal. Ordinarily we are not aware of karma. While we are certainly aware of physical cause and effect relationships, we are largely blind to the cognitive side of causality, which stems from our self-conception. In fact, it is not too much to say that the primary effect of karma is the construction of the self in all its obviousness, which in being obvious makes karma disappear from our awareness. The obviousness of the self is, therefore, inversely proportional to the obviousness of karma. The more we experience life from an ego-centered point of view—that is to say, in a personal way—the further away we stray from grasping karmic causality—in other words, the less obvious it appears.

Being ignorant of the nature of causality, we fail to see how our own actions and perceptions form behavioral pathways, which profoundly affect our future actions. The most consequential result of these behavioral patterns is our tendency to act from a first-person perspective and explain our experiential encounters in terms of the centrality of the ego. The more we attempt to make sense of our experiences in terms of the ego, the deeper we plant the illusion of the self. This circle of intentional action, whereby the ego differentiates itself from the very world it strives to makes sense of, is karma—a form of cognitive causality together with the habits of behavior and awareness it creates and perpetuates. With this in mind, it becomes clear why the old abbot's question about not being subject to causality is flawed. The question itself serves only to tighten the grip of the problem and cannot be answered without participating in an error of five hundred lifetimes. Hyakujō does, of course, provide an answer to the abbot but the reply he offers is to a different question. Keep in mind that karma never occurs outside the self.

Karma, then, is the name given to a self-generated pattern of actions that establish an inside, which manifests an outside in relation to which we are normatively related. The coemergence of inside and outside, and the dualism this manifests, is the root of karma, which is referred to in the literature as a form of ignorance because of the assumption we make regarding the independence of both domains. On the one hand, we posit a fixed external world, while on the other, we take for granted a permanent self. This cognitive structure effectively serves to generate the boundary conditions of the ego. From the Buddhist point of view, to say that the ego is empty is not to say that it does not exist, but is rather to recognize that what the ego is, is precisely this projected appearance of permanence, the causal effects of which are karma. To be enlightened, therefore, is not to end karma, but to alter our awareness so that karma and mind are no longer two things. Under these conditions we are no longer blind to karma and it begins to loosen its grip, releasing us from lingering mental states that perpetuate the cycle of rebirth and draw us from one life to the next.

When the mind wanders beyond itself, discriminating between an internal ego and an external world, it erroneously locates karma outside of itself as well, and in doing so fashions the notions of transmigration and rebirth, which are simply metaphors for the wandering mind itself. In his commentary on the Wild Fox kōan, Shibayama Rōshi skillfully invokes the subtleties of this point. "When a fox is really a fox, and not a thought of discriminating consciousness moves there, he is truly 'a former head of a monastery.' When an old man cannot be an old man and goes astray with his dualistic thinking, he is a fox. If the mind does not wander, there is in effect neither transmigration nor rebirth. This is awakening."[3]

Strictly speaking, then, to be enlightened is to stand in no relationship whatsoever to karma. Where there is no distance there is no relation. Our impulse, of course, is to try to figure out how we are related to karma, but to pose questions about the nature of the relationship between karma and enlightenment, as the old abbot does, is to race swiftly down the wrong path. When one is a fox, Shibayama Rōshi instructs, simply be a fox. When one is an old abbot, simply be an old abbot. Life, like the kōan itself, is simply not a question. And yet, like the old abbot, all too often we are taken in by the need to find an answer. Life—what Dōgen called *genjō* or presence—is the great kōan, and literary kōans are merely instruments assisting us in paying attention to it. No more, no less.

Looking ahead to the next section, we can now say that within *Shushōgi* repentance must be understood not as an act of contrition but as the first honest glimpse of ourselves as the source of karma—the first indication of our willingness to pay attention. Everyone participates in karmic causality, but in acknowledging this, in declaring openly, bluntly, and without shame that our sense of self is entangled in karmic causation, we take the first step toward mindfulness and toward disposing ourselves to awakening.

Repenting and Eliminating Bad Karma

9 *Shushōgi* Paragraphs 7–10

STEVE BEIN

The buddhas and ancestors, because of their limitless sympathy, have opened the vast gates of compassion in order to lead all beings to awakening. Among humans and devas, who would not enter?
—*From fascicle 1: "Bendōwa [On the Endeavor of the Way]"*

Although karmic retribution for evil acts must come in one of the three times, repentance lessens the effects, or eliminates the bad karma and brings about purification.
—*From fascicle 85: "Sanji no Gō [Karma in the Three Periods]"*

Therefore, we should repent before buddha in all sincerity.
The power of the merit that results from repenting in this way before buddha saves and purifies us. This merit encourages the growth of unobstructed faith and effort. When faith appears it transforms both self and other, and its benefits extend to beings both sentient and insentient.

The gist of repentance is expressed as follows: "Although we have accumulated much bad karma in the past, producing causes and conditions that obstruct our practice of the way, may the buddhas and ancestors who have attained the way of the buddha take pity on us, liberate us from our karmic entanglements, and remove obstructions to our study of the way. May their merit fill up and hold sway over the inexhaustible dharma realm, so that they share with us their compassion." Buddhas and ancestors were once like us; in the future we shall be like them.
—*From fascicle 10: "Keisei Sanshoku [Valley Sounds, Mountain Colors]"*

"All my past and harmful karma, born from beginningless greed, hate,
and delusion, through body, speech, and mind, I now fully avow."
—*From the* Kegon Kyō *(The Avataṃsaka Sūtra or Flower Garland Sutra)*[1]

If we repent in this way, we will certainly receive the mysterious
guidance of the buddhas and ancestors. Keeping this in mind
and acting in the appropriate manner, we should openly confess
before the buddha. The power of this confession will cut the roots
of our bad karma.
—*From fascicle 10: "Keisei Sanshoku [Valley Sounds, Mountain Colors]"*

I begin with an initial observation: at first glance, repentance is not an
easy concept to square with basic Buddhist metaphysics. If we take the
doctrine of impermanence[2] and the doctrine of non-ego[3] seriously, then
it seems that we must take repentance to be a convenient conceptual
fiction, but one that is, strictly speaking, nonsensical. Ultimately the
"me" that repents is not the "me" that committed the wrongdoing that
demands repentance. Thus the "me" that repents is repenting for someone else's wrongdoing, and that makes no more sense than my repenting
for your wrongdoing. It is easy to conceive of my apologizing for your
misbehavior, but not of my repenting for it. The doctrines of non-ego and
impermanence seem to entail that repentance, at least as we ordinarily
conceive of it, is no more than a mirage.

Thus when Dōgen speaks of repentance in *Shushōgi*, it is worthwhile
to pause and reflect carefully on what he might mean. Much work has
already been done on whether what *Shushōgi* says about repentance is
consistent with *Shōbōgenzō*, or whether it more accurately reflects the
voice of the Meiji era Sōtō Zen reformers who sought to counteract the
spread of Christianity.[4] That question is not my concern here. Rather, I
am interested in what Dōgen means by repentance, and also in how he
means it.

The seventh paragraph of *Shushōgi* encapsulates an idea that is central
both to *Shushōgi* and to the debate about whether or not this fascicle
really is an accurate distillation of Dōgen's thought:

Although karmic retribution for evil acts must come in one of
the three times, repentance lessens the effects, or eliminates
the bad karma and brings about purification.[5]

Setting aside the question of whether the passage more accurately reflects
Dōgen or Dōgen Zen,[6] we ought to first recognize that *Shushōgi* was primarily compiled for the laity, not for clergy, and that laypeople are not
expected to understand the Buddhist doctrine of the two truths in quite
the same detail as monks and nuns. Thus the metaphysical problem of
repentance might be lost on the intended audience. But the more strin-
gent concern is both an ethical problem and an interpretive problem:
namely, how ought we to read this passage, and what lesson ought we to
take from it?

According to Steven Heine, *Shushōgi* has been criticized in recent
years for its apparent endorsement of the doctrine of "repentance equals
the eradication of evil karma," or *sange metsuzai*, as a panacea for the
consequences of improper or sinful behavior.[7] Here Heine takes up the
question of whether *Shushōgi* corroborates or contaminates Dōgen's
teachings in *Shōbōgenzō*, but I contend that we cannot address this
question until we answer the more pressing question of whether we
ought to read *Shushōgi* this way at all. I think the answer to that question
is clearly "No."

Reading this passage to mean "repent so that you can receive a lesser
punishment" is not only simplistic but also openly egoistic. Repentance
in the name of self-benefit is no repentance at all. Even little children are
taught to mean their apologies, and not simply to apologize in order to
get a lighter sentence, so to speak.

This simplistic reading is connected to what I take to be an overly
simplistic reading of the *Shōbōgenzō* fascicle "Sanji no Gō [Karma in the
Three Periods]," though one that is very easy to accept at first glance. One
of Dōgen's projects in this fascicle is to address the question of why good
people are so often visited by suffering they do not seem to deserve. This
is the problem of evil that has long plagued theologians of the Abrahamic
traditions, who face an apparent logical contradiction if they contend
both that evil exists and that an omnipotent creator exists who is also

morally good. Buddhism does not posit the existence of such a being, but according to Dainen David Putney, the Buddhist must still come to grips with the problem of evil, and indeed the problem was pivotal in Dōgen's life: "For Dōgen, the problem of evil could be stated as follows: If all beings necessarily and inherently 'possess' Buddha-nature, why is there delusion and suffering?"[8]

According to the tradition, this is the question that ultimately drove Dōgen out of his comfortable Tendai monastery on Mount Hiei and across the Sea of Japan, ultimately to the doorstep of Tiantong Rujing.[9] In the end Dōgen offers multiple solutions to this problem,[10] but for present purposes I will focus only on "Sanji no Gō," where he makes two parallel claims:

> Bad karma like this must—whether it waits for continuance or skips continuance—inevitably suffer its effect.

> Good karma like this must—whether it waits for continuance or skips continuance—inevitably receive its effect.[11]

The easy reading of "Sanji no Gō" would have Dōgen answer the perennial question of the problem of evil by saying, in essence, "Don't worry, everything will work out for the best." But this is no solution at all; rather, it simply amounts to saying that there is no evil. I think it unlikely that Dōgen should be immortalized for empty platitudes such as this.

Recall the initial observation that the concept of repentance seems to be at odds with basic Buddhist metaphysics regarding the impermanence of the agent. In point of fact, the problem runs deeper, for the doctrine of karma and the doctrine of impermanence seem to leave us with a contradiction with regard to moral accountability. If all is impermanent, then if you kick me in the shin, the you that initiated the kick is already gone by the time the kick makes impact, and the you that landed the kick is already gone by the time my brain interprets the neural impulses from my shin as painful.

If the penalty for kicking someone in the shin is a slap on the wrist, who deserves to pay the fine? The "you" that currently exists is not the one that kicked me, and the "me" that currently exists is not even the "me" that got kicked. Given the impermanence of all things, it is hard to see how good behavior deserves praise, or how wicked behavior deserves punishment. And if that is true, then moral accountability—and with it, karma—is nonsensical.

This is just a gloss of the problem, but there can be no doubt that it is a problem, because some of the sectarian divisions in early Indian Buddhism arose out of this problem. The Pudgalavādins first posited the *pudgala*, or person, as a solution to this problem, and the Sarvāstivādin position regarding the reality of past, present, and future—which, incidentally, has echoes in the *Shōbōgenzō* fascicle "Sanji no Gō"[12]—is another attempt at a solution. Thus, "don't worry, it will all work out for the best" is not only an inadequate solution to the problem of evil; it also allows the problem of moral accountability to pass by more or less unnoticed. The same is true of "repent in order to get a lighter sentence."

Allow me to return to the passage that I am concerned about interpreting, and that Heine is concerned about rectifying with *Shōbōgenzō*:

> Although karmic retribution for evil acts must come in one of the three times [*sanji no gō*], repentance lessens the effects, or eliminates the bad karma and brings about purification.

The facile reading of this passage seems to hinge upon misreading two later passages from *Shushōgi*, the first of which is the ninth paragraph:

> Although we have accumulated much bad karma in the past, producing causes and conditions that obstruct our practice of the way, may the buddhas and ancestors who have attained the way of the buddha take pity on us, liberate us from our karmic entanglements, and remove obstructions to our study of the way.

Note that Dōgen is not talking about eliminating bad karma. He speaks only of disentangling ourselves from its effects long enough to properly study and practice the Way. In effect, bad karma from the past is a disturbance to present meditation, something like having a radio on when one requires peace and quiet, and here Dōgen says the function of repentance is to turn down the radio, that is, to silence the disturbance long enough that we can study and practice the Way.

Now there is a legitimate question regarding what "study and practice of the Way" means in *Shushōgi*. *Fukanzazengi* (*Universally Recommended Instructions for Zazen*) and *Shōbōgenzō* (*Treasury of the True Dharma Eye*) as a whole clearly indicate that the meaning of this is to sit zazen, while zazen is mentioned not once in the entirety of *Shushōgi*. That is a problem of its own, and I think it surely arises from the Meiji era reformers' interest in making Sōtō Zen more palatable to a public that was becoming increasingly enamored with Christianity. And because those reformers were responding to the spread of Christianity, it is all too easy to read the repentance they focused on in *Shushōgi* as mirroring the Christian notion of repentance. But Christianity has no doctrine of non-ego to contend with. Thus it is not only that Dōgen Zen does not conceive of repentance in the Christian sense; Dōgen Zen cannot conceive of repentance in the Christian sense.

The same idea appears in a second passage from paragraph ten of *Shushōgi*:

> "All my past and harmful karma, born from beginningless greed, hate, and delusion, through body, speech, and mind, I now fully avow." If we repent in this way, we will certainly receive the mysterious guidance of the buddhas and ancestors. . . . The power of this confession will cut the roots of our bad karma.

Here again it is easy to take the superficial reading, holding that "cut the roots of our bad karma" means "erase our bad karma." If this passage had come from a Christian monk instead of a Buddhist one, I think this reading would not be superficial at all. But Dōgen literally cannot mean what a Christian monk means in this context, for a number of reasons: sin is not the same thing as bad karma, to sully the soul is not the same thing as to entangle, and the mere idea of the soul excludes the idea of *muga* or non-ego.

The more important message here—and indeed in everything *Shushōgi* has to say about repentance—is that by repenting we admit and embrace our past wrongs, and that by doing this we can get free of them long enough to properly and mindfully practice the Way.

So in conclusion, the advice in *Shushōgi* regarding repentance is not so far from some of the mandates of a Twelve-Step Program: without taking ownership of one's own wrongdoings one cannot have sustained clarity. Now how does this solve the metaphysical problem in my initial observation? That is, how does it square repentance with the doctrine of non-ego and the doctrine of impermanence? Because this is not repentance as an act of contrition for real past wrongs; it is a meditation aid. Embracing the enduring self as a tenet of conventional truth is good enough; one need not fully realize that there is no such self on the level of ultimate truth.

Perhaps this sounds to you like a cop-out. Think of it instead as an instance of *upāya* or skillful means. Those who fully realize non-ego as an ultimate truth have no need for repentance as a meditative aid, but for laypeople who have not yet attained this level of realization, it remains a useful tool.

In any case I cannot see how we can make sense of reading Dōgen's *Shushōgi* as endorsing a conception of repentance that only makes sense in a theistic tradition. It is clearer to understand Dōgen's repentance in such a way that allows us to read *Shushōgi* as being consistent with *Shōbōgenzō*. At the same time we defend the nineteenth-century Sōtō reformers against the charge that they sold out Dōgen's teachings in order to promote a brand of Sōtō Zen that could better compete with Christian expansionism.

Receiving Precepts and Joining the Ranks

10 *Shushōgi* Paragraphs 11–14

JOHN C. MARALDO

Next, we should pay profound respects to the three treasures of buddha, dharma, and sangha. We should vow to make offerings and pay
respects to the three treasures even in the future lives and bodies.
—*From fascicle 94: "Dōshin [Heart of the Way]"*

This reverent veneration of buddha, dharma, and sangha is what the
buddhas and ancestors in both India and China correctly transmitted.
—*From fascicle 89: "Kie Buppōsō (or Kie Sambō) [Taking Refuge in
Buddha, Dharma, and Sangha]"*

Beings of meager fortune and scant virtue are unable even to hear
the name of the three treasures; how much less can they take refuge
in them. Do not, being compelled by fear, vainly take refuge in mountain spirits or ghosts, or in the shrines of non-Buddhists. Those kinds
of refuges do not liberate from sufferings. Quickly taking refuge in the
three treasures of buddha, dharma, and sangha will not only bring
release from suffering, it will lead to the realization of enlightenment.

In taking refuge in the three treasures, we should have pure faith.
Whether during the Tathagata's lifetime or after, we place our palms
together in gassho, bow our heads, and recite: "We take refuge in the
buddha, we take refuge in the dharma, we take refuge in the sangha."
We take refuge in the buddha because he is the great teacher. We
take refuge in the dharma because it is good medicine. We take refuge in the sangha because it is an excellent friend. It is only by taking
refuge in the three treasures that we become disciples of the buddha.
Whatever precepts we receive, they are always taken after the three

refuges. Therefore it is in dependence on the three refuges that we gain the precepts.

The merit of taking refuge in the buddha, the dharma, and the sangha is always fulfilled when there is a spiritual communication of supplication and response. When there is a spiritual communication of supplication and response, devas, humans, hell dwellers, hungry ghosts, and animals all take refuge. Those who have taken refuge, in life after life, time after time, existence after existence, place after place, will steadily advance, surely accumulate merit, and attain unsurpassed, complete, perfect enlightenment. We should realize that the merit of the threefold refuge is the most honored, the highest, the most profound, and inconceivable. The World-Honored One himself has already borne witness to this, and living beings should believe in it.

—*From fascicle 89: "Kie Buppōsō (or Kie Sambō) [Taking Refuge in Buddha, Dharma, and Sangha]"*

One way to understand the third section of *Shushōgi* ("Receiving Precepts and Joining the Ranks") is first to ask: Who is it that practices? We might assume that it is each of us, each person addressed by this scripture. *Shushōgi* begins with the imperative of clarifying the meaning of birth and death, and we are born and die as individuals. Is it not as individual practitioners that we are called upon to clarify the great matter of life and death? Is it not incumbent upon each one of us to practice and verify enlightenment? *Shushōgi* ends with a reminder that clarification of the great matter of birth and death comes about through continual daily practice. But then it implies that this practice is not a solitary endeavor; it is "the practice of the buddhas." Indeed, paragraph 30 states that the practice of the buddhas is manifested through our practice.

The reference to the Buddha, Dharma, and Sangha also indicates that one does not practice alone. On a superficial level, this means that awakening of the Buddha, the truth of the Dharma, and the communal bond of the Sangha serve to support the efforts of the individual practitioner, to guide her or him in realizing enlightenment. The individual does not practice alone. On an ideal level more deeply informed by Dōgen's *Shōbōgenzō*, the realization that comes through practicing enlightenment is not the achievement of the individual at all, even as supported by a community, its teaching, and the example of the Buddha. Realization is the work of Buddha-Dharma-Sangha actualizing itself.

Buddhist traditions call Buddha, Dharma, and Sangha the "Three Treasures," with the implication that these three facets of Buddhism represent the richness of its resources. Individual and family devotees can rely upon these treasures, and in turn the Sangha is supported by the devotion, labor, and monetary donation of its members. Making offerings and paying respect to these treasures ensure their continuing presence throughout the changes in one's own life and body. The text appeals to a devotee's sense of tradition and responsibility when it says that our models, the buddhas and ancestors from both West (India) and East (China), have taught us to venerate the Three Treasures. But what is the nature of that which we are to venerate?

Are the Three Treasures something outside us, objects handed down from the past, or perhaps resources hidden within each of us individually, that each of us already has? The fascicle of Dōgen's *Shōbōgenzō* that *Shushōgi* quotes in the following paragraphs, "Kie Buppōsō [Taking Refuge in Buddha, Dharma, and Sangha]," suggests that neither of these is the case. Rather, the Three Treasures and their benefits present themselves when a certain communion, communication, or connection is realized among those who practice the Way, and the act of veneration fosters this realization. Veneration then is a way to recognize the bond that exists among us as sentient beings and to begin their realization as buddhas. The three treasures name a communal reality.

As the next paragraph indicates, we are fortunate even to hear of the Three Treasures, this resource common to us; we need not be led astray. The "shrines of non-Buddhists" refers to the challenges and suppression faced by late nineteenth-century Japanese Buddhism when Sōtō Zen laypersons and priests compiled *Shushōgi*. Today devotees may read the passage in a different light. If we do not believe in mountain spirits or ghosts and do not haunt shrines devoted to them to seek protection, we may take the imperative more generally as a statement to point practitioners in the right direction with the right motivation. The imperative "do not seek refuge outside the Way but instead take refuge in the Three Treasures" is then simply a pointer to what truly has liberating power: Buddha, Dharma, and Sangha. In English, to take refuge has the connotation of seeking a place of security and resting in it. So to take refuge in the Three Treasures would mean to find in them a place where one can feel secure and at home. While we may understand the phrase in this modern sense, the connotation of the original medieval Japanese phrase was probably somewhat different: accepting [the Three Treasures] as something to rely on, entrusting oneself to them.

Starting in the era before Dōgen's time, Japanese aristocrats and other laypeople would take part in a ceremony of "taking refuge" over and over again, perhaps to accept and then renew their vows to keep the precepts. Taking refuge had a strong, perhaps predominantly ritual function. Engaging in rituals runs the risk of "going through the motions" absent-mindedly, but it may also become a practice of attending to the matter at hand, which in this case means the content of the precepts [see next chapter] and ultimately the "great matter of birth and death" that is "the most important issue of all for Buddhists," as the opening of *Shushōgi* proclaims. When one attentively engages in a ritual, as a public or communal ceremony the ritual actively connects one to other practitioners and to the communal nature of the practice. One becomes part of a community, and in the case of a ritual devoted to the Three Treasures, one participates in the realization of Buddha, Dharma, and Sangha. These three together embody *bodhi* or enlightenment, which then is not reduced to some psychic state of an individual. Taking refuge can have liberating power because it invokes the power of a spiritual connection with all beings as they realize buddhahood.

As indicated in the ensuing (thirteenth) paragraph, the appeal to the Three Treasures also indicates that Sōtō Zen places its teaching squarely in the conventional Buddhist tradition. Taking refuge in Buddha, Dharma, and Sangha has been a traditional way to commit oneself to the Buddhist path, and it is still used ritually in many Buddhist schools to publically declare this commitment and become a member of a community. Today the ceremony of *jukai* (formally receiving the precepts) is frequently the way practitioners officially announce their affiliation with a particular Zen teacher and community. *Shushōgi* presents taking refuge as the entrance to receiving the precepts, with pure faith or trust as the entrance to taking refuge. If taking refuge in the Three Treasures means entrusting oneself to them, as previously suggested, then its first step is an act of placing one's practice in the hands of the Buddha, relying on the truth of the teachings, and taking the community as one's own. Taking refuge is then the way to one's own practice becoming the practice of the Buddha, who communes with all beings to practice the truth. The text likens this truth to good medicine, in other words, what we need to help us realize enlightenment. It likens the Sangha to an excellent friend, someone with whom we can bond, so that again our practice is never simply the practice of an individual. The triple recitation to Buddha, Dharma, and Sangha voices our solidarity with these facets of Buddhism. The repetition of "we take refuge in" echoes the continual nature of our practice.

Relying on the act of taking refuge and entrusting ourselves to the Three Treasures, we are able to receive the precepts. As vows to live or act in a certain way, the precepts express their own kind of bond, that between the present and the future—but not as two unconnected times. Just as taking refuge reinforces the bond between oneself and other practitioners and transforms personal practice into communal practice, gaining the precepts connects this moment of practice with the next moment, on and on. The precepts bind practitioners to each present moment, and their fulfillment is performed moment by moment, not some time in the future. The precepts too take the form of an ongoing practice.

As indicated in the fourteenth paragraph, the Buddhist notion of merit is often interpreted as the benefits or karmic virtue gained by one or more beings that can be transferred to another being. Merit then is a kind of discrete and even quantifiable asset that measures the gainer's good deeds or the power of his or her ritual action. *Shushōgi* implies that the merit of taking refuge is not confined to a favor bestowed, to a benefit gained by one's own good deeds, or transferred to others by ritual. It is the benefit realized when one practices with others sympathetically responding to one another. Indeed, this responsive communication extends to all beings, no matter how advanced on the Way or how deluded they may be. "Devas, humans, hell dwellers, hungry ghosts, and animals" name those who in dwell in five of the six mythological realms of transmigration. The allusion here points to the comprehensive community of beings who benefit throughout time from the practice of the sangha; thus all can be said to take refuge when one enters into this bond of communal practice. Generated by constant, repetitive practice, the merit extends beyond any one individual, and any one time and place of practice, to benefit all. Ultimately all beings are liberated by the threefold refuge whereby one's practice is entrusted to the Buddha, the Dharma, and the Sangha and identified with their activity. "Unsurpassed, complete, perfect enlightenment"[1] names the ideal state of being, as it were, of this triple reality, and there can be no greater benefit than realizing this state. That it has indeed been realized is verified by the existence of the Buddha, the World-Honored One.

The story is told of the dramatic moment in Śākyamuni's awakening when Mara, the lord of demons and symbol of distraction, makes one last attempt to block his realization. Śākyamuni reaches down and touches the earth, calling on the earth goddess to testify to his lifetimes of dedication to the liberation of all beings. This story of the earth bearing witness to Śākyamuni places him in communion with all beings and once again testifies to the communal nature of Buddhist practice. We discover who it is that practices when we entrust ourselves to and rely upon the Three Treasures, and they in turn are realized in our shared practice.

11 *Shushōgi* Paragraphs 15–17

Michael Schwartz

Next we should receive the three sets of pure precepts:
the precepts of restraining behavior, the precepts of doing
good, and the precepts of benefiting living beings.
—*From fascicle 89: "Kie Buppōsō (or Kie Sambō) [Taking Refuge in
Buddha, Dharma, and Sangha]"*

We should then accept the ten grave prohibitions. First, do not kill;
second, do not steal; third, do not engage in improper sexual
conduct; fourth, do not lie; fifth, do not deal in intoxicants; sixth,
do not criticize others; seventh, do not praise self and slander others;
eighth, do not be stingy with the dharma or property; ninth, do not
give way to anger; and tenth, do not disparage the three treasures.
The buddhas all receive and uphold these three refuges, three sets
of pure precepts, and ten grave prohibitions.
—*From fascicle 95: "Jukai [Receiving the Precepts]"*

Those who receive the precepts verify the unsurpassed, complete,
perfect enlightenment verified by all the buddhas of the three
times, the fruit of the buddhahood, adamantine and indestructible.
Is there any wise person who would not gladly seek this goal?
—*From fascicle 87: "Shukke Kudoku [The Virtue of Home Leaving]"*

The World-Honored One has clearly shown to all living beings
that when they receive the buddha's precepts, they join the ranks
of the buddhas, the rank equal to the great awakening; truly they
are children of the buddhas.
—*From fascicle 89: "Kie Buppōsō (or Kie Sambō) [Taking Refuge in
Buddha, Dharma, and Sangha]"*

The buddhas always dwell in this, giving no thought to its various aspects; beings long function in this, the aspects never revealed in their various thoughts. At this time, the land, grasses and trees, fences and walls, tiles and pebbles, all things in the dharma realm of the ten directions, perform the work of the buddhas. Therefore, the beings who enjoy the benefits of wind and water thus produced are all mysteriously aided by the wondrous and inconceivable transformative power of buddha, and manifest a personal awakening. This is the merit of nonintention, the merit of nonartifice. This is arousing the thought of enlightenment.

—*From fascicle 1: "Bendōwa [On the Endeavor of the Way]"*

The first of the above paragraphs recommends that the practitioner heed the three collective precepts and the ten grave prohibitions. The following paragraph promises that by adhering to these precepts and prohibitions one will achieve buddhahood. And the final paragraph expounds on the unsurpassable qualities of nondual awakening.

It is stating the obvious that Dōgen recommends *shikantaza*, that is, zazen as the direct path of awakening. Putting aside philological debates about whether this section of *Shushōgi* adequately expresses Dōgen's view or not, we ask: what might be the value of taking up the three precepts and ten prohibitions for an awakened life? For even if zazen is the way, does this exclude the importance of adhering to the precepts and prohibitions? What might be the import of the precepts and prohibitions even if they are not centered as the fundamental practice of Sōtō Zen?

The precepts and prohibitions orient us toward awakening and empower awakened conduct. They are not awakened Mind itself, but rather are conventional expressions pointing us to Mind and its unsurpassable wisdom and compassion qualities. By taking up the three precepts of good conduct and sane motivation, our hearts open more readily into the ever-present compassion of our innate Buddha Nature, our whole being inspired toward fundamental practice—sitting becomes richer and more fruitful. Sitting now for all beings—sitting as all beings—innate goodness shines forth. We relax into the awakened Mind that is always already the case; the root *kleśas* of attachment, aversion, and ignorance therein unwind all by themselves, releasing our reified sense of a self that is solid and discrete, separate from others and the world. The three precepts are thus not to be understood as mere conventional codes—"conventional" in the Western sense of a fundamentalist wave of moral development—but rather are skillful aids in dehabituating our reified minds by releasing the obstructing *kleśas*, opening us to the innate goodness of our Buddha Nature.

When taken up skillfully and wisely, the ten grave prohibitions likewise enact their own special magic. To take them up in a moralizing and fundamentalist mode, which no doubt occurs within many Zen and Buddhist circles, is not the most mature way—or rather not the way that is going to benefit the majority of Western practitioners. Nor is ignoring or bypassing them a smart approach, one that unfortunately is adopted by many serious meditators who align themselves with Zen. Ken Wilber's discussion of "Boomeritis Buddhism" is instructive in this regard. Wilber, who has trained in the Zen and Tibetan Buddhist traditions (and whose realization has been authenticated by Buddhist lineage holders), sees Western psychology and the human potential movement of the past forty years as making important contributions to our understanding of the psyche. When asked in an interview in *Tricycle* magazine what was the difference between his realization and that of the Buddha, he responded with a playful smile that he, unlike the Buddha, could drive a Jeep. What Wilber was pointing to is that awakening does not automatically bring with it all human capacities and skill sets of body, speech, and mind. Beyond lineage myths and tales, one does not hear of someone awakening and then instantly start speaking for the first time, with no prior knowledge, twenty foreign languages in multiple local vernaculars; or, more ordinarily, never having seen a car before, getting into a Jeep and driving skillfully on the Autobahn. Many capacities of body, speech, and mind do not magically appear with awakening. These include, for Wilber, certain capacities that have been disclosed by developmental psychology and which unfold in a stage-like manner; where stages cannot be skipped, the growth from one stage to another in adulthood taking years, each new stage bringing forth novel capacities.

Bracketing the question whether these developmental waves are pan-cultural, they do seem to pertain to Westerners—and the evidence is striking. With reference to those Westerners taking up serious Zen practice, the developmental waves tend to be very high, having evolved beyond the conventional, "moralizing" uptake of norms and ethical codes. Premodern and traditionalist stages tend to be literalist, adopting such codes in a rigid manner, often as sacred absolutes that are the divine property of the group to which one belongs. Modern and post-traditional developmental waves also see and honor moral codes, but can in addition reflect on them, calling into question this or that norm or prescription; while seeing into how singular circumstances so often do not fit neatly into any given set of universal prescriptions or prohibitions.

Along with this gain in the capacity for moral reflection, there has been a downside to these developmental waves as they have taken shape in the boomer generation (and bequeathed to the wider culture): a regressive narcissism and egoistic inflation that can rear its head on the turn of a dime; it is the sentiment expressed in phrases like "nobody tells me what to do," "you are not the boss of me," and in contexts of decision making that "I must also have a say in all this." It is this mix of high moral development and regressive egoism that has come to inhabit many sectors of contemporary spiritual practice—justly prompting Wilber's phrase "Boomeritis Buddhism."

The ten grave prohibitions can thus prove baffling to the contemporary Western Zen practitioner. One approach for such a person is to force a kind of premodern, conventional adherence that is from the standpoint of the practitioner's own capacities felt at the core as inauthentic. Another is to exercise one's moral capacities of reflection, often leading to adjusting the prohibitions in ways that can readily activate the Boomeritis gene, the prohibitions coming to be treated as mere codes of a past and distant culture, thereby losing their guiding force. Fortunately, a third way is open to us that honors the wisdom of the prohibitions while leaving their meaning and sense open-ended as a matter of ongoing discovery.

In this third approach one contemplates one or another of the prohibitions in a mode of meditative inquiry, activating the discriminating wisdom of Mind to shine light upon and penetrate into the saying's sense.

This mode of inquiry is not confined to discursive mind but calls upon Mind itself to "see into" the phrase. It can be done during formal practice on the cushion or during one's everyday activities, and can include bringing our life circumstances into the inquiry. Energized by discriminating awareness, we look into the situation through the focusing lens of the prohibition, inviting insights to come forth at their own pace, in their own ways. The meaning of the prohibition comes alive for us with regard to our actual circumstances; it is the wisdom of Mind shedding light on skillful paths of action.

Nor does one so readily grow beyond paying attention to the prohibitions. For all we need to do is consider the repeated scandals in Buddhist circles of sex between teachers and students. To be sure, the sexual mores and practices of the contemporary Western world are not those of medieval Japan. But to think that one can simply bypass the third prohibition in the name of cultural difference or high levels of development (including citing one's grounding in awakened Mind) is to court the danger of inflicting needless pain through unwise and unskillful action (despite claims of "crazy wisdom"). Even lineage holders, who have been verified by the community of the competent to be awakened to their Buddha Nature, have time and again engaged in harmful sexual behavior with students, leading in some cases to damaging entire sanghas.

But how could this be so for an authenticated Zen master? Does not true awakening mean that wise and compassionate action spontaneously springs forth? Experience teaches us that someone can be deeply awakened, transmit Big Mind (and Big Heart), and still get caught up in specific kinds of egoistic habits and desires. While it does seem to be the case that some practitioners, as with great masters like Dōgen, awaken through a rigorous practice of zazen and come to embody an enlightened way of skillful living for all, there are others who awaken to "Big Mind" without question, yet karma does not simply burn off—or rather, certain strains of karma can still "catch" attention, or motivate action in an unconscious manner, leading to conduct that is less than skillful. From the side of the one who has awakened, all is perfection, all is beauty, even amid divine and boundless sorrow; yet from the side of other sentient beings, especially those who have not yet awakened, this awakened one's actions, when still caught in egoistic energy streams, impacts as harmful. Contrary to certain premodern religious myths, useful for inspiration but dangerous if taken up in an unquestioning precritical manner, awakening does not in all cases automatically mean that there are not some remaining "snags"—the record of humanity and its spiritual realizers proves this time and time again. The three precepts and ten prohibitions are thus a skillful set of contemplative phrases even for an awakened one.[1]

The ten grave prohibitions in this light are very special guidelines. They funnel us not only, as with the three precepts, in the direction of awakening but also prove to be wise checks about the depth of one's awakened action. Taking the prohibitions seriously, if not reductively, they allow us to check in about the skillfulness of our conduct—in the case of sex, whether all are served by such relations, or whether needless suffering is likely to be an outcome. The more we reflect on the third prohibition, empowered by the energy of our zazen practice, the more we see into what will be in a given circumstance the integrity of our sexual conduct. The result is not then a mode of moralized sexuality—it is a mature, wise, and loving way of sex appropriate for the singular situations in which we find ourselves.

Contemplating the precepts and prohibitions with a maturity fueled by our zazen practice, wisdom and compassion come to shine more and more through all domains of our conduct in the world.

Making the Vow to Benefit Beings

12 *Shushōgi* Paragraphs 18–20

Tetsuzen Jason M. Wirth

To arouse the thought of enlightenment is to vow to save all
beings before saving ourselves. Whether lay person or monk,
whether a deva or a human, whether suffering or at ease,
we should quickly form the intention of first saving others
before saving ourselves. . . . Though of humble appearance,
one who has formed this intention is already the teacher
of all living beings.
—*From fascicle 70: "Hotsu Bodaishin [Arousing the Aspiration
for Enlightenment]"*

Even a girl of seven is a teacher to the fourfold assembly,
a compassionate father to living beings. Do not make
an issue of male and female. This is a most wondrous principle
of the way of buddha.
—*From fascicle 9: "Raihai Tokuzui [Receiving the Marrow by Bowing]"*

After arousing the thought of enlightenment, even though we cycle
through the six destinies and four modes of birth, the circumstances
of this cycling themselves are all the practice of the vow of
enlightenment. Therefore, although until now we may have vainly
idled away our time, we should quickly make the vow before the
present life has passed.
—*From fascicle 10: "Keisei Sanshoku [Valley Sounds, Mountain Colors]"*

Even if we have acquired a full measure of merit, sufficient to become
a buddha, we turn it over, dedicating it to living beings that they may
become buddhas and attain the Way. There are some who practice

for countless kalpas, saving living beings first without themselves
becoming buddhas; they only save beings and benefit beings.
—*From fascicle 70: "Hotsu Bodaishin [Arousing the Aspiration for
Enlightenment]"*

The fact that *Shushōgi* is incontestably mired in the historical exigencies
of Meiji Japan and the politics of the Sōtō school tempts some lovers of
Dōgen to dismiss it out of hand. Despite its shortcomings, some of these
precious words in this section of *Shushōgi* indicate to me that this would
be a great loss.

This section opens with what is often called the bodhisattva vow:
the "vow to save all beings before saving ourselves." This vow is not a
mere resolve. It is the arousal of an aspiration to move beyond oneself
(one's ego-self) to an awakened self, which is simultaneously an affirmation in compassion of one's love for oneself as all beings and for all
beings as oneself. In "Hotsu Bodaishin,"[1] Dōgen writes that the meaning of arousing *bodhicitta* "is to endeavor without ceasing—in body,
speech, and thought—to help all sentient beings to arouse the aspiration for enlightenment. This leads them to the buddha way."[2] Indeed, it
is "to intend to awaken others before yourself."[3] Just as Dōgen had said
as early as his initial work, *Fukanzazengi* (*Universally Recommended
Instructions for Zazen*), when he advised negotiators of the Buddha
Way to have no mind on becoming a buddha, he again counsels: "Do
not think of yourself becoming a buddha by helping people to arouse
the aspiration to awaken others before awakening themselves."[4] One
also dedicates even that merit to awakening others. In the Mahāyāna
tradition, the bodhisattva ideal, awakening to oneself as dying to oneself by awakening to oneself as all others, is the awakening of the full
spectrum of the heart and mind, the realization of *bodhicitta*. For
Dōgen, the awakening of this aspiration does not come from within
oneself nor does it originate from the outside. The self with its interior
and its environmental exterior has simultaneously been cast away and
has fallen away to the awakening of the great earth itself. "However,
after arousing the aspiration, when taking up the great earth, all of it

turns into gold; when stirring the great ocean, it immediately turns into nectar."[5]

Bodhi[6] means awakened and is related to *buddha* (awakened one), while *citta*[7] means consciousness, the circulation of mind and heart broadly construed. In classical Mahāyāna, one can distinguish two non-dual and inseparable aspects of *bodhicitta*: the awakening of the desire to awaken, that is, the aspiration to awaken as the affirmation and cultivation of the bodhisattva ideal (the vow to save all others before oneself); and the consummation or realization or full awakening to the quality of consciousness already implicit in the desire to make the vow and to take up the way of the bodhisattva. For Dōgen, *bodhicitta* is the awakening of the great earth already as the awakening of the aspiration to practice. It is not the awakening of a desire to achieve something for oneself, to gain something new, because it is already the casting and falling away of body and mind,[8] the forgetting of the self. To practice the self is to forget the self and to forget the self is to be confirmed by the great earth. One does not practice the self for the sake of the self—have no mind on becoming a buddha and awakening is the awakening of the aspiration to awaken others. The aspiration to awaken oneself first so that one can subsequently awaken others is the counsel of demons and fraudulent teachers. "Never give up the vow of practice to awaken other sentient beings first. Know that any words that are against this vow are a statement of demons, those outside the way, or unwholesome friends."[9]

Even in washing one's face, Dōgen tells us in "Senmen [Washing the Face]," a fascicle that he returned to again and again, one is awoken to the aspiration to practice for others. "Do not make your scheming self a priority. Do not make your calculating self real."[10] By washing the face in the awakening aspiration that is *bodhicitta*, "you take up emptiness and wash emptiness"[11] and hence "washing the face is not merely removing filth; it is the life vein of buddha ancestors."[12] This is no less true, we learn in *Tenzo Kyōkun* (*Instructions to the Monastery Cook*)," for preparing rice. It is also no less true for how one wears one's robes, or how one greets another, or even how one wipes oneself after defecating outdoors because one had been practicing "under a tree or in an open field."[13]

Indeed, the awakening of the aspiration for awakening itself, the upsurge of *bodhicitta*, brings a sense of urgency to all activities. One practices as if one's life, indeed the earth itself, depends on it. "This may be the last day of your life,"[14] Dōgen warns, and as you awaken to the life of awakening, you may suddenly "have the sense of being a fish in a small puddle."[15] There is so little time and almost no water! Why have I wasted so much time and taken so many things for granted? Hence, echoing the fascicle "Keisei Sanshoku [Valley Sounds, Mountain Colors]," *Shushōgi* counsels: "Therefore, although until now we may have vainly idled away our time, we should quickly make the vow before the present life has passed."[16]

The nonduality of awakening to the aspiration to awaken and achieving awakening can also be seen in the great treasure of Indian Mahāyāna literature, the *Bodhisattvacharyāvatāra* (or *Bodhicaryāvatāra*), *The Way of the Bodhisattva*,[17] written sometime around the beginning of the eighth century of the common era by Śāntideva at the ancient Buddhist university Nālandā in what is now the northern Indian state of Bihar. The first aspect of *bodhicitta*, according to Śāntideva, is aspirational, *bodhicitta* "in intention," which makes possible "great results for those still turning in the wheel of life."[18] When *bodhicitta* is activated, when it is no longer merely aspirational, that is, as the heart and mind awaken, "willing to set free the endless multitudes of beings,"[19] then "a great and unremitting stream . . . rises equal to the vastness of the sky."[20] This is the flowing forth of itself of the bodhisattva ideal:

> May I be an isle for those who yearn for land,
> A lamp for those who yearn for light;
> For all who need a resting place, a bed;
> For those who need a servant, may I be their slave.[21]

It is critical to note that for Śāntideva both aspects are aspects of the nonduality of *bodhicitta*. Awakening to the aspiration to awaken and awakening as such are not separable and have no independent standing. In awakening to the desire to awaken one is already awake. One is awakening to the ongoing practice of awakening. It is only a matter of speaking that we say that full awakening issues from the awakening of the desire to awaken, as if this were a temporal succession of two separate states. It is part of the real genius of Dōgen to have articulated brilliantly and to have created new ways to express the nonseparation of these two aspects and to deny the delusional sense of temporality implied by the assumption that we are moving from one state to another state. We are not the reference point for time, moving from state to state through time. The awakening of *bodhicitta* as the aspiration to awaken others is the casting and falling away of oneself as a fixed point of reference for time itself.

This was also the question that had occupied Dōgen since his youth with his Tendai teachers on Hieizan: if we are already awakened, why do we have to practice? Or as he posed the question at the beginning of *Fukanzazengi*:

> The way is originally perfect and all-pervading. How could it be contingent on practice and realization? The true vehicle is self-sufficient. What need is there special effort? Indeed, the whole body is free from dust. Who could believe in a means to brush it clean? It is never apart from this very place; what is the use of traveling around to practice? And yet, if there is a hairsbreadth deviation, it is like the gap between heaven and earth.[22]

Although traveling to some exotic place is not required, this hairsbreadth deviation drove Dōgen to China where he realized that awakening is not an end state but the continuous life of practice, the "oneness of practice-realization."[23] Awakening is not hiding, waiting one day to show itself or for us to discover it. Running around looking for it is like running around looking for one's head. The ongoing quality of our realization is the ongoing quality of our practice. Dōgen consequently rejected as absurd the Kamakura Buddhist contention that we are living in the *mappō*, the degenerate third age in which we are incapable of realization. Dōgen countered in "Bendōwa" that the "Dharma is not divided into periods of truth, imitation, and decline. Instead it is taught that everyone attains the way by practice."[24] One does not practice in order to attain a temporally and spatially remote and presently detached state of awakening. One's practice is one's ongoing realization, indeed the elemental practice-realization of mountains and rivers and the great earth as such. The heart-mind right now is the Buddha (*soku shin ze butsu*), but the anticipation of the Buddha as elsewhere, waiting to intervene upon oneself or the earth was a heretical relationship to nature and the great earth. Practice is the ongoing realization of the great earth.

It is in this context of the bodhisattva vow and the arousal of the nonduality of *bodhicitta* that *Shushōgi*, like an immense breath of fresh air in a fetid tomb, counsels: "Do not make an issue of male and female." Indeed, the place of women in historical Buddha Dharma has largely been a debacle. It is true, however, that not making an issue of "male and female" runs the risk of further ignoring the voices of women, of disregarding the need to share in the work of constructing space and time for their action and for their voices to be heard here and now, and of failing to account for ancient and pervasive legacies of marginalization by making equality merely an issue of one's Buddha Nature, not one's social and political life. It is also true that *Shushōgi*, as we shall see, can and has been presented in this lamentable fashion. Nonetheless, one can also hear in these words something that remains precious: the echo of words that speak to a way out of this longstanding calamity.

Shushōgi begins its plea for inclusivity by presenting Dōgen's defense of the daughter of the dragon king, which is recounted by Mañjuśrī in the twelfth chapter of the *Lotus Sutra*. It tells the expedient narrative[25] of a seven-year-old girl who becomes fully awakened. "Her eloquence has no obstructions, and she is compassionately mindful of the beings as if they were her babies. Her merits are perfect."[26] Upon meeting her, Śāriputra is scandalized. "This is hard to believe. What is the reason? A woman's body is filthy, it is not a Dharma-receptacle. How can you attain unexcelled bodhi"?[27] The dragon girl proves Śāriputra wrong,[28] although the latter reflects an ancient (Buddhist) prejudice that a woman's body is too defiled to be purified or awakened in her lifetime.

Strikingly, Dōgen unequivocally rejects such misogyny as a fundamental betrayal of the Buddha Way. Already in the very early fascicle "Bendōwa" in the *mondō* or session of "questions and answers" that he presumably conducted with his beloved disciple and friend Ejō Koun, the thirteenth question is posed: "Should zazen be practiced by lay men and women, or should it be practiced solely by home leavers?" That is, is the practice of Zen only for monks and only to be practiced in monasteries? The answer is as concise as it is direct: "The ancestors say, 'In understanding buddha dharma, men and women, nobles and commoners, are not distinguished.'"[29]

This unequivocal critique is most powerfully present in the relatively early fascicle "Raihai Tokuzui [Receiving the Marrow by Bowing]," which is also the source for the defense of women in *Shushōgi*. "Why are men special? Emptiness is emptiness. . . . Both men and women attain the Way. You should honor attainment of the Way. Do not discriminate between men and women. This is the most wondrous principle of the buddha way."[30] He again takes up the grave mistake that Zen practice is the sole provenance of male monks and monastic life:

Hoping to hear dharma and leave the household does not depend on being female or male. Before becoming free from delusion, men and women are equally not free from delusion. At the time of becoming free from delusion and realizing the truth, there is no difference between men and women. If you vow for a long time not to look at women, do you leave out women when you vow to save numberless sentient beings? If you do so, you are not a bodhisattva. How can you call it the Buddha's compassion? This is merely the nonsense spoken by a soaking drunk shravaka.[31]

In Mahāyāna sutras like the *Lotus Sutra*, the śrāvaka is considered a mere auditor (the word means something like "voice hearer"). The śrāvaka learns the letter of the teachings but does not awaken to and embody them. Dōgen's implication is clear: a misogynist is ragingly drunk on fundamentalism, heartlessly asleep to the bodhisattva ideal. This toxic disposition included the reification of women into sexual objects. "Those who are extremely stupid think that women are merely the objects of sexual desire and treat women in this way. The Buddha's children should not be like this."[32] Referring to a practice already prevalent in Kamakura Japan, but which would get much worse in subsequent centuries, Dōgen also excoriated the prohibition of women or any other kind of laypeople from entering the vicinity of monastic practice, even when there were no monks present. Calling it a "ridiculous custom," he concluded, "if we laughed about it, our stomachs would be exhausted."[33] Indeed, who can in the final analysis stop women's awakening and hoard the Dharma to oneself, "who can try to block them and keep them from arriving at this stage" of "wondrous enlightenment"?[34] Sadly, Grace Shireson tells us that "despite Dōgen's writings about gender equality in the thirteenth century, discrimination against women persisted in the order he founded through the twentieth century. For example, around 1900 the Sōtō Zen school gave monks an average stipend of 180,000 yen a year in financial support, while nuns received on average only 600 yen a year."[35]

Critics like Bernard Faure charge that Dōgen early on talked the talk, so to speak, but he did not really walk the walk, remaining "if not fundamentally misogynist, at least very aware of the dangers that a feminine presence could bring to his community."[36] Faure is in the company of Japanese critics like Kasahara Kazuo, Hokoya Noriaki, and Tagami Taishū, as well as some western critics, who contend that while Dōgen may have defended women in his idealistic youth, the administrative demands and glories of Eiheiji eventually drove him to abandon these views. Despite scant textual or historical evidence, this speculation is now prevalent enough that it threatens to become the official account of this issue. Moreover, the accusation implies, almost meanspiritedly, that Dōgen, perhaps the most brilliantly philosophical of all of Zen's great teachers, was inconsistent or in the end just another venal and opportunistic Zen profiteer. Not only is the critique of Buddhist misogyny in the "Raihai Tokuzui" presented as fundamental to practice-realization—it is not an optional extension of the Dharma made in a moment of enthusiasm—but there is also no evidence that Dōgen sought to delete this fascicle from *Shōbōgenzō*. Given its unequivocal defense of women, this would have been an obvious thing to do when confronted with a dangerous "feminine presence." As Paula Kane Robinson Arai assesses the claim, which is largely based on a single line from "Shukke Kudoku [Leaving the Household]" that seems to have been taken out of context:

In the face of the sheer number of passages in Dōgen's texts that develop his positive view of women, versus the one sentence to the contrary—especially given that the sentence appears in a text revised after Dōgen's death—the case for Dōgen reversing his views on women is weak. To offer the compromise that Dōgen did not change his stance philosophically, but he just decided it was impractical to have women practicing at Eiheiji, does not resolve the issue. The historical record does not support such an interpretation.[37]

Arai cites evidence to the contrary, including Dōgen's first female disciple, Ryōnen, as well as a record of female disciples (and patrons) throughout the whole of his life as a teacher. I would add that, although it is certainly wise to avoid the trap of hagiography when it comes to our teacher ancestors, a serious study of *Shōbōgenzō* reveals a deeply ripening but always consistent wisdom and an unflagging, unapologetic, and fierce compassion. Most deeply, however, the depths of one's own practice verify the truth of Dōgen's defense of women. The point of practice is not to fixate on beliefs and submit to ideology. It is to open the true Dharma eye, to see more fully, to pluck out Bodhidharma's eye and make it one's own. It is not to resign oneself to the prevailing ideological hierarchies and grand idols of one's time. It is not that Dōgen was fairly enlightened for his time, but rather that the opening of the Dharma eye shatters the delusions of one's time, indeed, of ideological regimes of time as such.

Our betrayal through various forms of discrimination of the majority of our species, as well as our denigration of the earth and its many non-human coinhabitants, are symptoms of our toxic delusional ignorance[38] as well as our consequent greedy attachments[39] and hateful aversions.[40] Our hateful, self-serving, exclusionary views evince the somnambulance of the closed Dharma eye. Its refutation can today be seen in the extraordinary leadership and teaching of many contemporary women practitioners as well as the slowly emerging and much-needed emergence of a subterranean history of women's Buddhist awakenings.[41]

The so-called second founder and "mother" of Sōtō Zen, Keizan
Jōkin (1268–1325), shared Dōgen's commitment to gender inclusivity.
He "transformed Dōgen's preachings about women's equality into the
reality of authentic and independent women's practice and it was also
Keizan who transformed the Sōtō Zen school by including women and
laypeople more fully."[42] Even Faure admits that "he seems to have been
more ready to take a few risks in order to bring to pass this equality of
the sexes."[43] Keizan's mother, Ekan Daishi, had her own devout practice
and deeply influenced her son, who went on to do much for women's
practice, including conferring the first ever Sōtō Dharma transmission
to a woman, Ekyū, who then became a teacher in her own right. In 1322
Keizan built a monastery for women on his land adjacent to Yōkōji on the
Noto Peninsula and put his female disciple, Sonin, in charge.

William Bodiford has argued that not only must there "have been
many more nuns at medieval Sōtō monasteries than current records suggest,"[44] but there were also—unsurprisingly—significant gender dispari-
ties. He laments that the nonduality that clearly implies gender equality
remained largely on the theoretical plane and "medieval Sōtō teachers
did not advocate a status for women higher than that established by secular society. The equality of women was to be realized not in life, but in
death."[45] Later funeral rites sought to redeem women from the afflictions
of gender—one funeral sermon, for example, invoked the corpse to "shed
the defilement of the female body."[46] It would, however, get even worse in
the Tokugawa period (1603–1868), when Buddhist nuns suffered countless humiliations. They were, for example, unable to conduct funerals,
or ordain their own Dharma heirs, or even wear anything but the black
robes of a novice, regardless of how long they had been nuns.

The discrimination rampant in Buddhist practice has also become a
major theme for Critical Buddhists. They contend that the emphasis on
an original enlightenment relegates equality and inclusivity to an onto-
logically pure dimension while enervating any possible social critique
of—and even justifying—the many inequities of everyday life. The Buddha Dharma becomes reactionary, quietist, otherworldly, its own kind
of opiate of the people. This is an important critique, but even one of its
major proponents, Hakamaya Noriaki, recognizes that this position is

a betrayal of Dōgen. "Is it not ironic that this idea, criticized by Dōgen, has from his time up to the present been accepted as the mainstream of Japanese Buddhism, even among Sōtō believers who revere Dōgen as their founder?"[47] Hakamaya cites Dōgen's rejection in "Bendōwa" of the Senika[48] heresy: there is no eternal, abiding self, independent of the hold of time. It follows that writing off the many social injustices of contemporary life to karma and past wrongs is untenable. There is no eternal self subject to rebirth and therefore subject to karmic retribution. Nonetheless, this has been the trick: to move from an original oneness through karmic cause and effect to a justification of the inevitability of inequality. Hakamaya cites an exemplary Sōtō sermon on *Shushōgi*, which proceeds from "one reality, the same and equal" through karmic cause and effect so that it concludes with resignation "to the fact that the reason that we are born into this world and experience various and myriad punishments and rewards is entirely due to the causes and conditions of past lives."[49]

Hence, we have, using the terminology of Dongshan's influential "Five Ranks [*Goi*]," the ontological bifurcation of true (*shō*) unity and the inevitable provisional (*hen*) realm with all of its intractable disappointments.[50] As we have seen, Dōgen dismissed the very intelligibility of the separation of being into transcendent and immanent dimensions. There is no future enlightened realm to be one day attained through diligent practice and auspicious rebirth. Nonetheless, Hakamaya insists that the ideology of the absolute was what triumphed:

> No doubt the reason the very ideas that Dōgen criticized managed to become central to Sōtō lies in the fact that the mainstream of Japanese Buddhism itself has long been dominated by the doctrine of original enlightenment. Whether consciously or unconsciously, Sōtō simply allowed itself to be swept along with the current rather than follow Dōgen and swim against it. This resulted in a formulation of doctrine based on ideas like the "Five Ranks," which Dōgen himself had despised.[51]

The Five Ranks is an important teaching poem for both the Sōtō and Rinzai schools and it delineates the five relationships between *shō* (absolute unity) and *hen* (the provisional or relative realm). It is important to note, however, that, contrary to the reading that Hakamaya reports as prevalent, the highest rank has nothing whatsoever to do with a quietist abandonment of *hen* in favor of the attainment of *shō*; which amounts to what Hakuin diagnosed as Zen sickness, or *kūbyō*, a fixation with and attachment to emptiness. The highest (or fifth) rank is the complete nonduality and nonseparation of *hen* and *shō*. This is the consummation of the return to the marketplace in the famous oxherding poems and paintings and it is at the heart of Dōgen's insistence on the "oneness of practice-realization."[52] In his celebrated account of the practice of the Buddha Way in "Genjōkōan [Actualizing the Fundamental Point]" it is the final stage: "No trace of enlightenment remains, and this no-trace continues endlessly."[53] There is no separation between *hen* and *shō* but rather, as the Five Ranks puts it, the "attainment of their unity [*kenchūtō*]" in everyday life.

In a sense, one could say that the challenge of Zen practice, or perhaps any spiritual practice, is not awakening per se, but rather the transformation of one's modes of seeing, thinking, and acting in everyday life. Reflecting on his dual commitments to Zen practice and the Ignatian *Spiritual Exercises*, the former Jesuit Ruben Habito discerns a link between the threefold movement in the *Exercises* from purgation and repentance to illumination to the union with God in everyday life and the ongoing commitment to discernment of God in all things and the threefold movement in Zen from emptying (including presumably the emphasis in *Shushōgi* on repentance or *sange*) and enhancing one's capacity for concentration or *samādhi*[54] to *kenshō godō* (awakening to one's true face and realizing the Way) to *mujōdō no taigen* (activating the highest path), that is, the embodiment of Zen mind in everyday life and the ongoing cultivation of the way of the bodhisattva in all that one is and does. "The third stage is continually reinforced by the first two. In other words, we continue the process of bringing the disparate elements of our existential lives back to its center in the here and now. We also continue to receive new insights and ever deeper experiences of realization of what we have already come to know like the back of our hand."[55]

Yasutani Hakuun Rōshi called *mujōdō no taigen* "the actualization of the Supreme Way throughout our entire being and our daily activities. At this point we do not distinguish the end from the means. *Saijōjō*, which I have spoken of as the fifth and highest of the five types of Zen, corresponds to this stage.... Kensho when manifested in all of your actions is *mujōdō no taigen*."[56] We can infer that *mujōdō no taigen* is the fifth rank, Dongshan's "attainment of unity."[57] Yasutani chides the Rinzai sect for putting too much emphasis on *kenshō* at the expense of *mujōdō no taigen*. Although the Sōtō sect explicitly advocates *mujōdō no taigen*, Yasutani does not let them off the hook either. Their promotion of *mujōdō no taigen*

> amounts to little more than an accumulation of joriki, which ... "leaks" or recedes and ultimately disappears unless zazen is carried on regularly. The contention of the Soto sect nowadays that kensho is unnecessary and that one need do no more than carry on his daily activities with the Mind of the Buddha is specious, for without kensho you can never really know what this Buddha-mind is. These imbalances in both sects in recent times have, unfortunately, impaired the quality of Zen teaching.[58]

Yasutani had his finger on the pulse of an important aspect of the problem: the resistance to the full implications of the Buddha Way and its transformation into a way of being with others and the great earth.

Although it is not only right but also urgent to emphasize that the reading of the Five Ranks that reinforces phenomenal inequities by sequestering equality to an absolute realm is pernicious, it is not right to say that this was the actual force of the Five Ranks teaching.[59] Hakuin, for example, used it to profound effect against the somnolent Zen establishment.[60] He reminisced that one of the reasons that "Zen gardens of recent times are desolate and barren"[61] is because in the transmission of Dongshan's Five Ranks they "seemed to have discarded the words 'reciprocal interpenetration,' and to pay no attention to them. Thereupon the rhinoceros of doubt once more raised its head."[62] For Hakuin, the final stage was not merely the mutual integration of opposites, of emptiness and form, and the "effortlessness" in which one "lets the great uncaused compassion shine forth."[63] That is only the penultimate stage. For the final rank, "attainment of unity" (*kenchūtō*), Hakuin lets Dongshan's words speak for themselves: "All men want to leave / the current of ordinary life, / but he, after all, comes back / to sit among the coals and ashes."[64] Hakuin rails against the "blind" students who do not appreciate a genuine practice and study of the Five Ranks and "cannot get out" of the "mud of heterodox views . . . until death overtakes them."[65] "It is," Hakuin sternly concluded, "of the utmost importance to study and pass through the Five Ranks, to attain penetrating insight into them, and to be totally without fixation or hesitation."[66]

Nor is it true to say that Dōgen "despised" the actual teaching of the Five Ranks. He unequivocally opposed a reading of the Five Ranks that did not open the true Dharma eye, and he clearly denounced the misreading of the Five Ranks (and many other Chan teachings) that threatened to occlude the Dharma by holding that the absolute was elsewhere or that Buddha Nature[67] was found otherwise than in the now and here or that the Buddha Nature was an escape from the dust of everyday life rather than a radical awakening to it. Everyday life for the awakened heart and mind is a great miracle:[68] "Causing water to spout out of the head is a practice of the Lesser Vehicles. It is merely a minor miracle. On the other hand, fetching water is a great miracle," writes Dōgen in "Jinzū [Miracles]."[69] For this, however, one must not exclusively study the way with one's head or latch onto positions and enforce beliefs. It requires complete *shinjin gakudō*, study with body and heart-mind, practice and thinking.[70]

In "Butsudō [The Buddha Way]," not only does Dōgen consign the very idea of a Zen school to "demons who violate the buddha way,"[71] but he warns against grasping the teaching of the Five Ranks—or any other canonical teaching for that matter—dogmatically and consequently losing "genuine practice in the way of clouds and water."[72] In "Bukkyō [Buddha Sutras]," he defends Dongshan's teaching of the Five Ranks, but admonishes that it requires the "body and mind of the buddha dharma"[73] to be appreciated, claiming that such teachings are "not in the realm to be known by hasty people," although they have been "authentically transmitted."[74] In "Shunjū [Spring and Autumn]," Dōgen calls these "hasty people"—alas the legacy too often of Buddha Dharma, including Sōtō—"peasants or stray cats who have never understood the inner chambers of Dongshan."[75] The inner chamber is an awakening to the great earth. "Do not mistakenly say that Dongshan's buddha dharma is the Five Ranks of oneness and differentiation."[76] As we already could see in the "Raihai Tokuzui [Receiving the Marrow by Bowing]," justifying discrimination by adhering to the letter of some teacher's words or to the mere inertia of tradition or to the disengaged quietism that regards everything as fine because everything reflects the Buddha Dharma does not receive the marrow. We receive the marrow by bowing to all of the Way-seeking beings and do not discriminate by gender, age, race, class, creed, sexual persuasion, or even species. Awakening is receiving the great marrow of the earth itself with its myriad wondrous, singular beings. It is our vow and dedication to awaken to the great earth as the buddha lands.

Nonetheless, we hasty ones have often spoken of the Five Ranks in mistaken ways. In this respect, Hakamaya, in defending Dōgen, asks the hard question of Shushōgi: "Where shall we locate Shushōgi within Sōtō once we have understood that the preachers who worked from the text used it to foster social discrimination based on the doctrine of original enlightenment and counter to the ideas of Dōgen?"[77] Hakamaya admits that this is a "vexing" question for Sōtōshū.

In the world of Western Zen, however, Shushōgi has not had the same impact. It is rarely memorized or chanted and the discrimination and injustice endemic to Western capitalist cultures have their own respective genealogies. In the midst of the great earth crisis that modern and postmodern culture has wrought, we can see that we are starving in a sea of wealth. Rather than awaken to ourselves as a part of the earth's exuberant interdependence, we fear that we will never have enough and insanely hold that our economies can and should grow in perpetuity, regardless of the ruinous nature of that growth. We fill the bottomless well of ourselves with monstrously unjust habits of hoarding and consuming that harm most all creatures, not just the majority of the human population. Nonetheless, the faint call to awakening, the stirring of our hunger for a new earth and the coming of the buddha lands, can already be heard in the courageous and compassionate refusal in *Shushōgi* of its era's prerogatives as it, hearkening back to Keizan's generosity, reaches out to laypeople, and, most importantly, allows us to hear the Buddha voice and sense the Dharma eye of Dōgen by insisting: "Why are men special? Emptiness is emptiness. . . . Do not discriminate between men and women. This is the most wondrous principle of the buddha way."[78] That is the awakening to the great earth with all of its wondrous—and wondrously distinct—buddha voices.

13 *Shushōgi* Paragraph 21

LEAH KALMANSON

There are four kinds of wisdom that benefit living beings:
giving, kind speech, beneficial deeds, and cooperation.
—*From fascicle 70: "Hotsu Bodaishin [Arousing the Aspiration
for Enlightenment]" and fascicle 2: "Maka Hannya Haramitsu
[Mahā-Prajñāpāramitā]"*

These are the practices of the vow of the bodhisattva. "Giving"
means not to covet. In principle, although nothing is truly one's
own, this does not prevent us from giving. Do not disdain even
a small offering; its giving will surely bear fruit. Therefore, we
should give even a line or a verse of the dharma, sowing good
seeds for this life and other lives. We should give even a penny
or a single blade of grass of resources, establishing good roots
for this world and other worlds. The dharma is a resource,
and resources are the dharma. Without coveting reward or
thanks from others, we simply share our strength with them.
Providing ferries and building bridges are also the perfection
of giving. Earning a living and producing goods are fundamentally
nothing other than giving.
—*From fascicle 46: "Bodaisatta Shi Shōhō [The Bodhisattva's Four
Methods of Guidance]"*

The underlying assumption is that "merit" is a magical,
superstitious, or at best symbolic kind of thing that no rational,
scientifically minded person could take seriously as actually existing.
In the East Asian Buddhist tradition of which Japanese Zen is a part,
however, people do believe in merit. It is as real to them as, say,
money—that other symbolic, magical thing that has no substantial
existence but nevertheless serves to organize human societies
and get things done. There is no doubt that the main purpose
of sutra-chanting services in Zen is the production of merit
and that the formal dedication of that merit
is the performative heart and defining moment of the ritual.
—T. Griffith Foulk

Visitors to Sōtō Zen monasteries in Japan may be surprised to see how much of the monks' time is taken up with daily rituals and devotional ceremonies. For example, in sutra-chanting rituals, sacred verses are chanted to produce beneficial karma or "merit," and that merit is then dedicated to aid a variety of beings, from the dead ancestors of parishioners, to the monastery's patrons, to all sentient life. Indeed, at the local Sōtō temples scattered throughout Japan, the presiding priest's main task is to perform the rituals that generate merit for the benefit of the surrounding community, while the practice of zazen, either on the part of the priest or the local parishioners, is optional.[1]

Influential American Zen teacher Philip Kapleau recounts in his diaries his shock at seeing Japanese monks chanting and bowing before statues of the Buddha:

What a weird scene of refined sorcery and idolatry: shaven-headed black-robed monks sitting motionlessly chanting mystic gibberish to the accompaniment of a huge wooden tom-tom emitting otherworldly sounds, while the roshi, like some elegantly gowned witch-doctor is making magic passes

and prostrating himself again and again before an altar bris-
tling with idols and images.²

Watching these rituals of "sorcery and idolatry," which differed so strikingly from Kapleau's assumptions about Zen, he wondered to himself: "Is
this the Zen of Tanka, who tossed a Buddha statue into the fire? Is this the
Zen of Rinzai, who shouted 'You must kill the Buddha'"?³

This story of Kapleau's bewilderment highlights the fact that, outside
of Japan, Zen is often viewed as an alternative to traditional "organized"
religions, and the Zen teachings on mindfulness and meditation are often
read at the exclusion of instructions to perform seemingly superstitious
rituals such as the transfer of karmic merit. Yet in the *Shōbōgenzō* fascicle
"Bodaisatta Shi Shōhō [The Bodhisattva's Four Methods of Guidance],"
Dōgen notes that the monastery maintains intimate ties with parishioners who visit seeking to participate in merit-making rituals:

> The Buddha said, "When a donor comes into the monastic
> assembly, people admire him." You should know that the mind
> of such a person communicates subtly with others. Therefore,
> give even a line or a verse of the Dharma as an offering, sowing
> good seeds for this life and other lives."⁴

Dōgen's instructions to "give even a line or a verse of the Dharma" echo
the opening lines of the twenty-first paragraph of *Shushōgi*, in which
Dōgen reflects on the meaning of giving. Indeed, in these passages the
dedication of sutra verses is Dōgen's first example of what it means to
"give." Only secondarily does he mention giving money and material
resources.

Through this ordering I do not think that Dōgen upholds the transfer of karmic merit at the expense of more palpable forms of charity.
Rather, I think that he teaches us that the attitude cultivated through
merit-transfer rituals is the spirit of generosity in which all charity must
be carried out, else our charitable acts risk becoming self-serving bonds
of further attachment. Dōgen's commentary on giving touches on basic
questions at the heart of Buddhist philosophy and morality: If there is no

"self," then who is compassionate, who gives compassionately to others, and to whom are such gifts given? Let us take a look at a few of the relevant passages from the *Shōbōgenzō* fascicle "Bodaisatta Shi Shōhō [The Bodhisattva's Four Methods of Guidance]" with these issues in mind.

Here Dōgen makes it clear that giving should be not thought of simply as transferring something that I own to someone else. Giving cannot be measured in this way. His teachings remind us of the link between ego-identity and the accumulation of property. Occupying our minds with the objects that we own or desire to own easily feeds into the delusions of I-consciousness and subject-object duality. We reassure ourselves: "Surely I exist! Just look at all this stuff I have!" From this perspective, giving something away becomes an affront to the self's integrity. It is as if we lose a part of ourselves when we lose a part of our property. When we identify so strongly with our stuff, how can we possibly give freely and compassionately to others? To the contrary, we can only mete out our gifts stingily, making sense of them as bargaining chips, passing our stuff around to each other in a collective attempt to overcome our impermanence.

Dōgen says: "Whether we give a gift of Dharma or of material things, the act is endowed with the merit that accords with giving. Even though we own nothing, that is no reason not to give."[5] His point—that ownership has nothing to do with what I can give to another—is aimed directly at the calculating mind that can only imagine gifts as justified according to the everyday economics of ownership and exchange. He notes: "When treasure is left just as treasure, treasure becomes giving."[6] When we leave treasure as treasure, we do not limit things by imposing on them our stingy categories of "mine" and "not mine." Through this, we rediscover the abundance or "treasure" of things, and this abundance becomes giving. In other words, for Dōgen, freeing the self from the delusion of ownership is, in the same moment, the act of giving. When I own nothing, then all that I am and all that I have becomes endowed with the merit of giving: "having a body and giving up the body are both giving; making a living and producing things are nothing other than giving."[7]

Dedicating the merit of our acts to others, then, is a paradigmatic example of what it means to give: merit is limitless and does not belong to me, so it can't be "given" in the usual sense, and yet our generosity benefits ourselves and others now and in the future. Indeed, almost all activities inside a Japanese Sōtō monastery are dedicated to help others, which is to say, almost all monastic practices are acts of giving—the merit generated by practicing zazen, the merit of a monk's enlightenment, even, is not kept to aid the monk but is ritually dedicated for the sake of others. American meditators who are taught to practice zazen without the merit-transfer aspect may miss out on this crucial link between practice, enlightenment, and compassionate generosity.

Dōgen continues in "Bodaisatta Shi Shōhō": "We give 'self' to ourselves, and we give 'other' to others. The power of the causal relations of giving reaches to devas, human beings, and even enlightened sages. When giving becomes actual, such causal relations are immediately formed."[8] Here we see that even the apparent duality of self and other becomes a gift when the relations that sustain self and other are forged in the wellspring of compassion. The very act of giving enacts these relations, or, as Dōgen says, gives "self" to self and "other" to other.

Let us consider this gift of self and other in light of our earlier question: If there is no "self," then who is compassionate, who gives compassionately to others, and to whom are such gifts given? The act of giving does indeed draw lines from self to other whose causal effectiveness can be felt concretely. As Dōgen says above, "When giving becomes actual, such causal relations are immediately formed." In other words, when I give a gift, this act marks me as the "giver" and the other as the "recipient," and my gift may become the cause of various positive consequences. As we see, then, Dōgen does not speak of the merit that accords to giving in terms of overcoming the duality of self and other; rather, he seems to suggest that this merit has to do with redrawing the boundary of self and other on more compassionate lines. Generosity is our most powerful tool for bringing these lines into focus.

I would like to suggest that, as practitioners of Zen in the West, we can cultivate this generosity by giving to Zen a deep appreciation of the full range of its doctrinal, religious, and ritual practices—for example, by giving to Zen the open-mindedness to allow ourselves to take merit and merit-transfer seriously. In increasing numbers, Zen centers in the United

States, Canada, Latin America, Europe, and elsewhere are incorporating Buddhist merit rituals into their regular activities. For example, the Rochester Zen Center has held an "earth relief ceremony" that includes chanting, prostrations, and monetary donations. Afterward, the merit of the event is ritually transferred to designated recipients: "Tonight we have offered candles, incense, fruit, and tea / Chanted sutras and *dharani.* / Whatever merit comes to us from these offerings / We now return to the earth, sea, and sky."[9] Similarly, the Vermont Zen Center holds a variety of poverty and hunger relief ceremonies that combine merit-transfer rituals with the ceremonial collection of food and monetary donations from participants.[10]

Certainly these innovative Zen rituals, rooted in American soil, are in accord with Dōgen's views on giving. As he teaches, when we model all of our acts of giving on the paradigm of merit-making, we give freely and compassionately, unbound by the stinginess of the ego and its constant wheeling and dealing. In doing so, we enact a reality of compassion, whose lines of cause-and-effect will reverberate outward, "sowing good seeds for this life and other lives."

14 *Shushōgi* Paragraphs 22–23

Jien Erin McCarthy[1]

"Kind speech" means, when meeting living beings, to think kindly
of them and offer them affectionate words. To speak with a feeling
of tenderness toward living beings, as if they were one's own infant,
is what is meant by kind speech. We should praise the virtuous and
pity the virtueless. Kind speech is fundamental to mollifying one's
enemies and fostering harmony among one's friends. Hearing kind
speech to one's face brightens one's countenance and pleases one's
heart. Hearing kind speech indirectly leaves a deep impression.
We should realize that kind speech has the power to move the
heavens. . . . "Beneficial deeds" means to devise good ways of
benefiting living beings, whether noble or humble. Those who
encountered the trapped tortoise and the injured bird simply
performed beneficial deeds for them, without seeking their reward
or thanks. The foolish believe that their own interests will suffer if
they put the benefits of others first. This is not the case. Beneficial
deeds are one, universally benefiting self and others.
—*From fascicle 46: "Bodaisatta Shi Shōhō [The Bodhisattva's Four
Methods of Guidance]"*

The root of kind speech for Dōgen is compassion. In its attendant passage
in *Shōbōgenzō*, the first instruction in kind speech is not speech at all, but
first "to feel compassion" for other living beings and then to "offer them
caring and loving words." Compassion is a warm, deep feeling of empathy for others, akin to love, combined with the desire to relieve their suffering.[2] Here in *Shushōgi*, Dōgen encourages us to use not just kind but
affectionate words to express love and compassion for all living beings.

This might seem a simplistic phrase at first. A friend of mine who went to see the Dalai Lama came back greatly disappointed because, "All he said was be nice to people."

But what Dōgen (and I am sure the Dalai Lama, too) asks us to do here goes far beyond just "being nice." We are to treat others with the compassion we give babies, and not just any babies, but our own offspring. This counsels an intimacy that we usually reserve only for those in our closest circle—and perhaps we don't even always use loving and affectionate words with them either because offering such words requires really letting go of self so that we can speak from a state of compassion. Treating others from this place of intimacy also requires vulnerability on our part, which leaves us open to being taken advantage of. As Thomas P. Kasulis puts it: "Compassion breaks the shell of the ego so that the pain of others enters our own being."[3] And if we were not recipients of kind, caring words as babies or children, it not being automatic that parents always speak with kindness and affection to their children (and in some cases never), our ability to offer that affectionate care and kindness might well be damaged. As Dōgen points out in *Shōbōgenzō*, there is a direct link between compassion and kind speech: "Remember, kind speech arises from a loving mind, and the seed of a loving mind is compassion."[4] Here, by "loving mind," we understand *kokoro*, heart-mind—"the subjective side of the whole human state, not only intellectual consciousness."[5] The root of kind speech, which comes from a loving heart-mind, is being in a loving subjective state. This is compassion—to be in the world in such a way that we offer all living beings the same affection and kind words that we would offer to our babies. Japanese philosopher Watsuji Tetsurō, whose book *Shamon Dōgen*[6] was pivotal in the revival of Dōgen in Japan, writes about Dōgen's perspective on compassion:

> The greatest force obstructing love is selfishness, which takes root in what Dōgen calls body-mind; this can be nothing other than attachment to self. When one throws away all desires to preserve one's body-mind, empties the self, and lets oneself enjoy coming into contact with others, then love freely flows with the force of one's whole personality.[7]

In true Zen paradox, this personality empty of self is a greatly expanded personality—linked ever more deeply to others because the egocentric perspective has been dissolved. And yet, when thinking about speaking to the other as though they were an infant, we need to be careful, for what can appear to be kind words and care may prove on closer inspection not to involve care or compassion at all, and indeed to be the opposite—not a matter of caring for the other, but for meeting one's own needs or soothing one's own anxieties—something that is self-referential and even selfish.[8] This is why it is crucial that Dōgen's practice of kind speech and compassion be linked to the other practices that cultivate selflessness.

This idea of treating all living beings we encounter as if they were our own children also reinforces the idea of nondual interconnectedness that permeates *Shōbōgenzō*. In his *Ethics*, Watsuji holds up the relationship between mother and baby as the model for such an interconnectedness:

> So far as physiological bodies are concerned, they can be spoken of as easily as individual trees. But this is not the case with bodies viewed as expressions of the subjective or as persons in their concrete qualities. A mother and her baby can never be conceived of as merely two independent individuals. A baby wishes for its mother's body, and the mother offers her breast to the baby. If they are separated from each other, both look for each other with all the more intensity. Since ancient times in Japan, any attempt to isolate two bodies such as these from each other has been described by the aphorism "to wrench green wood." As is evident, a mother's body and her baby's are somehow connected as though one. . . . This power of attraction, even though not physical attraction alone, is yet a real attraction connecting the two as though one.[9]

Here, Watsuji provides an example that illustrates Dōgen's nondual interconnectedness evoked through the metaphor of the infant—the intimacy where the boundaries between self and other are collapsed. It is precisely, I think, the kind of love he writes about in his Dōgen book where he tells us that "Dōgen teaches of the possibility of a broad, all-encompassing love within the transparent world, from which attachment to self and love of fame are banished."[10] And yet we must be careful not to overpress the metaphor of the mother-child at work here, for such connections and relations have been used to oppress women and limit their freedom, and at the same time pay close attention to the fact that it is this unique connection between the mother's and child's bodies that is being held up as the model for ethics. What role might the gendered body play in reaching the state of nonattachment . . . in order, as we see here, to love that much more freely than we can when tethered to the self?

While thinking of all other living beings as our infants may not seem natural to us, Dōgen challenges us even further in the next part of the passage. Here, he asks us to give up our grudges and self-centered perspectives when he further advises us to bring this same kind, affectionate speech not only to one's friends but also to one's enemies. Easy enough to do for those we love, for our friends—in fact we get joy from brightening the faces of those we love. We can see disappointments lifted, hurts healed, harmony restored through kind speech among those we love, and this is deeply satisfying. Yet keeping this in the circle of those we love is not enough—we need to extend our affectionate words to "mollify our enemies" as it is stated here in *Shushōgi*, or "defeat our adversaries" as he puts it in *Shōbōgenzō*. The latter is a more challenging formulation of the *Shushōgi* passage. In "Genjōkōan," Dōgen reminds us that all things are Buddha Dharma . . . even our adversaries. This seems like an impossible task even in day-to-day life once we start to take it seriously. Caring tenderness for the colleague who cut me off at the knees in the last meeting? Kind, caring, tender speech toward someone who has wounded me emotionally? And yet if we can manage this—if we can do what Dōgen exhorts us to do, he promises us that we can change the world.

This sounds at first like a very naive view. "So we should have compassion and kind words for Saddam Hussein? For the people who are oppressors? For the person who abused me?" we might quite rightly ask. The compassion at the root of kind speech that Dōgen encourages here is not a naive panacea for the world's problems. In fact, looking to Dōgen for a system of ethics or to compassion as a solution for the world's problems, from a layperson's perspective in particular, will doubtless leave us dissatisfied:

> Dōgen does not try to alleviate the social unrest of the sec-
> ular world by means of secular excellence. After all, the root
> of social unrest arises from craving. The only salvation from
> this unrest is the way of the patriarchs, who cut away the root
> of this unrest. . . . Dōgen did not try to criticize things like
> the disputes over land, which were frequent in his day, or the
> severe oppression of farmers at the hands of landowners who
> had just gained power.[11]

This is puzzling. Does not compassion require us to want to relieve the suffering of those who are being oppressed? A question too broad to address here, but worth raising: What might a Dōgen-inspired response to such social injustice look like? For surely we are not to just let oppression flourish.

While his response to social-political problems may leave us wanting more, what Dōgen does offer us is an orientation for living, a way of being-in-the-world. First of all, the kind of compassion encouraged here is compassion for the suffering of the entire interconnected world—it doesn't mean that we have to condone actions, such as oppression, that do harm and cause suffering. Secondly, what this does mean is that we have to recognize that harmful acts and suffering do not happen in a vacuum. There are almost always innumerable interconnected causes that, when looked at from the perspective of nondual interconnectedness and compassion bring to light the fact that we cannot place blame for oppression or suffering simply on any one individual. Thirdly, we see that the compassion out of which kind speech arises provides a way to approach the problem of suffering or pain—one that demands we do not approach it from a self-centric perspective, but one that sees the web of interconnectedness and shared responsibility for suffering.

The attitude with which we encounter the other sets the tone for the encounter and everything that follows from it. If I rage at the colleague who continuously seems to undermine me, I am likely to not speak kind words to the clerk at the checkout at the grocery store who is dealing with a long line of people impatient to get home, and then when I get home myself, how likely am I to leave that anger and impatience at the door? Yet if we think of even our adversaries as our own infants, the anger and impatience in both ourselves and the other can begin to dissolve. For a parent, how selfless does one need to be at certain moments? Finding that place where we let go of our selves and find compassion even for our adversary, whether it is a baby who won't sleep, or someone standing in the way of something we want, or an oppressor, if we can let go of our ego-self and meet the other in the space of nondual betweenness, or interconnectedness, where compassion and kind speech meet, Dōgen promises us that we can change the world.

A kind word, for example, to someone who expects a confrontation is powerful; it "has the power to move the heavens." If we bring compassion and tenderness to a situation where before we might have brought indignation, the tenor of the encounter has the potential to change entirely. When anger arises, Dōgen asks us to stop and examine ourselves: "Why am I feeling like this?" we might ask, instead of giving in to the rush of anger. Even if we find the anger justified, responding from a Dōgen-inspired perspective requires us to then not hold on to that anger, but to see what kind of suffering it might be causing and find a way to relieve it. Taking a minute or two to be compassionate to ourselves, really examining our motives, might allow us the space to find compassion and kind words for the other. Dōgen also tells us, "Hearing kind speech indirectly leaves a deep impression." Returning to the metaphor of the baby or child, we know the power of this. Children unconsciously emulate those around them; as any parent knows, the very worst of one's language gets repeated in public by the child . . . so if we think of other beings as impressionable babies, yet not in the controlling way mentioned above, and consciously use kind speech and affectionate words that we want to be repeated, they will leave an impression. While this may seem hopelessly naive, and impossible to actually achieve, holding it as a goal seems essential.

The next paragraph is dedicated to beneficial deeds, which are like the jewels in Indra's net—what is reflected in one facet of one jewel is reflected in all the other facets in all of the other jewels in the net stretched across the infinite sky. In *Shōbōgenzō*, Dōgen tells us, "Benefit self and others alike. If you have this heart, even beneficial action for the sake of grass, trees, wind, and water is spontaneous and unremitting."[12] Beneficial deeds cause endless ripples of benefit to flow infinitely outward.

In the paragraph from *Shushōgi*, Dōgen evokes animals mainly because of their wordlessness. When we spontaneously respond to animals in need we are responding from a place of compassion, from *kokoro*. Animals cannot tell us what they need with words; we need to listen from a different place, from our heart-mind. We need to gaze into their eyes, listen to their breathing, watch how they move, and listen to them differently from how we listen to words. Where I used to live, in the late spring, snapping turtles tried to cross the road. They often seemed to get stranded on the two-lane highway—yet in those twelve years I can count on one hand the number of times I passed one stranded, alone, in the middle of the road. More often than not, someone had stopped to help the by now very frightened and defensive turtle get to the other side so that she might reach her destination, usually coming from or going to lay her eggs. I never once saw one hit or witnessed anyone veering to try to hit one. The spontaneous response of the person to the distressed tortoise evoked in Dōgen's example, or the snapping turtles in the North Country, is not about the needs of the person doing the beneficial deed. An angry snapping turtle does not seem in the least grateful for the help, in fact! Unlike our relationship with our pets, from whom we do expect love and affection, helping animals we come across in the wild or on the road or in the backyard, we truly expect nothing at all in return—they can't say thank you or promise us anything—there is no expectation of reciprocity here. Putting a fallen baby bird back in its nest, gently blowing the sand out of a ladybug's wings so she can fly again, helping the snapping turtle cross the road, these actions come from the place of compassion where our concern is only for the well-being of the other. Dōgen's compassion, whether for people, or animals, or water and trees, cannot be read as an ethical "system"—we will not find rules or imperatives here. Rather, we find an orientation from which to frame the problems—an orientation from which to figure out what the right thing is to do . . . and this will be exceedingly difficult, given that the nondual interconnectedness of everything means that "us" versus "them" or "wrong" versus "right" or "good" versus "evil"—the very frameworks we most often use to work out the "right" thing, the "beneficial" deed—must be abandoned.

However, this same interconnectedness that makes figuring out the "right" deed to do so terribly complex also brings back those deeds to benefit us, when performed from a place of selflessness, from the prereflective consciousness that one attains through zazen, which enables us to respond with an ethics of spontaneous responsiveness.[13] And responding from this place of selflessness allows the action to benefit us too as Dōgen evokes with his examples. The reference to the tortoise is from a Chinese chronicle that tells the story of Koyu, a man who saved a tortoise in distress and subsequently became governor of Yofu.[14] The story of the sparrow, from *Zokuseikaiki* (*Tales from Sei, Part Two*) recounts how a nine-year-old boy, Yoho, cared for an injured bird: "The sparrow repaid him with four white rings, which led Yoho to assume the three top official posts in the land."[15] The interconnectedness of everything, expressed in dependent origination, means that these deeds done for others also benefit ourselves—compassion shown to others, as with kind words, influences others to do the same and so our deeds come full circle.

As he himself recognizes, some may dismiss Dōgen's view as naive—and simply to say "do beneficial deeds and they will come back to you" may not be particularly profound . . . but to pursue such an attitude of compassionate responsiveness, where there are no signposts but your own heart, is anything but trite.

15 *Shushōgi* Paragraphs 24–25

DAINEN DAVID PUTNEY

"Cooperation" means not to differentiate; to make no
distinction between self and others. It is, for example, like
the human Tathāgata who was the same as other human beings.
There is a way of understanding such that we identify others
with ourselves and then identify ourselves with others. At such
times self and other are without boundaries. The ocean does
not reject any water; this is cooperation. It is because of this
that water collects and becomes an ocean.
—*From fascicle 46: "Bodaisatta Shi Shōhō [The Bodhisattva's Four
Methods of Guidance]"*

In sum, we should calmly reflect on the fact that the practice
of the vow of arousing the thought of enlightenment has such
principles; we should not be too hasty here.
—*From fascicle 10: "Keisei Sanshoku [Valley Sounds, Mountain Colors]"
and fascicle 25: "Bukkyō [The Buddha's Teaching]"*

In working to save others, we should venerate and respect the
merit that allows all living beings to receive guidance.
—*From fascicle 9: "Raihai Tokuzui [Receiving the Marrow by Bowing]"*

Dōji is the fourth kind of wisdom necessary for the Vow to Save All
Beings, the essence of the mind of enlightenment.[1] This is the vow not
to cross over to the "other side" (not to attain enlightenment or buddhahood) until one has helped all other beings attain buddhahood and nirvana. Among the four kinds of wisdom included in the vow, the first is

"giving," the second is "kind speech," the third is "beneficial deeds." These
have already been discussed. The fourth is "cooperation."

"Cooperation" is one possible translation of *dōji*, which literally means
"same" and "thing, matter, or task." Yokoi Yūhō[2] translates *dōji* as "identification" or "purpose." Nishijima and Cross note that *dōji* could also
be translated as "identity of task or purpose."[3] The text tells us that *dōji*
means "not different": not different in terms of self and not different in
terms of others[4]—in other words, "to make no distinction between self
and other."

We must be careful, however, not to misunderstand *dōji* in terms of
absolute identity. Throughout *Shōbōgenzō*, Dōgen discusses the fundamental Buddhist teaching of "no-self"[5] and "emptiness."[6] As Nāgārjuna
points out, *śūnyatā* is essentially "interdependent arising."[7] According to
the Buddha Dharma, there are no permanent and atomic (independent)
selves or entities. All dharmas (entities)[8] are interrelated and interconnected. All dharmas arise because of other dharmas. Thus, there can be
no absolute distinction between self and other. Every aspect of the self is
thoroughly interrelated with every other: its environment, other beings,
and other dharmas.

Beings are neither identical nor distinct. Dōgen is emphasizing their
close interrelationship, and thus their cooperation, their common task.
Dōji is the nondifference among beings and ultimately even the Buddha and the people to whom he preached the Buddha Dharma. The text
asserts that the Tathāgata[9] (Buddha), when he taught among humans,
was not essentially different than those humans. The teaching of *dōji* tells
us how we should identify and cooperate with one another.

Dōgen clarifies that self and others are without boundaries since they
are in constant and thorough interaction with one another through interdependent arising (*pratītyasamutpāda*). The ocean, he says, does not
reject water; this is interaction. This is why the water gathers together to
form the oceans.

The text for this passage is from Dōgen's *Shōbōgenzō* fascicle "Bodaisatta Shi Shōhō [The Bodhisattva's Four Methods of Guidance]," which
focuses on the four social relations discussed above. Here Dōgen tells
us that "the task of cooperation means, for example, concrete behavior,

a dignified attitude, and a real situation."[10] Dōgen is telling us that the real task of cooperation is not abstract but is always related to a concrete task. Dōgen clarifies that "There may be a principle of, after letting others identify with us, then letting ourselves identify with others. [All relations between] self and others are depend on the [particular] occasion."[11]

Dōgen quotes from the Daoist *Guanzi* (Jp. *Kanshi*): "The sea does not refuse water; therefore it is able to realize its greatness. Mountains do not refuse earth; therefore they are able to realize their height. Enlightened rulers do not hate their people; therefore they are able to realize a large following." Near the close of this fascicle Dōgen writes: "Thus the truth of cooperation exists both for enlightened rulers and for ignorant people and this is why cooperation is the conduct and the vow of a bodhisattva. We should face all things only with gentle faces."[12]

The ensuing paragraph relates to Dōgen's *Shōbōgenzō* fascicle "Keisei Sanshoku [Valley Sounds, Mountain Colors]," which expresses another facet of arousing the thought of enlightenment, teaching us in poetic terms that the whole world expresses the Buddha Dharma, including "rivers and valleys and mountains." All of nature is truth and therefore expresses the Buddha Dharma. This is another facet of *dōji*, cooperation.[13]

Also consider the *Shōbōgenzō* fascicle "Bukkyō [The Buddha's Teaching]," where Dōgen teaches us that all of the Buddha's sutras express the entire Buddha Dharma. Dōgen writes: "Remember, when one phrase is authentically transmitted, the authentic transmission of the whole dharma takes place. When one phrase has been authentically transmitted, there is the transmission of mountains and the transmission of waters."[14] This is another example of cooperation. Zen has been widely known as the "transmission outside the scriptures," but Dōgen reaffirms the teaching that each and every phrase and character (letter) in the scriptures teaches the entire Buddha Dharma. Dōgen continued teaching the transmission from master to disciple. Both are modes of cooperation.

There is also the *Shōbōgenzō* fascicle "Raihai Tokuzui [Receiving the Marrow by Bowing]," where Dōgen writes: "When you meet teachers who expound the supreme state of bodhi, have no regard for their race or caste, do not notice their looks."[15] Dōgen goes on to insist that, if they have attained supreme wisdom, we should venerate not only monks but also nuns, householders (laypeople), children, and any other kind of being.[16] He continues by pungently ridiculing all forms of sexual discrimination, especially the widespread bias against the idea that women can attain full and complete wisdom.[17] Dōgen's insistence on the veneration of all beings who have attained supreme wisdom is another example of *dōji*. It is the actualization of the Four Kinds of Wisdom: giving, kind speech, beneficial deeds, and *dōji*.

Practicing Buddhism
and Repaying Blessings

16 *Shushōgi* Paragraphs 26–28

STEVEN HEINE

Arousing the thought of enlightenment is mainly something
that human beings in this world should do.
—*From fascicle 70: "Hotsu Bodaishin [Arousing the Aspiration
for Enlightenment]"*

Should we not rejoice that we have had the opportunity to
be born in this land of the Buddha Shakyamuni and to have
encountered him?
—*From fascicle 10: "Keisei Sanshoku [Valley Sounds, Mountain Colors]"*
and fascicle 61: "Kenbutsu [Seeing the Buddha]"

We should calmly consider that if this was a time when the
true dharma had not yet spread in the world, we should not
be able to encounter it, even if we vowed to sacrifice our very
lives for it. We who have at present encountered the true
dharma should make such a vow.
—*From fascicle 31b: "Gyōji, Part Two (ge) [Continuous Practice]"*
and fascicle 10: "Keisei Sanshoku [Valley Sounds, Mountain Colors]"

Do we not know that the Buddha said, "When you meet a
teacher who expounds supreme enlightenment, do not consider
his family background, do not regard his appearance, do not
dislike his faults, and do not think about his conduct.
Simply, out of respect for wisdom, bow to him three times daily,
honor him, and do not cause him any grief."
—*From fascicle 9: "Raihai Tokuzui [Receiving the Marrow by Bowing]"*

That we are now able to see the Buddha and hear the dharma is due to the blessings that have come to us through the practice of every one of the buddhas and ancestors. If the buddhas and ancestors had not directly transmitted the dharma, how could it have reached us today? We should be grateful for the blessings of even a single phrase; we should be grateful for the blessings of even a single dharma. How much more should we be grateful for the great blessings of the treasury of the eye of the true dharma, the supreme great dharma. The injured bird did not forget its blessings, but showed its thanks with the rings of three ministries. The trapped tortoise did not forget its blessings, but showed its thanks with the seal of Yubu.
—*From fascicle 31b: "Gyōji, Part Two (ge) [Continuous Practice]"*

If even animals repay their blessing, how could humans ignore them?
—*From fascicle 13: "Kesa Kudoku [The Power of the Kesa]"*

To elucidate the meaning of these passages, let us briefly review the teachings of *Shushōgi* regarding the relation between self and other, or individual spiritual realization and the all-encompassing quality of the Buddha Nature that embraces all living beings. Whereas the doctrine of the universality of Buddha Nature has an orientation that is naturalistic and transcends anthropocentrism, an emphasis on the personal quest for attaining enlightenment, which is a potential only available to human beings, focuses on people-based endeavors.

The opening section in *Shushōgi* puts an emphasis on the anthropocentric notion of self-understanding and self-realization gained through clarifying the all-important matter of birth and death. Fortunately born as humans with the opportunity to encounter the Buddha Dharma, yet nevertheless bound by the law of karmic causality and the omnipresent threat of retribution for misbehavior to be suffered in present and future lives, people must not waste time or forsake responsibility by leaving their fate to the whims of impermanence. Instead, taking refuge in the Three Treasures through ongoing repentance and receiving the sixteen precepts, which makes anyone equal to the buddhas, represents the beginning of the sacred path. At this stage, human selfhood is in the process of being cultivated and polished.

Once it is understood that the self has been spiritually purified, the last two sections of *Shushōgi* tend to reverse—or, as seen from another angle, supplement—the focus on the inner path. The stress is put in the need to give back to others for the benevolence and blessings bestowed through compassionate and cooperative deeds or forms of expression. Full realization, according to the fourth section on "Making the Vow to Benefit Beings," requires steadfast dedication to serving all living beings without seeking reward, personal gain, or thanks. This stage can be manifested in the everyday life of a householder who builds bridges and produces goods in order to earn a living that provides for the whole family. These occupations expand human awareness to encompass the community and to have an impact on nature, which can in turn function as a resource for enhancing human life.

The passages at the beginning of section five make it clear that an additional layer of other-directionality based on dismantling anthropocentrism is required to complete the journey through developing the attitude of expressing gratitude[1] to the Buddha for awakening humans to the spiritual law that is followed by all forms of life. *Shushōgi* emphasizes that an attitude of grateful appreciation, rather than simply awe and veneration, is not to be considered separate or cut off from the demands of ordinary existence. Nakane Kandō, the founder of Tsurumi University located in Yokohama near Sōjiji temple, which was established by Keizan (the fourth ancestor of the Sōtō school), states that an outlook of profound gratitude for the educational opportunity and respect for the institution and its members' functions is an essential ingredient of the university's Zen-based creed. This outlook is to be followed consistently by faculty, administrators, and students alike.

Like the previous division's section of *Shushōgi*, this section of the text combines selections from the "old" or 75-fascicle *Shōbōgenzō* known for its emphasis on metaphysical doctrines, such as "Gyōji, Part Two (ge) [Continuous Practice]," "Keisei Sanshoku [Valley Sounds, Mountain Colors]," "Kenbutsu [Seeing the Buddha]," and "Raihai Tokuzui [Receiving the Marrow by Bowing]," and the "new" or 12-fascicle *Shōbōgenzō* known for its attention to precepts and behavioral issues, such as "Hotsu Bodaishin [Arousing the Aspiration for Enlightenment]" and "Kesa Kudoku [The Power of the *Kesa*]." The message is that people should learn from and try to emulate the deeds of animals that manifest a selfless and noble demeanor. One of the main features of this standpoint concerns how various creatures that have been celebrated traditionally in Chinese myths and legends were incorporated, over time, into Buddhist folklore as a way of teaching moral lessons. Humans have the advantage of knowing and trying consciously to overcome their karma, but nonhumans are special in that they are innately selfless and, therefore, in a fundamental sense, their deeds are pure in a way that can offer guidance to people.

The opening of section five retains a strong degree of anthropocentrism by highlighting that human beings alone are able to arouse the aspiration to attain an experience of awakening and must be grateful for this status. According to the biographical writings in *Hōkyōki* (*Record from the Baoqing Era*) and "Kenzeiki [The Record of Kenzei]," when Dōgen traveled to China he often reflected on the good fortune of his coming from a remote island country like Japan and, in reaching the mainland, was hosted by the head abbots of the leading Zen temples of the Song dynasty. He also scoffed at native Chinese practitioners who were lax in their training regimen for abandoning the gift of the Dharma they had been offered more readily than outsiders. When Dōgen returned to Japanese soil, his teaching method quickly became well known for its strict emphasis on puritanical discipline and an unwavering adherence to Buddhist ethics. In the Edo period, rituals of gratitude[2] to ancestors, including Dōgen, became a common form of ceremonial practice throughout the Sōtō sect.

While the uniqueness of humanity is noted in paragraph 26, the passages following this give moral weight to the role of nonhumans as instructive and inspirational. First, in a startling assertion from the fascicle "Raihai Tokuzui [Receiving the Marrow by Bowing]," which was previously cited in paragraphs 24–25 for its emphasis on the equality of women, all teachers who are effective in embodying and imparting wisdom regardless of background, appearance, or any apparent shortcomings must be venerated and honored without partiality or exception. This is a universal category that apparently encompasses all living beings, and while drawing on premodern supernaturalism that finds a sympathetic resonance between human and insentient beings, it also has a resonance with contemporary ecological ideals. As a result, people need to be aware and alive to the potential that the truth of the Buddha Dharma can appear in the flash of a moment, at any time and from every direction. In that sense, a single phrase or one dharma can, in an instantaneous moment, be sufficient to trigger awakening, just as a drop of water causes ripples that are felt throughout the waterway.

Beyond developing sensitivity to these ever-present possibilities, according to *Shushōgi*, humans can learn from the tales of an injured bird and a trapped tortoise, which appear as classic Chinese stories integrated into the Buddhist tradition, an important lesson about the need to demonstrate the depth of their gratitude. In the first example, a boy who helped an injured sparrow recover from debilitation eventually received four silver rings as recompense and this led to his being appointed to three high government positions during his lifetime. In the next instance about a man who rescued a tortoise, when the animal went on its way, it looked back over its shoulder to its benefactor, as if to acknowledge its indebtedness, and sometime later the man rose to a high official position. The seal of his office miraculously appeared in the form of a tortoise turning its head, and efforts to recast the object to try to remove the image did not work because it would nevertheless continue to reappear on the seal. The man realized that somehow the tortoise had played a part in his having received the appointment, so he kept the seal intact out of his reciprocal sense of gratitude.

This story recalls another classic Chinese account in which a tortoise is instructional but in a different way. The early Daoist thinker Zhuangzi was asked by a king's officials to become a head administrator. Holding onto his fishing pole without turning his head, he said, "I have heard that there is a sacred tortoise in Zhu that has been dead for three thousand years. The king keeps it wrapped in cloth and boxed, and stores it in the ancestral temple. Now would this tortoise rather be dead and have its bones left behind and honored? Or would it rather be alive and dragging its tail in the mud?" The two officials replied that it would rather be alive dragging its tail in the mud, to which Zhuangzi said, "Go away! I'll drag my tail in the mud!"[3]

Whereas the tortoise is passively instructive in the Zhuangzi anecdote, in the moral tales with their mythological underpinning, Dōgen cites the nonhuman being as more exalted. This is because the nonhuman being purposefully expresses its appreciation with conviction and commitment that extends over the course of time. Is this story intended as a heuristic device that has metaphorical significance and nothing more, or does it convey an animistic worldview preserved in the doctrine of the universal Buddha Nature that Dōgen wishes to explore? How would these implications have been interpreted by the audience for *Shushōgi*, which primarily consisted of lay Zen followers in late nineteenth-century Japan who were influenced by modernism, and in what ways should the imagery be appropriated by a global readership today?

The answers to these hermeneutic queries are no doubt better left in the mind's eye of the beholder. In any case, according to the opening passages contained in the final section of *Shushōgi*, it is clear that embracing an approach based on transcending anthropocentrism by learning from the behavior of altruistic animals operates as a crucial factor in the human quest to attain spiritual realization. This requires reciprocity of gratefulness, which occurs between ancestors and disciples, and teachers and students, as well as humans and nonhumans.

17 *Shushōgi* Paragraph 29

GRAHAM PARKES

Our expression of gratitude should not consist in any other practices;
the true path of such expression lies solely in our daily practice of
Buddhism. This means that we practice without neglecting our lives
day to day and without being absorbed in ourselves.
—*From fascicle 31b: "Gyōji, Part Two (ge) [Continuous Practice]"*

You wake up in the morning. It is a new day. A new life, in a way. A
wonder to be here again, since it is never certain that we will wake up
the next morning. In fact, what is certain is that there will come a next
morning when we do not wake up: one day it will all be over. "Even if you
make hundreds of plans," Dōgen writes, "and create thousands of means
to save yourselves, in the end you will turn to dust in the tomb."[1] There is
no denying that: we are now able to survey a far vaster range of human
history than was available to Dōgen, and we can definitively say that the
death rate for human beings has held steady since the beginning—at
exactly 100 percent. So, unless things are now going really miserably, this
waking up this morning is something to be grateful for. As Nietzsche's
Zarathustra says: "Whoever is of the rabble wants to live gratis; we others,
however, to whom life has given itself—we are always wondering what
we can best give in return!"[2] For Dōgen, what we can best give in return
is practice: "Continuous practice, day after day, is the most appropriate
way of expressing gratitude."[3] Not just sitting alone, then, but engaged
practice that's not only "for our own sake"—physical, somatic practice,
which prevents the body's being taken over by "that horrendous robber,
the demon of fame and gain."

But just sitting as well. And for those of us who are not home-leavers it may make sense to begin the day's thanking with some sitting without thinking, before continuing the practice. Because one thing we learn from attending to the breath is its finitude, our finitude. A few centuries before Dōgen, the Chan master Yunmen[4] was always telling his disciples to wake up and pay attention: "Hurry up! Hurry up! Time does not wait for anyone, and breathing out is no guarantee of breathing in again! Or do you have a spare body and mind to fritter away?"[5] This is the lesson from those moments between the end of the exhalation and the beginning of the inhalation: that some day there will come, for the first time in our lives and as an end to them, an exhalation that is not followed by an inhalation. At one level the point of practice for Dōgen is actually very simple: to enable the confrontation with, and embrace of, impermanence—the world's impermanence, but more immediately our own. In talking to the "Students of the Way" in his monastery, he says:

> When you truly see impermanence, egocentric mind does not
> arise, neither does desire for fame and profit. Out of fear that
> the days and nights are passing quickly, practice the Way as
> if you were trying to extinguish a fire enveloping your head.[6]

If your hair is ablaze, you do not waste time speculating, or planning how to increase your income or your chances of fame: you cannot take it with you, and before too long even the most renowned figures sink into oblivion. So you practice, in this very moment, since it is the only one there is. Like the in-breath and out-breath but instantaneous, arising and perishing, moment after moment. It is a pity when we miss it.

Sitting goes well when there is settling, like the settling, in the old days, of a newly built house onto its foundations, as the frame gradually adjusts to the weight and gets aligned with the forces of gravity and the contours of the ground. But they say the most important moments are those when you lift your bottom off the zafu and assume the standing posture that will carry you through the day. For that is the opportunity to make the practice continuous, and for the home-dweller the next phase is crucial—and more easily negotiated, in my experience, if there is a brief period during which one can be alone and pay full attention to one's activities in silence.

Here, in Japan, now that winter is almost over, it is the season of the satsuma tangerine. The color: orange—indeed the perfect example of orange color—like the rising or setting of the winter sun. It is a blessing, at this darker time of year with its abundance of root vegetables and their generally muted colors, to have a burst of bright orange as a reminder of sunnier times. The skin is mottled, with countless dark dots (oil glands) randomly spaced but with an even distribution overall, like a galaxy full of dark suns suspended in orange space. Its texture is smooth to the touch, and malleable, caressable like soft flesh; the fragrance somehow sweet, but indefinable—except by the word "tangerine." Likewise for the tangy taste: to know it you have to taste it (like the water in the Zen saying) for yourself.

The tangerine is one of the easiest fruits to eat because you can peel it without getting your fingers covered in juice. No need for anything as formal as a plate (the skin when peeled can form two small bowls), but best to sit down and relax, for if you eat it "on the run," or while preparing some other item of breakfast, you are likely to miss the richness of the experience. Much simpler to peel than an orange, since the skin lies more loosely on the flesh. A shallow bite with the incisors is a good way to start, and provides a foretaste that's slightly bitter, thanks to the flavor of the rind. But the sound of the rind tearing and coming away from the flesh inside is a unique delight: a subdued crackling, as the inner spheroid is revealed. Sometimes a puff of fragrant mist escapes. The color within is muted by comparison with the orange of the outside, striped and blotchy with the soft creamy hue of the pith.

Twelve segments typically, rarely more and sometimes eleven or ten, it is easily pulled apart. The teeth sink gently through the inner skin and into the succulent flesh, releasing a soft burst of juice and flavor, sometimes on the tart side but also sweet. The taste turns slightly tarter as you swallow the flesh and chew the remaining skin and pith, which often takes a fair amount of grinding. Apparently the balance in taste between the sweeter flesh and tarter pith reflects the way something in the pith counteracts the acid of the juice.

One's enjoyment of this noble fruit is enhanced by the knowledge of the wealth of nutrients and other health-giving substances it contains: various vitamins and acids and enzymes and fiber, and above all "nobiletin," a phytochemical that has been found to have antioxidant, anticancer, anti-inflammatory, and cholesterol-lowering properties, to reduce obesity, counteract memory loss and dementia, and help prevent heart disease, diabetes, and stroke. How wonderful that something that good for you should taste so delicious.

Given the traditional sleeping arrangement in Japan (on futons on the floor of a room fitted with tatami mats), to clear a space for the day's activities one has to put the bedding away—an exercise that involves a bit more than simply making the bed. This could be construed as a superfluous chore to be performed before proceeding to the more important things that need to be done. From the perspective of the western household, where, if time is short, one can shut the door on the bedroom without even making the bed, the Japanese arrangement is inefficient. But we might well question the priority we tend to give to efficiency as a measure for ordering or evaluating our lives—the Nazis, after all, were paragons of efficiency. How valuable efficiency is depends entirely on the nature of the activity and its larger context.

If we think about it, the way we so often structure our experience and activities—we distinguish fulfilling ends from burdensome chores in order to achieve our goals—this condemns us to a great deal of drudgery. If we refrain (as Dōgen would encourage us to do) from dividing the world up into means and ends; for example, if we approach the clearing of the sleeping area as an occasion for enjoying life, would that not shift the perspective and enrich our experience? Part of what makes tasks like this into chores is the perception that we are having to do the same thing over and over again—whether it is making the bed, washing the dishes, or cleaning the room. But it does not take prolonged reflection to realize that things are always different every time, and each situation is in fact unique. It is just that we tend to overlook this because our eye is on some future purpose.

The task—in the positive sense of the word, meaning a piece of work that has to be done—is to clear the rice-straw matted decks. Best to let the bedding air for a while, which provides an opportunity to wash the face and clean the teeth. Dōgen has a great deal to say about making those two activities into consummate practice.[7] Assuming my wife can be persuaded to get up for it, the question is how best to go about this task. How can we get better at it, so much better that we are doing our very best, making the best of something that needs to be done? The first thing is to open one of the sliding doors of the cabinet along the side of the room, which has been specially constructed for the purpose of storing the bedding.

There are many ways for me to open the door, some better, some worse. But what is it that makes one way better and another worse—and does it really matter? There may be a branch of physiology that deals with the human musculoskeletal system at work, but we do not need it for answering this question if we simply suppose that the worse ways lead to pain and suffering and the better to full enjoyment. This particular door is older and heavier than most, and inclined to stick, perhaps because it is slightly warped. For a body such as mine, with longer than average limbs, successful sliding requires careful attention to the body's posture and center of gravity, and the relative positions of hands and feet, if muscles are not to be strained or ligaments overstretched. By paying such attention we acquire an implicit understanding of the biomechanics of muscle leverage. Too much force applied, and to a wrong point on the edge of the door, can suddenly send it sliding into the post with a thud loud enough to wake the neighbors. A finger pinched, shoulder muscle strained, or lower back thrown out—all are indications that this way of opening the door is worse rather than better.

What is interesting here is not just that the better ways tend to be those that take less effort and use less energy: they also feel better as you perform the movements, and they no doubt look better, too, if anyone happens to be watching. The better ways are distinguished by their style and grace, and the pleasure they afford.

So, if we do not want this first shared task of the day to be a chore, we can make it into something more like a dance, which requires not letting it lapse into merely habitual activity and leads to a lot more fun. It was clear early in our marriage that we would never be the next Fred Astaire and Ginger Rogers, but we still hold out hope for some distinction in the far less competitive field of bedding storing. The order of dance moves that naturally suggests itself is one where the last things to go into the cabinet should be the first to come out in the evening, when you lay the bedding down on the floor again. But within that framework there is plenty of room for creative improvisation.

In folding the sheets, once you synchronize your actions with those of your fellow folder, the well-coordinated interaction becomes a joy to participate in. It is less a matter of efficient body movement than of avoiding unnecessary exertion and postures that produce strain: that way the motions flow easily and smoothly, and on a cold morning the exercise has a pleasantly warming and tonic effect. The enjoyment becomes richer as you learn not only to harmonize your movements with your partner's but also to adjust them to the size and weight and texture of what you are folding, responding to the sheet or blanket as a third participant in the early morning dance.

In our dealings with bigger things there is sometimes a tendency (for men, at least) to manhandle them: intent on our own goals, we misjudge the weights or positions or pliabilities of things, and we end up making one obstruct another, or even hurting ourselves with them, which in turn promotes an unhelpfully antagonistic attitude. But when putting away the futons becomes more spontaneous with practice, you lose the sense that you are the one performing the movements and gain a feeling for the unfolding of the activity from a center that is somehow between or among the participants. You know where the futons, once folded, belong; and things go better if, instead of your having to heave them into place, you simply help them get to where they need to be. This is an instance of what Dōgen calls "turning things while being turned by things," and it is through practice that we develop a sense of both how things are turning so that we can align ourselves aright, and how our turning them is in turn affecting what is going on.[8] Helping the futons get to where they need to be depends on their having their appropriate places to begin with, but these do not need to be determined by a plan thought out in our heads beforehand and then implemented "on the ground." Rather, the suitabilities—where the various items of bedding best belong—are actually suggested by the things themselves, as long as we remain open and responsive to them.

Dōgen reports that the Chan master Changqing[9] practiced for almost twenty-nine years, wearing out twenty sitting mats, before "he suddenly had great awakening while rolling up a bamboo shade."[10] You can be sure that Changqing wasn't daydreaming about breakfast while he was performing that everyday task.

The German philosopher Immanuel Kant famously wrote that we should treat humanity, whether in others or in our own person, never as mere means to our own ends, but always, out of respect, as ends in themselves. If we were to extend this "categorical imperative" to animals and inanimate things, we might well find that things get better for all of us.

But now it is time to leave for work, which is fortunately within walking distance. Pity the poor commuters who have to sit in their cars for hours, stuck in rush hour traffic on congested freeways: that is one of the tougher tests of one's ability to engage in continuous practice. But the workplace is also a site rich in challenges to our ability to practice "without being absorbed in ourselves." "You practice continuously," Dōgen writes, "without wasting a single day of your life, without using it for your own sake. Why is it so? Your life is a fortunate outcome of continuous practice from the past."[11]

We did not make our bodies or create our lives but received them from the ancestors, and so we should be grateful. And since we have them only "on loan," as it were, rather than as permanent possessions, we can express our gratitude by working for the benefit not only of our contemporaries but also of those to come. "Thinking upon the time when your body will turn to dust or mud, you should care about future generations without self-concern."[12] But since most of us in the developed world at the beginning of the twenty-first century are totally uninterested in thinking about such a time, our self-concern has become so huge that the last thing we care about is future generations—as evidenced by our perverse unwillingness to do anything about slowing global warming or the ongoing destruction of the natural environment. Considering the ethos of the United States at this point in its history, it would be hard to imagine anything more diametrically opposed to what motivates Dōgen to advocate continuous practice. But the fact that, nevertheless, Dōgen's spirit is very much alive in that same, vast country (albeit for only a tiny percentage of the population) shines a small ray of hope through this dismal situation. Perhaps, through continuous practice, that ray can be broadened and extended.

18 *Shushōgi* Paragraph 30

MARK UNNO

Time flies faster than an arrow, and life is more transient than
the dew. With what skill means or devices can we retrieve even a
single day that has passed? A hundred years lived to no purpose
are days and months to be regretted. It is to be but a pitiful bag
of bones. Even if we live in abandon, as slaves to the senses for
the days and months of a hundred years, if we take up practice
for a single day therein, it is not only the practice of this life of a
hundred years, but also salvation in the hundred years of another
life. The life of this day is a life that should be esteemed,
a bag of bones that should be honored. We should love and
respect our bodies and minds, which undertake this practice.
Depending on our practice, the practice of the buddhas is manifested, and the great way of the buddhas penetrates everywhere.
Therefore, the practice of a single day is the seed of the buddhas,
the practice of the buddhas.
—*From fascicle 31a: "Gyōji, Part One (jō) [Continuous Practice]" and
fascicle 31b:"Gyōji, Part Two (ge) [Continuous Practice]"*

At its heart, this passage from the "Gyōji" fascicle of Dōgen's *Shōbōgenzō*
is very simple. Life is fleeting. One should not waste it chasing after illusory objects of desire. Rather, one should take good care of this precious
human body as the vehicle of great practice, in order to awaken to the
truth of the Dharma. If only one would follow this simple teaching, then
one could fully realize one's Buddha Nature, emptiness, the oneness of
all reality.

Yet our very delusions make it difficult to follow such a straightforward, simple teaching. Thus, Dōgen kindly provides an elaboration that elucidates the dynamic workings of the Dharma as it unfolds from moment to moment. In this regard, one may note that there are three facets to this passage: human life within the bounds of relative time, which can be considered historical time of sorts; philosophical truth, which is unconditioned and transcends finite time, and is thus timeless (but does not exist apart from temporality); and the subjective awareness of the Buddhist practitioner, which unfolds in the present moment. It is this latter facet of subjective awareness that unites historical time and timeless philosophical truth, without which both time and philosophy remain mere abstractions. True awareness unfolding in the present moment of practice necessarily takes place within historical time and expresses the timeless truth of the Dharma.

Human beings live in historical time, and for much of our time, we are mired in delusion. We live "in abandon, as slaves to the senses for the days and months of a hundred years." One becomes too easily upset if even two meals are missed in a day; agitated if even two nights of sleeplessness occur in succession; resentful if one's "generosity" goes unnoticed or unreturned even after one week. This is the historical reality, the person who lives in time, this pitiful bag of bones.

The philosophical truth of the Dharma lies beyond the grasp of such attachments and delusions. The great Way of the buddhas, which is the way of emptiness and oneness, lies before and beyond human attempts to pigeonhole reality according to one's preconceptions of what reality is or should be. The point at which we begin to break with the historical time of slavish desires is the moment in which one recognizes that it is a waste of time, and there is not time to waste. In this impermanent world, we jump from one burning ship onto another as we futilely attempt to fulfill our desires. When we recognize our futility, we also recognize that time is precious: "Time flies faster than an arrow, and life is more transient than the dew."

At some level we sense that true fulfillment comes to us through our awareness that we are deeply connected to all other beings, and to fully realize this is the path to liberation. The true subject is not the single, finite human being who is chasing objects of desire. Rather, the true subject lies in intersubjectivity, such that the buddha-self is the buddha-cloud, buddha-sky, buddha-stars, sun, and moon, where "the great Way of the buddhas penetrates everywhere."

The path of practice is to realize this great Way of the buddhas while living in this historical world. It is to live in this world but not be of it. Yet the secret is not to stand aloof from the world. Rather, it is to be fully immersed in it: "The life of this day is a life that should be esteemed, a bag of bones that should be honored." This is the transformation of awareness, from the body of desire, this "pitiful bag of bones," to the body of practice, "a bag of bones that should be honored."

Delusions are interminable; practice is limitless. Thus, each moment is the moment of transformative practice: "If we take up practice for a single day therein, it is not only the practice of this life of a hundred years, but also salvation in the hundred years of another life." To practice for a single day, or even a single moment, is to break the cycle of delusion. The heart of this practice is the simultaneous awareness of delusion and awakening, blind passions and the compassionate practice of the Buddha, which is bequeathed to us through time, in history, but from beyond time, from Buddha Nature itself.

Seated meditation in the lotus posture is the form bequeathed to us in history, but it is a manifestation of the Buddha Nature that is its source beyond time; just this seated meditation, *shikantaza* (sitting-only), is the Buddha-seal of transmission. To take the lotus posture is to return to the source, both in the historical sense of returning to the original practice of the Buddha Śākyamuni and in the philosophical sense of returning to the source of the self in emptiness and oneness. The practitioner, taking the lotus posture, manifests the king-of-*samādhis-samādhi*,[1] which is the true body of practice, but which does not exist apart from the body of delusion. In fact, the suffering body of delusion becomes suffused with the great ease of *samādhi*; this is the meaning of blind passions being none other than awakening.[2]

All of this is rendered meaningless unless one realizes this in the present moment. Thus, the key to practice is to realize that the one who lives "in abandon, as [a] slave to the senses" is oneself, in the here-and-now.

Yet the moment of this recognition is also the moment of awakening; one is enabled to see the dark shadow of one's delusion because the light of Buddha Nature illuminates it.

This is just as Dōgen states in the "Genjōkōan [Actualizing the Fundamental Point]" fascicle of *Shōbōgenzō*: "Flowers fall always amidst our grudging; weeds flourish in our chagrin."[3] In the opening paragraph of the "Genjōkōan," this is the culmination of Dōgen's logic of practice because it is what brings the practitioner as reader into the present moment of awareness. It is like the alcoholic for whom the most critical moment is the first moment of recognition: "I have a problem." Until that moment, the alcoholic is in denial. The very moment he sees his own delusion, he is also freed from his delusion. It is the critical turning point, just as taking the lotus posture is the critical turning point for the Buddhist practitioner. Although the alcoholic may fall off the wagon many times, just as the practitioner may become lost in her delusions many times, once one has truly had one's delusions illuminated by the light of the Dharma, the seed of awakening has been planted; it will eventually flourish.

The seed and the fruit are one, cause and effect are simultaneous. "Therefore, the practice of a single day is the seed of the buddhas, the practice of the buddhas." When the addict looks back upon her past, she sees that everything essential to her recovery was given to her in the moment of recognizing her addiction; the recognition came to her from a larger awareness free from the bondage of addiction. Likewise, the practitioner looking back on the path of practice sees that everything essential was bequeathed in the moment of "sitting-only" in which her delusions were brought into relief by the illumination of Buddha Nature. Because the truth of this illumination is what sustains the path of practice, and this Buddha Nature is the true reality of the self in each moment of practice, seed and fruit, cause and effect, are simultaneous. The timeless body of the Dharma, the *dharmakāya*, supersedes the historical body in time. Nevertheless, there is a ripening and maturation of practice in historical time that is continually nourished by the timeless *dharmakāya*. Every time that the alcoholic falls off of the wagon, and every moment that the practitioner becomes lost in delusion, there is great suffering. Yet within each moment of delusion, there is also a moment of awakening;

unless this is also the moment of practice, the moment of awakening goes unrealized.

Although delusion by itself is meaningless, delusion illuminated by awakening brings awareness of the suffering of all beings, not just one's own; thus, one's realization of the oneness of all-reality is immeasurably enriched and deepened, and one receives the moment of practice-as-awakening with profound gratitude, as the gift of the Buddha's great compassion. Nothing is wasted. The deeper the delusion, the brighter the illumination of awakening; the more tenacious the blind passions, the greater the realization of compassion. This is the real significance of Dōgen's statement: "if we take up practice for a single day therein, it is not only the practice of this life of a hundred years, but also salvation in the hundred years of another life."

Just as the addict must be able to practice his recovery everywhere, even when others are partaking of alcohol, so, too, must the Buddhist practitioner harness the power of Buddha Nature beyond the form of seated meditation. Yet without the power of "sitting," there is no "only," that is, just this activity, whether it be chopping carrots, weeding the garden, or having tea. All forms of practice only become true practice when they are empowered by the *samādhi* of seated meditation. *Shikantaza* (sitting-only) is the portal through which the Dharma beyond time shines brightly in this world, like one bright shining pearl.

For Dōgen, the framework of the precepts supports the primacy of *shikantaza*. As in the case of seated meditation, the precepts are understood in historical as well as philosophical senses, both brought to life in the present moment of practice. That Dōgen valued the *Dharmaguptaka Vinaya* of the Buddha Śākyamuni demonstrates the return to the historical source. That he also formulated all of the other monastic regulations, which came to be known as *Eihei Shingi*, or the Pure Rules of Eihei, shows Dōgen's philosophical fluidity in expressing the source as the Buddha Nature of oneness: "With what skillful means or devices[4] can we retrieve even a single day that has passed?" That Dōgen cited the Ten Precepts and the Three Pure, Collective Precepts elucidates the basis for the precepts in the spirit of awakening which above all is embodied in *shikantaza*.

When one first learns that "time flies faster than an arrow, and life is more transient than the dew," there is a feeling of sorrow. When the veil of immortality is pierced, and one recognizes the impermanence of life, one feels the sadness of separation, just as Dōgen must have felt at the loss of his parents. Yet the real significance of impermanence is that life is more transient than the dew. It is briefer than we can know, like a flash of lightning in the night sky. In the great, great arc of the universe, even the life of a star is but a fleeting existence; how much more so one human life. Each life, unique, never to be again, flashes in and out of existence like a single twinkling of a star.

At the same time, we are not alone. Birds and insects, trees and grasses, the rivers, mountains, and stars—all are our mothers and fathers, brothers and sisters in the timeless process of birth and death. In the great compassionate awakening of the Buddha's practice in this moment now, each of us receives the precious gift of the seed and the fruit, practice-as-awakening. As Dōgen states, "Completely letting go and forgetting body and mind, one entrusts oneself to the realm of the Buddha, and practice unfolds from the side of the Buddha; when one simply follows in this way, one is released from the cycle of life and death and attains buddhahood without exerting any force or mental effort."[5]

> In the spring cherry blossoms, in the summer the cuckoo.
> In autumn the full moon, in winter the snow, clear, cold.
> —Dōgen

19 *Shushōgi* Paragraph 31

SHŪDŌ BRIAN SCHROEDER

These buddhas are the Buddha Shakyamuni. The Buddha Shakyamuni is "mind itself is buddha." When buddhas of the past, present, and future together fulfill buddhahood, they always become the Buddha Shakyamuni. This is "mind itself is buddha."
—*From fascicle 6: "Sokushin Zebutsu [Mind Here and Now Is Buddha]"*

We should carefully investigate who is meant when we say "mind itself is buddha."
—*From fascicle 81: "Ō saku Sendaba [King Seeking the Saindhava]"*

This is how we repay the blessings of the Buddha.
—*From fascicle 9: "Raihai Tokuzui [Receiving the Marrow by Bowing]"*

Outside the entrance to many zendos one finds often written on the *han*, the wooden board that is struck with a mallet to announce the start of zazen, the following words:

> Great is the matter of birth and death
> Life slips quickly by
> Time waits for no one
> Wake up! Wake up!
> Don't waste a moment

The gravity and sense of urgency is readily apparent. This is the guiding thought for those who enter the dragon gate of "nonthinking [*hi-shiryō*] . . . the essential art of zazen," as Eihei Dōgen writes in *Fukanzazengi*

(*Universally Recommended Instructions for Zazen*). Drawing to our attention "the great matter" of Zen Buddhism, thereby connecting beginning and ending, birth and death, in the cycle of existence that is samsara, *Shushōgi* (*The Meaning of Practice and Verification*) opens with the following words:

> The most important issue of all for Buddhists is the thorough clarification of the meaning of birth and death. If the buddha is within birth and death, there is no birth and death. Simply understand that birth and death are in themselves nirvana; there is no birth and death to be hated nor nirvana to be desired. Then, for the first time, we will be freed from birth and death. To master this problem is of supreme importance.

In his own way, Dōgen is articulating Nāgārjuna's famous realization some one thousand years earlier that nirvana and samsara are, while not identical, inseparably bound on this plane of existence.[1] From this perspective, if samsara can be affirmed as buddha as much as nirvana can, then freedom from birth and death is realizable here and now. It is a matter of not just understanding but actualizing the concluding thought of *Shushōgi*, namely, "mind itself is buddha."[2]

The phenomenon of mind has a rich and complex understanding in Buddhist thinking. Early Buddhism interpreted the Buddha Dharma primarily from what today we would term a psychological standpoint, and while this understanding was carried into the later Mahāyāna, there was also an increased emphasis on the relation between the phenomenal and intellectual aspects of existence. According to the *Ratnamegha Sūtra* (*Cloud of Jewels Sutra* or *Precious Clouds Sutra*), which was introduced to China by the northern Indian monk and Yogācāra scholar Bodhiruci,[3] and is generally considered to be the first sutra translated into Tibetan:

> All phenomena originate in the mind, and when the mind is fully known, all phenomena are fully known. . . . The bodhisattva, thoroughly examining the nature of things, dwells in

ever-present mindfulness of the activity of the mind, and so one does not come under the mind's power, but the mind's power comes under one's control. And with the mind under one's control, all phenomena are under one's control.[4]

"Control" here does not refer to either a coercion or manipulation, but rather to discipline in the sense of right action, right mindfulness, and skillful means.[5] This sutra, which was received in China, has clear resonances with the Daoist teaching of the Way[6] as soft and yielding. Control is the disciplined activity of not forcing the mind to construct reality, but rather yielding to its active passivity, so that the illusory distinction between the mind and the body is ultimately abandoned, and with it any false sense of inherent independence. This is the Buddha Mind, which is also no-mind,[7] not in the sense of being nonexistent but rather impermanent. It is the Buddha Mind that realizes the true nature of self and existence in general—in other words, Buddha Nature. As Dōgen teaches, "impermanence is itself Buddha Nature."[8]

In characteristic fashion of the Mahāyāna tradition, Dōgen employs "mind" in a variety of ways. He concludes with the following declaration:

> The Buddha Shakyamuni is "mind itself is buddha." When buddhas of the past, present, and future together fulfill buddhahood, they always become the Buddha Shakyamuni. This is "mind itself is buddha." We should carefully investigate who is meant when we say "mind itself is buddha." This is how we repay the blessings of the Buddha.

The development of Zen was influenced in part by the Yogācāra, or Mind-Only, school. Drawing on that, Dōgen also identifies mind with various levels of consciousness (for example, the mental activities of intellect, feeling, and will). However, just as he expands the notion of Buddha Nature to include both sentient and nonsentient forms of existence, Dōgen also extends the notion of mind to include the exterior world. In the *Shōbōgenzō* fascicle "Bendōwa [On the Endeavor of the Way]," he writes: "All things and all phenomena are just one mind—

nothing is excluded or unrelated. It is taught that all the dharma gates are equally one mind, and there is no differentiation.[9] For Dōgen, mind is simultaneously knowledge and reality, subject and object, idea and phenomenon, and yet transcends these distinctions. This is why he can state, "the Buddha Shakyamuni is 'mind itself is buddha.'" Dōgen here is simultaneously referring and not referring to the historical Buddha. In realizing his own awakening, Śākyamuni becomes the proper name of all other manifestations of awakening. But since Śākyamuni awakens to the realization of his own empty nature, there is then no more Śākyamuni. The Buddha Śākyamuni is simply the nondifferentiated event or process of "seeing" with "true Dharma eye" that all is mind, that everything is fundamentally interconnected and codependently arising. The emptiness of mind is therefore the thusness of mind[10] and vice-versa. This is the actualization of the teaching in the *Heart Sutra* that form and emptiness are interchangeable in meaning.

"To study the way of enlightenment is to study the self," writes Dōgen in one of his most famous passages.

> To study the self is to forget the self. To forget the self is to be actualized by myriad things. When actualized by myriad things, your mind and body as well as the bodies and minds of others drop away. No trace of realization remains, and this no-trace continues endlessly.[11]

Śākyamuni Buddha teaches that only non-ego[12] is the standpoint from which "one" (and not necessarily the individual one either) realizes the truth of the Dharma as dependent origination. Awakened beings continually practice because practice is itself the way. To do otherwise, though it too is the way, is not to realize the way. Without the realization that comes from practice, the mind does not "drop away," and Buddha Nature is not "seen."

The transmission of Dōgen Zen differs from other schools of Buddhism by emphasizing "going beyond Buddha."[13] It leaves behind rational conceptualization or reliance on the sutras as the means by which ones comes to this realization. The fullness[14] and emptiness[15] of the Buddha Dharma is communicated mind to mind. Bodhidharma writes, "in India, the twenty-seven ancestors only transmitted the imprint of Mind. And the only reason [I came] to China [was] to transmit the instantaneous teaching of the Mahāyāna: *This mind is the Buddha.*"[16] Elsewhere, he states: "This mind is the Buddha. . . . Beyond this mind you'll never find another Buddha. To search for enlightenment or nirvana beyond this mind is impossible. The reality of your own self-nature, the absence of cause and effect, is what is meant by mind. Your mind is nirvana."[17] This is the same meaning as Dōgen's opening declaration in *Shushōgi* that "birth and death are in themselves nirvana." Just as there is nothing beyond or outside birth and death—which is life itself—so also is there nothing beyond mind.

But what exactly is meant by "mind" here? Although he acknowledges the inadequacy of this distinction, the ninth-century Chinese Chan master Huangbo Xiyun (also referred to as Huang Po) draws a critical distinction between the One Mind and mind:

> All the Buddhas and all sentient beings are nothing but the One Mind, beside which nothing exists. This mind, which is without beginning, is unborn and indestructible. . . . The One Mind alone is the Buddha, and there is no distinction between the Buddha and sentient things, but that sentient beings are attached to forms and so seek externally for Buddhahood. By their very seeking they lose it, for that is using the Buddha to seek for the Buddha and using mind to grasp Mind.[18]

Huang Po's main point here is that the Buddha Mind, and thus Buddha Nature, is not something that can be located in a source other than ourselves. His teacher, Mazu Daoyi, taught that the ordinary mind is the way. Śākyamuni was a buddha, but he was only just Śākyamuni. Although we refer to him as the Buddha, this does not mean that he is the source. This is why another Chan master, Huang Po's student Linji Yixuan,[19] says, in one of Zen's most well known declarations: "If you see the Buddha on the way, kill him!" In other words, if one thinks that the One Mind is an external reality, or assign to it a metaphysical stature, then one turns it into something, in which case it cannot be Buddha Nature, which is always empty.

In his typically direct, bare-bones style, Bodhidharma describes the emptiness of the Buddha Mind in the following way:

> The nature of [a buddha's] mind is basically empty, neither pure nor impure. He [or she] is free of practice and realization. He [or she] is free of cause and effect. . . . A buddha is someone who does nothing, who can't even focus his [or her] mind on a buddha. A buddha isn't a buddha. Don't think about buddhas. If you don't see what I'm talking about, you'll never know your own mind. People who don't see their nature and imagine they can practice thoughtlessness all the time are liars and fools. They fall into endless space. They're like drunks. They can't tell good from evil. If you intend to cultivate such a practice, you have to put an end to rational thought. To attain enlightenment without seeing your nature is impossible.[20]

The question is how to "see" one's nature if that nature is not some external thing that can be "seen." This is what is meant by "mind," which is emptiness itself and can only be transmitted as mind to others mind-to-mind. This is why Zen insists on the close relation between a teacher and student, which has been the practice since Śākyamuni.

Now, Huang Po emphatically declares that the only Dharma is that there are no Dharmas. And yet the Buddha Dharma is only One Mind. He poses this dialectic:

> Q: If there is no Mind and no Dharma, what is meant by transmission?
> A: You hear people speak of Mind transmission and then you talk of something to be received. So Bodhidharma said:

> > The nature of the mind when understood no human speech can compass or disclose. Enlightenment is naught to be attained and he that gains it does not say he knows.

If I were to make this clear to you I doubt that you could stand up to it.[21]

Elsewhere, Huang Po writes:

> This Dharma is Mind, beyond which there is no Dharma; and this Mind *is* the Dharma, beyond which there is no mind. Mind in itself is not mind, yet neither is it no-mind. To say that Mind is no-mind implies something existent. Let there be a silent understanding and no more. . . . This Mind is the pure Buddha-Source inherent in all [people].[22]

Language is an altogether inadequate vehicle for understanding the Buddha Dharma and is not the road to transmission. Dōgen too was continually aware of the limitations of language. But we are also linguistic beings and language is as much a part of the Buddha Dharma as is the "practice-realization" that is emphasized in *Fukanzazengi*. In the fascicle "Uji [Being-Time]," Dōgen addresses the relation between language and mind:

> Both mind and words are the time being. Both arriving and not-arriving are the time being. . . . Mind is the moment of actualizing the fundamental point; words are the moment of going beyond, unlocking the barrier.[23]

Awakening to this realization is the heart of enlightenment, and this is something that occurs on the everyday level, which is the true "oneness of practice-realization."[24]

Bodhidharma's words in the "Wake-up Sermon" both capture the dilemma and express the way out:

> If you use your mind to study reality, you won't understand either your mind or reality. If you study reality without using your mind, you'll understand both. Those who don't understand, don't understand understanding. And those who

understand, understand not understanding. People of true vision know that the mind is empty. They transcend both understanding and not understanding. The absence of both understanding and not understanding is true understanding. Seen with true vision, form isn't simply form, because form depends on mind. And mind isn't simply mind, because mind depends on form. Mind and form create and negate each other.[25]

The mutual creation-negation of mind and form is the expression of the movement of *Dao*, the philosophy of which permeates the thinking of Bodhidharma, Huang Po, and Dōgen. Remembering this fundamental ground of thinking and existing is what gives us insight into the great matter of birth and death, and into the Buddha Mind. There is only the unity of the "now," the time-being, which is to say being-time.[26] This being-time is what Dōgen refers to when he writes: "When buddhas of the past, present and future together fulfill buddhahood, they always become the Buddha Shakyamuni. This is 'mind itself is buddha.'"[27]

PART III

FUKANZAZENGI—TEXT AND COMMENTARY

Fukanzazengi
(Universally Recommended Instructions for Zazen)

This translation of Dōgen's *Fukanzazengi* is taken from the *Soto School Scriptures for Daily Services and Practice*, ed. and trans. Carl Bielefeldt and T. Griffith Foulk, with the Rev. Taigen Leighton and the Rev. Shohaku Okumura (Tokyo: Sotoshu Shumucho and the Soto Zen Text Project, 2001).

The way is originally perfect and all-pervading. How could it be contingent on practice and realization? The true vehicle is self-sufficient. What need is there for special effort? Indeed, the whole body is free from dust. Who could believe in a means to brush it clean? It is never apart from this very place; what is the use of traveling around to practice? And yet, if there is a hairsbreadth deviation, it is like the gap between heaven and earth. If the least like or dislike arises, the mind is lost in confusion. Suppose you are confident in your understanding and rich in enlightenment, gaining the wisdom that knows at a glance, attaining the way and clarifying the mind, arousing an aspiration to reach for the heavens. You are playing in the entranceway, but you are still short of the vital path of emancipation.

Consider the Buddha: although he was wise at birth, the traces of his six years of upright sitting can yet be seen. As for Bodhidharma, although he had received the mind-seal, his nine years of facing a wall is celebrated still. If even the ancient sages were like this, how can we today dispense with wholehearted practice?

Therefore, put aside the intellectual practice of investigating words and chasing phrases, and learn to take the backward step that turns the light and shines it inward. Body and mind of themselves will drop away, and your original face will manifest. If you want to realize such, get to work on such right now.

For practicing Zen, a quiet room is suitable. Eat and drink moderately. Put aside all involvements and suspend all affairs. Do not think "good" or "bad." Do not judge true or false. Give up the operations of mind, intellect, and consciousness; stop measuring with thoughts, ideas, and views. Have no designs on becoming a buddha. How could that be limited to sitting or lying down?

At your sitting place, spread out a thick mat and put a cushion on it. Sit either in the full-lotus or half-lotus position. In the full-lotus position, first place your right foot on your left thigh, then your left foot on your right thigh. In the half-lotus, simply place your left foot on your right thigh. Tie your robes loosely and arrange them neatly. Then place your right hand on your left leg and your left hand on your right palm, thumbtips lightly touching. Straighten your body and sit upright, leaning neither left nor right, neither forward nor backward. Align your ears with your shoulders and your nose with your navel. Rest the tip of your tongue against the front of the roof of your mouth, with teeth together and lips shut. Always keep your eyes open, and breathe softly through your nose.

Once you have adjusted your posture, take a breath and exhale fully, rock your body right and left, and settle into steady, immovable sitting. Think of not thinking. Not thinking—what kind of thinking is that? Nonthinking. This is the essential art of zazen.

The zazen I speak of is not meditation practice. It is simply the dharma gate of joyful ease, the practice-realization of totally culminated enlightenment. It is the kōan realized; traps and snares can never reach it. If you grasp the point, you are like a dragon gaining the water, like a tiger taking to the mountains. For you must know that the true dharma appears of itself, so that from the start dullness and distraction are struck aside.

When you arise from sitting, move slowly and quietly, calmly and deliberately. Do not rise suddenly or abruptly. In surveying the past, we find that transcendence of both mundane and sacred and dying while either sitting or standing have all depended entirely on the power of zazen.

In addition, triggering awakening with a finger, a banner, a needle, or a mallet, and effecting realization with a whisk, a fist, a staff, or a shout—these cannot be understood by discriminative thinking; much less can they be known through the practice of supernatural power. They must represent conduct beyond seeing and hearing. Are they not a standard prior to knowledge and views?

This being the case, intelligence or lack of it is not an issue; make no distinction between the dull and the sharp-witted. If you concentrate your effort single-mindedly, that in itself is wholeheartedly engaging the way. Practice-realization is naturally undefiled. Going forward is, after all, an everyday affair.

In general, in our world and others, in both India and China, all equally hold the Buddha-seal. While each lineage expresses its own style, they are all simply devoted to sitting, totally blocked in resolute stability. Although they say that there are ten thousand distinctions and a thousand variations, they just wholeheartedly engage the way in zazen. Why leave behind the seat in your own home to wander in vain through the dusty realms of other lands? If you make one misstep, you stumble past what is directly in front of you.

You have gained the pivotal opportunity of human form. Do not pass your days and nights in vain. You are taking care of the essential activity of the Buddha Way. Who would take wasteful delight in the spark from a flintstone? Besides, form and substance are like the dew on the grass, the fortunes of life like a dart of lightning—emptied in an instant, vanished in a flash.

Please, honored followers of Zen, long accustomed to groping for the elephant, do not doubt the true dragon. Devote your energies to the way of direct pointing at the real. Revere the one who has gone beyond learning and is free from effort. Accord with the enlightenment of all the buddhas; succeed to the *samādhi* of all the ancestors. Continue to live in such a way, and you will be such a person. The treasure store will open of itself, and you may enjoy it freely.

20 The Enlightening Practice of Nonthinking: Unfolding Dōgen's *Fukanzazengi*

KANPŪ BRET W. DAVIS

Those who see the Way, practice the Way.
—*Benjing, quoted by Dōgen in "Bendōwa"*[1]

The practice of Zen (*sanzen*) is seated meditation (*zazen*).
—*Dōgen, "Zazengi"*[2]

Think of not-thinking. How do you think of not-thinking?
Nonthinking. This is the essential art of zazen.
—*Dōgen, Fukanzazengi*[3]

Body and mind of themselves will drop away, and your original
face will manifest.
—*Dōgen, Fukanzazengi*

When just one person does zazen even one time, he becomes,
imperceptibly, one with each and all of the myriad things and
permeates completely all time, so that, within the limitless universe,
throughout past, future, and present, he is performing the eternal
and ceaseless work of guiding beings to enlightenment.
—*Dōgen, "Bendōwa"*[4]

UNIVERSAL RECOMMENDATION OF ZAZEN

There are two texts by Dōgen that are recited daily by many Sōtō Zen practitioners: *Fukanzazengi* (*Universally Recommended Instructions for Zazen*) and *Shushōgi* (*The Meaning of Practice and Verification*). The former is Dōgen's revised version of the first text he wrote after returning from China in 1227, having received the seal of Dharma transmission from his teacher Rujing.[5] The latter text was compiled in the late nineteenth century by the Sōtō sect and consists of selected passages from various fascicles of Dōgen's major work, *Shōbōgenzō* (*Treasury of the True Dharma Eye*).[6] It is meant to serve as a compendium of Dōgen's key teachings, especially for laypeople. Yet many of the passages selected were written near the end of Dōgen's career, and the text as a whole reflects his stress at that time on such matters as karmic causality, repentance, and taking the precepts. Remarkably, the practice of zazen (seated meditation) is not mentioned at all in *Shushōgi*. This is particularly odd, given that zazen is, by nearly all accounts, a core practice of Buddhism and especially of Dōgen's Zen.[7] Hence, for all its importance as a concise summary of teachings stressed in Dōgen's later years that have not yet not received their due attention in the West, for a more comprehensive introduction to Dōgen's Zen, reflection on *Shushōgi* needs to be prefaced and supplemented by reflection on an early programmatic text such as *Fukanzazengi*.

It is significant that the first major text Dōgen composed upon returning from China, *Fukanzazengi*, is a universal recommendation of zazen. In another seminal early text, "Bendōwa [Discernment and Wholehearted Practice of the Way],"[8] Dōgen advocates "zazen only," which he defines as "the *samādhi* of self-enjoyment and employment [of enlightenment],"[9] as the right entrance to the Buddha Dharma, and as the "wonderful means . . . passed on directly from Buddha to Buddha."[10] This emphasis on zazen is repeated throughout subsequent collections of practical teachings, such as *Gakudō Yōjin-shū* (*Guidelines for Studying the Way*)[11] and *Shōbōgenzō Zuimonki* (*Transcription of Talks on the Treasure of the True Dharma Eye*).[12] The latter contains the following passages:

> In Zen the practice that has been handed down by the Patriarchs is essentially zazen. This practice is suitable for all people.
> . . . If you clarify the great matter through just sitting (*shikantaza*), you will have unlimited ways to guide others, even if you may not know a single word. . . . Zazen is the practice

of the Buddhas, and is thus without artifice. It is indeed the
true embodiment of the self. The buddha dharma is not to be
sought outside of this.[13]

Nor is this emphasis on zazen confined to Dōgen's early period. As Steven Heine remarks, "Dōgen's commitment to just sitting (*shikantaza*) . . .
remains consistent throughout his career."[14] In *Shōbōgenzō* fascicles such
as "Kai-in Zammai [Ocean Mūdra Samādhi],"[15] "Zazengi [Instructions
for Zazen],"[16] "Zazenshin [The Point of Zazen],"[17] and "Zanmai-ō-zanmai
[King of Samādhis],"[18] as well as in numerous talks gathered in the *Eihei
Kōroku*,[19] Dōgen never tires of stressing the importance and singing the
praises of zazen.[20]

On occasion Dōgen goes so far as to claim that "you no longer have
need for incense-offerings, bowing, calling on the name of Amida Buddha,[21] penance disciplines, or reading sutras. Just sit in zazen and cast
off your body and mind,"[22] and he ascribes this exclusive emphasis on
zazen to his teacher, Rujing.[23] To be sure, such statements where Dōgen
promotes the practice of zazen to the exclusion of other practices of
Buddhism need to be tempered and counterbalanced by attending to the
manner in which he does in fact affirm, interpretively adapt, and promote
these other disciplines.[24] Nevertheless, that zazen is the most important
practice for Dōgen can hardly be disputed. The pioneer Dōgen scholar
in the West, Hee-Jin Kim, suggests that "Dōgen's whole works—written
or otherwise—are simply footnotes on zazen-only."[25] And a contemporary Sōtō teacher, Shohaku OKUMURA, has not only called *Fukanzazengi*
Dōgen's "most important writing" but has even suggested that "all of the
Shōbōgenzō and Dōgen's other writings . . . can be seen as commentaries"
on this brief yet extremely rich text.[26]

The present essay attempts to unfold the implications of *Fukanzazengi*,
using it as a touchstone and springboard for reflecting on key elements
of the practice and philosophy of Dōgen's Zen. In particular this essay
attempts to elucidate two core teachings of *Fukanzazengi* that are reit-
erated and elaborated on elsewhere in Dōgen's writings: "the oneness of
practice and enlightenment"[27] and "nonthinking."[28] In order to understand the profound significance of the former idea, however, we need to

begin with a consideration of Dōgen's great faith and his great doubt—a consideration that will also allow us to clarify some key doctrinal commonalities and methodological differences between the Sōtō and Rinzai schools of Japanese Zen.

GREAT FAITH AND GREAT DOUBT

The opening section of *Fukanzazengi* presents—and is meant to evoke in us—the great quandary that Dōgen struggled with as a young monk, a quandary that drove him to leave the Tendai monastery on Mt. Hiei, to practice under Eisai's successor Myōzen at Kenninji, the first Zen temple in Japan, and ultimately to go to China in search of an answer. In his traditional Sōtō biographies, the young Dōgen was deeply troubled by the following question.

> Both esoteric and exoteric Buddhist teachings proclaim that "one's own embodied self-nature is naturally from birth the original Dharma-nature." If this is so, why do the Buddhas of the past, present and future aspire to and pursue enlightenment?[29]

In other words, if the Tendai teaching of *hongaku*, "original enlightenment" is true—that is, if from the start we are enlightened beings—why is there a need for us to practice the various disciplines of Buddhism, such as zazen? While the mature Dōgen neither affirms nor rejects the term *hongaku*, he does frequently employ very similar terms such as *honshō*, and his confident affirmation of a kind of "original enlightenment" seems evident in the opening lines of *Fukanzazengi*:

> The Way is basically perfect and all-pervading; how could it be contingent upon practice and enlightenment? The true vehicle is self-sufficient; what need is there for special effort? Indeed, the whole body is free from dust; who could believe in a means to brush it clean? It is never apart from this very place; what is the use of travelling around to practice?

"The Way" translates *dao*[30] in Chinese, a concept borrowed by early Chinese Buddhists from Daoism and used to translate, among other Sanskrit terms, "*bodhi*, which means awakening or enlightenment, as in one of the translations of *anuttarā samyak-saṃbodhi*, supreme awakening, *mujōdō*."[31] Dōgen's affirmation of an all-pervading Way can thus be understood as an affirmation of an original enlightenment that pervades all of reality. This affirmation is iterated in his famous "creative rereading" of the pivotal lines from the *Mahāparinirvāṇa Sūtra*, normally understood to mean "all sentient beings without exception have the Buddha Nature." According to Dōgen, "the words entire being [*shitsu-u*] mean both sentient beings and all [other] beings; and so, [what the *Sūtra* means to say is that] entire being is the Buddha Nature [*shitsu-u wa busshō nari*]."[32]

However, this radical affirmation of a ubiquitous Buddha Nature—an all-pervading Way—can all too easily mislead us into a self-satisfied acceptance of our status quo state of delusion. As Kim points out, "Dōgen did not question the truth of original enlightenment but believed it with his whole heart and mind," and yet at the same time he was keenly aware that such doctrines could become "dangerously indistinguishable from a crude and irresponsible acceptance of whatever existed in the world, at the sacrifice of spiritual exertions."[33] Dōgen's teacher Rujing clearly warned him against misunderstanding or misuse of the teaching of original enlightenment: "If one says all sentient beings are from the first Buddhas, this would be the same as the heresy of naturalism (*jinen-gedō*)."[34]

For Dōgen, even if there is a sense in which we are always already enlightened, there remains the necessity of awakening to, realizing, manifesting, or verifying[35] this universal Way or ubiquitous Buddha Nature. As Dōgen succinctly puts this crucial point in "Bendōwa":

> Although the Dharma amply inheres in every person, without practice, it does not presence; if it is not verified, it is not attained.[36]

In "Shinjin Gakudō [Study of the Way with Body and Mind]" Dōgen stresses: "The Buddha Way is not attained without making the effort to practice it, and without making the effort to learn it, it becomes ever more remote."[37] Dōgen affirms many ways to practice with the body and the mind, but first and foremost he recommends the practice of zazen. In response to the misunderstanding of this practice of seated meditation as "sitting idly"—the conflation, we might say, of "just sitting"[38] with "just sitting around"—Dōgen responds: "This is as profound an illusion as to declare there is no water when you are sitting in the midst of the ocean."[39] In other words, to declare that one is already enlightened so there is no need to do anything is just as erroneous as to think that enlightenment is a distant goal, a special state of being far removed from the here and now.

In his *Zazenwasan* (*Song in Praise of Zazen*), the eighteenth-century Rinzai Zen master Hakuin also speaks of "crying out in thirst while standing in the midst of water." Not unlike Dōgen's *Fukanzazengi*, Hakuin's *Zazenwasan* begins with a firm declaration of original enlightenment: "Sentient beings are originally Buddhas"; and it ends with the claim: "This body is none other than Buddha."[40] Both Dōgen and Hakuin thus affirm a sense of innate buddhahood or what Buddhism (especially East Asian Mahāyāna Buddhism) often refers to as the "inherent purity of the mind,"[41] and they would agree that this is not a matter of a disembodied spiritual substance but entails rather what Dōgen refers to as "the oneness of body and mind."[42]

And yet there are indeed important differences between Dōgen's and Hakuin's approaches to the practice of verifying this innate buddhahood.[43] On the one hand, Hakuin's Rinzai Zen stresses the need to awaken to one's original Buddha Nature by way of using a kōan to first of all arouse the "great ball of doubt"; one must then resolve this doubt by breaking through the "gateless barrier" or "checkpoint without a gate"[44] of this "initial barrier"[45] kōan and, in an abrupt experience of *kenshō*, arrive at a direct realization of one's Buddha Nature.[46] Dōgen's Sōtō Zen, on the other hand, stresses the need to "just sit" with a firm "faith"[47] in one's inherent buddhahood. Dōgen tells us, "Only a person of great capacity and true faith is able to enter [the realm of buddhas]."[48] One must sit with the firm conviction that, from the start, zazen is a "practice based on enlightenment";[49] it is not a practice leading to enlightenment, but is itself "the wondrous practice of original enlightenment."[50] John Daido

Loori Rōshi (who taught using both kōan and *shikantaza* methods) writes: "*Shikantaza* . . . is zazen based fundamentally on faith—faith in the Buddha's enlightenment, faith in one's own Buddha Nature, faith in the process of practice itself."[51]

The *Zengakudaijiten* (*Large Dictionary of Zen Studies*), produced by the Sōtō school's Komazawa University, suggests that in Zen one finds two notions of "faith": one at the beginning of the path, as "the necessary state of mind for entering the gate of the Buddha Way," and one at the end of the path, as "the ultimate state of mind attesting to the truth (*shōshin*)."[52] It may be better to speak of this as a continuum rather than as two separate senses of faith; that is to say, it may be better to think in terms of a process through which "belief" deepens into "confidence." Yet for many there are, and may indeed need to be, decisive moments of "conversion," here in the sense of "turning the light around"[53] and seeing for oneself what one had heretofore merely believed on the basis of testimony.

Dōgen may be understood as offering a Zen version of St. Anselm's Christian dictum *credo ut intelligam* ("I believe so that I may understand"), insofar as a kind of faith is necessary to engage in the practice that enables one to recognize the enlightenment that was already there. This is neither faith in an unknowable Other nor belief in one's ability to come to understand this Other, but rather trust in one's innate ability to awaken to one's own "original face." Linji[54] also suggests that our fundamental ignorance, our failure to know ourselves, is bound up with a kind of faithlessness, namely what he calls a "lack of faith in yourself" or "lack of self-confidence."[55] Enlightenment may entail cultivating "trust/faith in the mind,"[56] as the third patriarch Sengcan puts it, or "awakening faith/trust in the Mahāyāna,"[57] where "Mahāyāna" indicates the Suchness of the One Mind.[58] In any case, generating a true faith, trust, conviction, or confidence in one's Buddha Nature may be, and may indeed need to be, experienced as a paradoxically transformative homecoming event of realization (in the double sense of "becoming aware of" and "actualizing")—as if finally becoming who one in truth has always already been.

As we have said, despite their profound doctrinal commonalities, there are significant differences between Dōgen's Sōtō and Hakuin's Rinzai methods of zazen. The Sōtō method is that of "just sitting" with firm faith in one's Buddha Nature, so that this faith can give way to confidence as this Buddha Nature "silently illuminates"[59] itself. The Rinzai method of "looking at phrases,"[60] on the other hand, employs kōans that confound and thus push one beyond dualistic discrimination.[61] A kōan such as Hakuin's "the sound of one hand" is used to generate what Wumen calls "the great ball of doubt," which is compared to a hot ball of iron that one can neither swallow nor spit out. Concentrating with one's "360 bones and 84,000 pores" such that, after "inside and outside have naturally become welded into a single block . . . all of a sudden it will break open, and you will astonish heaven and shake the earth."[62] Hakuin writes, "the study of Zen makes as its essential the resolution of the ball of doubt. That is why it is said: 'At the bottom of great doubt lies great awakening. If you doubt fully you will awaken fully.'"[63]

Nevertheless, we should bear in mind that, along with a "great feeling of doubt"[64] and a "great determination,"[65] the third requisite in Hakuin's Rinzai method is a "great root of faith,"[66] namely, faith that "sentient beings are originally Buddhas" and that one has the innate capacity to "see one's original nature." And for his part Dōgen, as we have seen, found it necessary to pass through a great doubt on the way to his own ego-shedding experience of "dropping off of the body and mind."[67] His teaching of "just sitting," moreover, is not a matter of just sitting around, lackadaisical in one's self-assurance that one is already enlightened; Dōgen repeatedly urges us to "arouse the *bodhicitta*" and meditate with wholehearted intensity, "as if putting out a fire on your head."[68]

A key section near the end of *Gakudō Yōjin-shū* (*Guidelines for Studying the Way*) reveals how Dōgen understands the relation between faith (or "trust," as *shin* is here translated) in our original inhabitance of the all-pervading Way and the need to realize, to awaken to, and to actualize this inhabitance through the practice of zazen.

> Those who practice the Buddha Way should first of all trust in the Buddha Way. Those who trust in the Buddha Way should trust that they are in essence within the Buddha Way,

where there is no delusion, no false thinking, no confusion, no increase or decrease, and no mistake. To arouse such trust and illuminate the Way in this manner, and to practice accordingly, are fundamental in studying the Way. You do this by sitting, which severs the root of thinking and blocks access to the road of intellectual understanding. . . . If once, in sitting, you sever the root of thinking, in eight or nine cases out of ten you will immediately attain understanding of the Way.[69]

We will return to the point that zazen involves stepping back beneath intellectual thinking. Before that, we need to see how the resolution of Dōgen's great doubt—that is to say, his ability to arouse great faith or confidence in, and to attain a holistic understanding of, his and our original inhabitance of the Buddha Way—was attained through the practice of zazen, and specifically through an experience of zazen as an exemplary instance of "the oneness of practice and enlightenment."

ONENESS OF PRACTICE AND ENLIGHTENMENT

We have seen how *Fukanzazengi* begins with a confident declaration of the ubiquity of the Buddha Way. We are already standing in the midst of the water, in the midst, that is, of the "Ocean of Buddha Nature."[70] But Dōgen immediately goes on to indicate the great problem:

And yet, if there is a hairs-breadth deviation, it is like the gap between heaven and earth; if the least like or dislike arises, the mind is lost in confusion.

When composing these lines Dōgen surely must have had in mind *Inscription on Trust in the Mind*, the great poem by the third patriarch, Sengcan, which begins:

The ultimate Way is not difficult. It only avoids picking and choosing.

If you just refrain from greed and hate, it is wide open,
   bright and clear.
Yet if there is the slightest distinction, it is as distant as
   heaven is from earth. . . .
Perfect all around like vast empty space, with nothing lack-
   ing and nothing extra.
It is indeed just our grasping and rejecting that make it
   seem otherwise.[71]

Later on in *Fukanzazengi* Dōgen says that, in the practice of zazen, one should "not think in terms of good or bad. Do not judge true or false." This echoes the sixth patriarch Huineng's teaching that, in order to awaken to one's "original face," one must "think neither good nor evil."[72]

The root problem at issue here is what Śākyamuni Buddha called the "three poisons" or "three unwholesome roots" of greed, hate, and igno-rance. Having misunderstood one's self as a fixed ego-substance dualis-tically separated from other persons and things in the world, one views these "others" in the bivalent terms of either that which gratifies the ego, that which one accordingly craves to pull toward oneself and possess, or that which disturbs the ego, that which one accordingly craves to push away and be rid of. Our discriminatory judgments of "good and evil" or "right and wrong" are proximally and for the most part rooted in these egoistic drives to pull toward and push away, in these volitional impulses of greed/attachment and aversion/hate, which in turn are rooted in our fundamental ignorance regarding the nature of ourselves and our rela-tion to other beings. Our egoistic value judgments inform, then, our intentional, discriminative thinking,[73] whether we are calculating how to satisfy a sexual desire, how to avoid an annoying person or unpleasant task, how to obtain a higher salary, or how to acquire a position of pres-tige and power over others.

Even the very practice of Buddhism itself is not immune from this calculative thinking, even when, or perhaps especially when, we attain to enlightening experiences. Indeed, the example of such problematic thinking given in *Fukanzazengi* is not that of an immoral or irreligious person, but rather that of an accomplished practitioner of Zen:

Suppose you are confident in your understanding and rich in enlightenment, gaining the wisdom that glimpses the ground [of buddhahood], attaining the Way and clarifying the mind, arousing an aspiration to reach for the heavens. You are playing in the entranceway, but you still are short of the vital path of emancipation.

Dōgen acknowledges that, in the course of one's practice, one might have powerfully enlightening experiences, "gaining the wisdom that glimpses the ground [of buddhahood]." Yet in such cases one has, at best, climbed to the top of a hundred foot pole, where it is easy to get stuck, ironically gloating in one's accomplishment, attached to one's own sense of liberation, tied up with "golden chains."

While sharply critical of the problems that can beset thinking in terms of "original enlightenment," especially the error of thinking that there is nothing to gain and therefore no need for practice, Dōgen also warns against problems involved in the idea of "acquired enlightenment,"[74] which include not only failing to recognize the all-pervading nature of the Way, but also thinking of enlightenment as a privileged experience and possession of a proud few. Dōgen repeatedly stresses that a true experience of enlightenment always gives way to wiping away the "traces of enlightenment."[75] In "Genjōkōan [The Presencing of Truth]" he writes: "There is laying to rest the traces of enlightenment, and one must ever again emerge from resting content with such traces."[76] A true Buddha is always "going beyond Buddha."[77] In Gakudo Yōjin-shū (Guidelines for Studying the Way) Dōgen writes: "Though practice varies—initiated by faith or Dharma knowledge, with emphasis on sudden or gradual enlightenment—you always depend on practice to go beyond enlightenment."[78] In an Enlightenment Day Ceremony Dharma Hall Discourse, he urges: "Right now awaken the way and see the bright star. This is exactly the place where the Tathāgata eats porridge."[79] And yet Dōgen would certainly agree with Zhaozhou when he says, if you have eaten your morning porridge, that is, if you have had your initial experience of awakening, "wash your bowl"—get rid of the residues, and the "stench," of enlightenment.[80]

Zhaozhou's instruction to "wash your bowl" can also be understood to indicate that enlightenment is ultimately to be found right in the midst of everyday life. The utmost importance of wholeheartedly engaging in seemingly mundane duties such as preparing meals is something Dōgen first learned in China from his encounters with two monastery cooks.[81] Together with the revolutionary idea that practice is not a means to the end of acquired enlightenment but rather an expression of original enlightenment, this was the key to Dōgen's solution to his great doubt, that is, to the contradiction he had felt there to be between his great faith in original enlightenment and his keen sense of the necessity of practice. Dōgen codified this solution in one of his signature phrases: "the oneness of practice and enlightenment."[82]

This idea is indicated in *Fukanzazengi* where, in order to stress the need for ongoing practice, even after initial realization, he refers to the "six years of upright sitting" of Śākyamuni Buddha, "even though he was [already] wise at birth," and to Bodhidharma's "nine years of facing a wall" sitting in zazen, even after he came to China as an enlightened master.

Dōgen first spells out this key idea of the oneness of practice and enlightenment in "Bendōwa" as follows:

> To think practice and enlightenment are not one is a non-Buddhist view. In the Buddha Dharma, practice and enlightenment are one and the same. As your present practice is practice within enlightenment [*shōjō no shu*], your initial wholehearted engagement in the Way is in itself the whole of original enlightenment [*honshō*]. That is why from the time you are instructed in the way of practice, you are told not to anticipate enlightenment apart from practice. It is because practice points directly to original enlightenment. Since it is from the very first the enlightenment of practice [*shu no shō*], enlightenment is endless. Since it is the practice of enlightenment [*shō no shu*], practice is beginningless. . . . It is practice that from the outset is inseparable from enlightenment, and, fortunately, we [practitioners] all transmit a portion of wondrous practice ourselves; our wholehearted engagement in the

Way with the beginner's mind thus obtains a portion of original enlightenment on the ground of nonwillful naturalness
[*mu-i*]. You should know that, in order to keep from defiling
this enlightenment that is inseparable from practice, Buddhas
and patriarchs teach unceasingly that we must not allow our
practice to diminish.[83]

The Way is always right there under our feet; and yet we are constantly
"defiling" or "tainting" it with our egoistic discriminations. It helps to
recall that the Sanskrit word for the afflictions that tether us to samsara
is *kleśa*, meaning the "impurities" or "coverings" that conceal us from
the purity of our true nature. These "defilements" cover over and cloud
the original luminosity of our enlightening minds, smoldering the warm
glow of our originally compassionate hearts, and as a result we suffer
from, and cause others to suffer from, "agonizing worries."[84] Zazen does
not make us into anything we are not already. Rather, it lets us become
what we truly already are. Zazen is "the Dharma gate of peace and bliss"
simply because it returns us to the "undefiled practice-enlightenment"[85]
that is the natural activity of our original face, our Buddha Nature.[86] The
Buddha Nature is ubiquitous, the Buddha Way is all-pervading; we just
need to undertake the radical "backward step"[87] so as to discover our
place of participation—our "Dharma position"[88]—in it. What is already
there needs to be verified (a more literal translation of Dōgen's favored
word for enlightenment, *shō*); it needs to be realized.

"Genjōkōan" ends with the following story, which poignantly illustrates the oneness of practice and enlightenment or verification:

> As Chan Master Baoche of Mount Mayu was using his fan, a
> monk came and asked, "It is the wind's nature to be constantly
> abiding and there is no place in which it does not circulate.
> Why then, sir, do you still use a fan?"
>
> The master said, "You only know that it is the nature of the
> wind to be constantly abiding. You don't yet know the reason
> [more literally: the principle of the Way] that there is no place
> it does not reach."

The monk said, "What is the reason for there being no place in which it does not circulate?"

At which time the master just used his fan.

The monk bowed reverently.

The verifying experience of the Buddha Dharma and the vital path of its true transmission are like this. To say that if it is constantly abiding one shouldn't use a fan, that even without using a fan one should be able to feel the wind, is to not know [the meaning of] either constantly abiding or the nature of the wind. Because it is the nature of the wind to be constantly abiding, the wind of the Buddha household lets the great earth presence as gold and ripens the Milky Way into delicious cream.[89]

The questioning monk, like the young Dōgen, is wondering why, if the "wind" of the Buddha Way is all-pervading, one needs to make the effort to practice. If everything is already as it should be, why work to improve anything? Should not the master be content with the heat as it is? Is he not trying to change reality by cooling himself with a fan? These questions betray a separation, an abstraction, of the self from the world. In truth, there is no essential difference between the wind naturally blowing and the master naturally fanning himself. In fact, refusing to fan himself would be artificial inactivity; that would reveal a misunderstanding of "nondoing"[90] as mere passivity or lack of activity, rather than as action (or inaction) done naturally, in accord with the situation, in accord with the Way.

Enlightenment is not a static end of activity, but rather a dynamic Way of being ever under way. What constantly abides is not an eternal substance but rather an ever-circulating "wind." The end of practice is to realize that there is no end of practice. The end of practice is to realize that endless practice is an end in itself. Linji would say that it is to be at Home while on the Way, and on the Way while at Home.[91] There is a Calm in the midst of the Wind, a still eye in the midst of even the stormiest activities of life. And to find this calm, to awaken to this immovable still-ness that is not opposed to but rather enables the most dynamic movement, Dōgen, along with the rest of the Zen tradition, recommends the practice of zazen.

In the practice of zazen, writes Dōgen in *Fukanzazengi*, we must "have no designs on becoming a Buddha. . . . The zazen I speak of is not meditation practice" in the sense of a technique for attaining something one does not already have or becoming something other than what one already is. Rather, "It is simply the Dharma gate of peace and bliss, the practice-enlightenment of totally culminated awakening. It is the truth realized [*kōan genjō*]." In the "Zazenshin [The Point of Zazen]" and "Kokyō [Ancient Mirror]" fascicles of the *Shōbōgenzō*, Dōgen pursues this issue further by taking up the story of Nanyue, who responds to Mazu's claim that he is "practicing zazen with the aim of making a Buddha" by engaging in the apparently futile action of "polishing a tile with the aim of making a mirror." This story is generally understood as underscoring the "original enlightenment" point that, since one is already a Buddha, one should not practice meditation in order to "acquire enlightenment." This reading can be taken to underscore Dōgen's teaching of the oneness of practice and enlightenment. Yet it might also be misunderstood to imply that there is no need to practice, which would plunge us back into the heresy of naturalism.[92] Dōgen thus turns the point of the story over once more and claims: "Polishing a tile to make a mirror definitely has a reason; it is not a hollow statement but rather the presentation of a universal truth [*genjō no kōan*]."[93] "When polishing a tile becomes a mirror, Mazu becomes a Buddha. When Mazu becomes a Buddha, Mazu immediately becomes Mazu. When Mazu becomes Mazu, zazen immediately becomes zazen." Hence, Dōgen goes on to say, "there is an ancient mirror made from a tile, and when this tile is polished it has never been defiled. The tile is not defiled; just polish it as a tile."[94] In other words, Buddha Nature is manifested precisely in wholehearted practice; this involves first of all engaging in zazen as a "practice of becoming a Buddha," not in the sense of aiming at a state or status to be attained at a later date, but rather in the sense of becoming a Buddha in and as each moment of this very practice. Being a Buddha is becoming a Buddha; it is a matter of always being on the Way of becoming a Buddha. Practice is enlightenment. Enlightenment is neither a distant goal nor an established state and status; it is a never-ending practice of enlightening. It is the realization of being at Home on the Way and on the Way at Home.

If we thoroughly engage in the practice of zazen in this manner, we are no longer self-conscious of doing the practice; the residual thought of "I am just sitting" drops off such that only an undefiled "just sitting" remains. This is practice-enlightenment being naturally undefiled. This is original verification, "the *samādhi* in which one receives and employs" the enlightening Way of the Buddha Nature. This reception-and-employment is Life living itself through one, and it issues forth in a wholehearted and traceless engagement in our everyday activities. There is no longer any trace of separation between practice and enlightenment, such that the one gives way completely to the other. "When we cast off the wondrous practice, original enlightenment fills our hands; when we transcend original enlightenment, wondrous practice permeates our bodies."[95]

In truth, all of life is practice. Since the Way is all-pervading, the practice of the Way should pervade all of one's life. Dōgen thus taught not only the proper way to "just sit," but also the proper way to mindfully just eat, use the toilet, go about one's work in harmonious community with others, brush one's teeth, fold one's robes, and get into bed. Sōtō Zen is often said to be characterized by the dictum formulated by the third abbot of Eiheiji, Gikai: "Dignified manner is the Buddha Dharma; decorum is the essential teaching."[96] In *Tenzo Kyōkun* (*Instructions to the Monastery Cook*) Dōgen teaches that Zen is a matter of wholehearted engagement in the mundane activities of life: cooking, tending to the garden, cleaning, taking out the garbage, and so on, all performed with the health and happiness of everyone in the community (ultimately the community of all sentient beings) in mind.

Zazen is a touchstone practice for such a life. Yet it should not be thought of as a sacred ritual separated from the profane activities of the rest of one's daily routine. All of life's activities are sacred. Bodhidharma goes still further and, in order to free us entirely from the snares of dualistic discrimination, tells us that the most sacred teaching of Zen is "vast emptiness; nothing sacred."[97] The Buddha Way does not take us beyond an engagement in the mundane activities of life; rather, as Nanquan says, "Everyday mind is the Way."[98] In *Fukanzazengi*, Dōgen says that one should practice zazen (seated meditation) with the understanding that it is not "limited to sitting or lying down." And yet, in order to find our way back into this Way of life as the oneness of practice and enlightenment, Dōgen universally recommends the specific practice of seated meditation. To paraphrase my own former teacher, Tanaka Hōjū Rōshi of Shōkokuji: zazen really means to let the heart-mind be seated, at all times, no matter what one is doing; folding the legs and meditating in the seated position is just the best way to go about learning how to do this.

THE HEART OF ZAZEN: NONTHINKING

Instructions in zazen generally proceed in three steps: one is first of all to attend to bodily position,[99] then to the breath,[100] and finally to the mind.[101] In *Fukanzazengi* Dōgen provides fairly detailed guidance on physical preparation and posture. Regarding the breath, though, he merely says that one should begin by "taking a breath and exhaling fully" and then should "breathe softly through one's nose." He does not go on to say, for example, that one should breath down into and up out of the *tanden*, the psychosomatic center of meditative concentration located one or two inches beneath the navel.[102] Nor does he suggest using the methods of "counting the breaths"[103] or "following the breaths"[104] on the way to "just sitting."[105]

Regarding the mind, Dōgen's instructions are terse, even cryptic, yet also pregnant and precise. We are told to

> put aside the intellectual practice of investigating words and chasing phrases, and learn to take the backward step that turns the light and shines it inward. . . . Give up the operations of the mind, intellect, and consciousness; stop measuring with thoughts, ideas, and views.

Although his prolific commentaries in *Shōbōgenzō* and *Eihei Kōroku* attest to his high regard for the Buddhist sutras and especially for the kōan literature of the Zen tradition, he evidently discourages "looking at phrases"[106] while sitting in zazen. It is true that, as Kim and Heine have compellingly demonstrated,[107] Dōgen stands out among Zen masters for his repudiation of a simplistic understanding of Zen as a tradition "not founded on words and letters." Remarkably and repeatedly, he radically affirms the liberating potential of the so-called "entangling vines"[108] of language, literature, and philosophy to serve as "expressive attainments of the Way."[109] Nevertheless, it is also clear that Dōgen's instructions regarding zazen as a practice of "just sitting" involve taking a temporary step back from discursive thinking.

Rather than focus on the central term or phrase[110] of a kōan, as we settle into "steady, immovable sitting," Dōgen instructs us to: "Think of not-thinking. How do you think of not-thinking? Nonthinking." These pithy words are taken from a dialogue between Yaoshan (745–827) and a monk. The importance of this dialogue for Dōgen's understanding of the practice of zazen is reflected in the fact that he cites it in "Zazengi [Instructions for Zazen]" as well as in *Fukanzazengi*, and he comments on it in "Zazenshin [The Point of Zazen]" as well as in two Dharma Hall Discourses.[111] The dialogue reads:

> Once, when the Great Master Hongdao of Yaoshan was sitting [in meditation], a monk asked him, "What are you thinking, [sitting there] so fixedly?" The master answered, "I am thinking of not-thinking." The monk asked, "How do you think of not-thinking?" The master answered, "Nonthinking."[112]

The word translated as "thinking" here is *shiryō*.[113] The first character of this compound covers a wide range of operations of the mind. Not unlike Descartes' *cogitare*, it can mean: to think, expect, judge, consider, believe, feel, regard, expect, imagine, intend, desire, care for, and so on. The second character means to weigh, measure, calculate or estimate. The term *shiryō* thus connotes a kind of discriminative thinking that calculates and evaluates. We can understand it to convey a sense of the basic "intentionality" or directedness of the *ego cogito* (the "I think") away from itself and toward things, things which it represents as objects standing over against itself as subject, objects which it then weighs, measures, calculates, and evaluates according to its interests, preferences, and plans.

When Dōgen instructs us to turn the light of the mind around on itself, he is not just asking us to become aware of this stream of discriminative, calculating thinking. The deeper lesson is to become aware of the source of awareness itself. But can the subject become aware of itself without turning itself into just another object of awareness? This would be like asking the eye to turn around and see itself, not indirectly as it is reflected back to itself from the outside, as in a mirror, but directly, nondually. However hard it tries, the grasping mind cannot, as Huike recognized, grasp itself; as the *Diamond Sutra* says, the mind is ungraspable. The calculating mind can only weigh and measure things by first of all holding them at a distance. When it turns around on itself, it is confounded by its own weightlessness, its own immeasurability, its own—emptiness. How is one then to proceed?

In Rinzai Zen, one is instructed to begin by "counting the breaths."[114] Before going cold turkey, a minimal amount of "mind candy" is offered—a bare and bland object for the subject to focus on as it begins the self-emptying descent beneath subject-object duality as such, the descent into a nondual awareness that underlies the polarity of intentional consciousness. The mind, the number, and the breath gradually merge as one enters the unified state of concentration called *samādhi*.[115] Then, when one is ready, a kōan is offered as a doorway—or rather as a "gateless barrier"—though which one must pass in order to reach absolute nonduality. Further kōans are then employed, not just to deepen this experience of nonduality, but also to free one from even the duality of duality and nonduality, and to train one to exercise this freedom in responsible and compassionate ways in a world in which subject and object, self and other, this and that, are "not one and not two."

Yet Dōgen's Sōtō Zen instructions in zazen from the start tell us to "just sit." Teachers in the Sōtō tradition often explain this *shikantaza* as a matter of neither paying attention to thoughts nor trying to get rid of them; rather, one should just let passing thoughts and feelings come and go as they will and, naturally, they will cease to command one's attention, cease to entice one to chase after them. Their force and frequency will dissipate and they may even disappear altogether for extended periods of time. Shunryu Suzuki teaches, "Do not try to stop your mind, but leave everything as it is. Then things will not stay in your mind for so long. Things will come as they come and go as they go." He goes on to say that "eventually your clear, empty mind will last fairly long."[116] Yet just as the sky or the ocean remains there, regardless of whether or not there are passing clouds or waves, the nonthinking mind remains there, regardless of whether or not we are thinking, not-thinking, or thinking of not-thinking.

As Loori puts it, nonthinking is "the boundless mind of *samādhi* that neither holds on to, nor lets go of, thoughts."[117] Becoming directly aware of—or rather, simply becoming—this clear, empty, open, untainted mind is the core of just sitting. This mind is at bottom neither an activity of thinking nor an object of thought; it is an open field of nondual aware-ness that embraces and enables both thinking and not-thinking as well as thinking of not-thinking. In terms of thinking, it can only be called "non-thinking" or *hi-shiryō*. The "non" (*hi*) here expresses neither privation nor opposition; nonthinking is not to be conflated with not-thinking,[118] that is, with an absence or suppression of thought. *Hi-shiryō* is sometimes more freely translated as "beyond thinking"—yet, in keeping with the orientation of a radical "backward step" to what Nishitani Keiji calls "the absolute near-side," it would be better understood as "beneath thinking." In any case, nonthinking is radically other than thinking—so radically other that it is not in any way at odds with or in opposition to thinking, and so it can be nondually "not one and not two" with it. Nonthink-ing is neither thinking nor the mere absence or suppression of think-ing. Whereas "not-thinking" can be thought of as a contentless object of thinking, nonthinking lies on the absolute hither side of the very duality of thinking and not-thinking.

Thinking is always aimed outward, in other words, it is always "step-ping forward." Thinking of not-thinking can be understood as a paradox-ical practice that short-circuits this outward orientation of the intentional mind and occasions the "backward step" into the nondual awareness of nonthinking as the ground—or rather empty field—of both thinking and not-thinking. In thinking of not-thinking, we are aiming our intentional mind at its own ground, at nonthinking, and thus turning it into a contentless object of thought, into a kind of relative or privative nothingness. But nonthinking is in truth an "absolute nothingness" in the sense of an essentially indeterminate field of nondual awareness, a field which underlies or encompasses the determinations of thinking, not-thinking, and thinking of not-thinking.

But how do we get from here to there? How do we cease to identify ourselves with the "monkey mind" of our obsessive trains of calculative thinking and begin to think (or not-think) from the clear, empty mind of nonthinking? Dōgen, following Yaoshan, tells us to "think of not-thinking." If one is told "not to think," the first thing one does, the only thing one knows how to do, is to think about not thinking. Yet, as we have said, when Dōgen tells us to "turn the light around," he is not telling us to make the mind into a mental object, the seer into something seen, awareness into an object of awareness. Nevertheless, we may indeed have to go through this detour, the "wall gazing" impasse of "thinking of not-thinking," in order to occasion the "backward step" with our whole being to a direct experience of what we can only call, in the language of thinking, "nonthinking."[119]

To repeat, nonthinking is not simply not-thinking, understood as either the suppression of thought or a contentless object of thought; nor does it exclude either not-thinking or thinking. Nonthinking is not opposed to thinking. It is the ultimate "where-from" and "where-in" of thinking; it is the open field of awareness that encompasses and engenders thinking. This is a crucial point that needs to be emphasized, since Zen is often mistaken—by misguided proponents as well as mistaken opponents—as entailing and even promoting an anti-intellectualism. Dōgen himself, we need to bear in mind, was a remarkably creative and critical thinker as well as an avid reader and prolific writer of texts, while at the same time being an advocate of regularly stepping back from these activities to just sit in nonthinking. Such just sitting does not replace but rather enables just reading and just thinking. As Kim points out, Dōgen does not simply disparage discriminatory thinking; he indeed explicitly speaks of "correct discrimination."[120] Whereas we normally discriminate on the basis of our egoistic cravings and attachments, "discriminative activities, once freed of substantialist, egocentric obsessions, can function compassionately and creatively."[121]

At one point Dōgen even identifies nonthinking with the "right thinking"[122] of the Eightfold Path; although he presumably means that what is traditionally understood as "right thinking" is rooted in the nonthinking of zazen, since he goes on to say that "right thinking is [sitting immovably in zazen to the point of] wearing through a meditation cushion."[123] In other words, "right thinking," as the second element of the Eightfold Path, is rooted in a correct understanding of the eighth element, "right concentration." Here Dōgen is presumably reiterating Huineng's claim that "Meditation itself is the substance of wisdom; wisdom itself is the function of meditation."[124] While this wisdom can and should animate discursive knowledge, it is rooted neither in discursive knowledge nor in obtuse ignorance. As Nanquan says, "The Way [Dao] does not belong to knowing or to not-knowing. Knowing is illusion; not-knowing is blankness."[125] The Way is realized through a peculiar and profound kind of nonknowing or nonthinking.

"When Buddhas are truly Buddhas," Dōgen writes in "Genjōkōan [The Presencing of Truth]," "there is no need for them to be conscious of themselves as Buddhas."[126] When Bodhidharma was asked who he is, he answered, without hesitation, without doubt, "I don't know" or, more literally, "not knowing."[127] This was not a mere confession of ignorance; it was a pure self-presentation of the original face, that is, of the formless, ungraspable self, of the self that has, as Dōgen goes on to say in "Genjōkōan," studied itself to the point of forgetting itself in its pure openness to the myriad things of the world. That pure openness of heart-mind[128] is nonthinking.

Let us be clear about this important and often misunderstood point: On the one hand, no amount of zazen on its own can replace philosophical thinking; on the other hand, no amount or kind of philosophical thinking—be it analytical, dialectical, hermeneutical, or even phenomenological—can substitute for the practice of zazen. Yet zazen no more opposes or delegitimizes philosophical thinking than it opposes or delegitimizes politics or poetry. Zazen should be understood as enabling philosophical thinking, just as it enables moral action and artistic creation; it clears the way for a free and responsible engagement in these activities. The point is *not only* that we must learn to think *on the basis of nonthinking*, to discriminate *on the basis of nondiscrimination*; the point is *also* that we must learn *to think* on the basis of nonthinking, *to discriminate* on the basis of nondiscrimination.[129] We must step back from thinking (and not-thinking) to nonthinking, not in order to avoid the privilege and responsibility of thinking, but in order to think well, that is, in order to not just spin the wheels of our egocentric discriminating minds without being rooted in a clear perception of, and non-egocentric participation in, the dynamically interconnected and perspectivally multiguous nexus of reality. And this entails discovering and maintaining the pure awareness of the open heart-mind of nonthinking.

Dōgen is often, and justifiably, lauded as the most intellectually brilliant and hermeneutically creative figure in the Zen tradition. Yet despite the strikingly philosophical quality of much of Dōgen's writing, along with the rest of the Zen tradition he too often points beyond the ken of discursive reason and speech. This is especially the case when he is prompting us to become aware of that which underlies thought, of that which enables thought but which, in the end, cannot be grasped in thought as an object of thought. In *Fukanzazengi* he refers to famous cases where Zen masters have raised a finger, held up a fist, or given a shout, and says that these nondiscursive actions, which "cannot be understood by discriminative thinking," present us with "a standard prior to knowledge and views." In order to understand these direct "presentations of truth,"[130] "intelligence or lack of it is not an issue." What matters is that "you concentrate your effort single-mindedly . . . wholeheartedly engaging the Way." What matters most is that one learn to engage in the undefiled practice-enlightenment, that is, in the enlightening practice of nonthinking—and thinking and acting from there.

Sky, Mirror, Ocean: Metaphors for the Open Mind

As Dōgen stresses in *Fukanzazengi*, and as I have stressed throughout this essay, the pivotal practice of Zen is zazen. Yet Dōgen never tires of exercising his philosophical and poetic powers to the fullest in order to speak out of and back into the meditative silence of just sitting. Accordingly, let us conclude by attempting to speak, at the very limits of language, of that which underlies and encompasses all discursive distinctions. Let us try to speak metaphorically of nonthinking and its relation to thinking and not-thinking, and indeed do so with three metaphors that are frequently employed by Dōgen himself, as well as by other Zen figures and by the Mahāyāna Buddhist tradition more generally, namely: sky, mirror, and ocean.[131]

The originally open heart-mind is like a clear sky. We should note that "sky," *sora*, is written with the same character as *kū*, "emptiness" or *śūnyatā*. And we should note that *kokū*, "empty space" or "vacant sky," is also a primal metaphor in Mahāyāna Buddhism, one that is often used synonymously with *kū*.[132] *Awakening of Faith in Mahāyāna* states:

> The essence of the mind is free from actual thoughts. The characteristic of being free from thoughts is to be like the realm of empty space, everywhere yet not in any one place, the one single characteristic of reality, the undifferentiated dharma-body of the Buddha.[133]

Because the "One Mind" is like empty space, it does not obstruct, but rather makes room for, the myriad phenomena in their dynamic interrelatedness. Dōgen takes up this metaphor in "Kokū [Empty Space]," the first fascicle of *Shōbōgenzō* to be delivered at Daibutsuji (later renamed Eiheiji). In this text he effectively equates empty space with nonthinking when he says that "thinking is to be realized by means of empty space, and not-thinking is to be realized by means of empty space."[134] Both thinking and not-thinking take place within the empty space of nonthinking.

But first we must awaken to the clear sky of this underlying nonthinking. Most of the time the mind is a cloudy sky, the clouds being analogous to our intentional, perspectival, and discriminatory thoughts, desires, and emotions, and to the bits of the world interpretively experienced through, or tainted by, the karmic filters of this mostly egocentric stream of consciousness. Although our basic awareness is that of the open sky, we are so wrapped up in the passing clouds that we identify ourselves with these clouds and identify things with our cloudy images of them.

The mirror, which reflects things as they show themselves without distortion, is another central metaphor for the originally enlightened mind in Mahāyāna Buddhism. Dōgen takes up this metaphor especially in the "Kokyō [Ancient Mirror]" fascicle of *Shōbōgenzō*, which begins: "What all the Buddhas and Patriarchs have received, maintained, and passed down, person to person, is the ancient mirror."[135] Harada Sogaku Rōshi explains nonthinking in terms the nonjudgmental quality of a mirror that reflects things as they are without "picking and choosing according to our [egocentric] likes and dislikes."[136] Dōgen quotes Shitou's response to a question concerning the fundamental meaning of the Buddha Dharma: "Not to attain, not to know." When pressed further, Shitou responds: "The vast sky does not hinder white clouds from flying."[137] This nonhindering, however, does not mean standing aloof, but rather being totally engaged in the vicissitudes of life with all its ups and downs and, yes, with all its demands for discriminatory thinking. Only now, in this "total activity"[138] issuing from the open heart-mind, one discriminates on the basis on nondiscrimination,[139] that is, on the basis of impartial compassion, rather than on the basis of egoistic craving and loathing.

How do we get from here to there, or rather, how do we "step back" from there to here, that is, to the "absolute near-side" of the open heart-mind? As we have seen, the answer is zazen, and the method we are given is that of "thinking of not-thinking." When we are told to "think of not-thinking," we, who in our delusion identify ourselves with the stream of cloudy consciousness, are being asked to turn our attention to the sky, which cannot but first appear, from the perspective of the cloudy discriminating mind, as a contentless, formless void. But as we engage in the "backward step," as we disidentify with, detach ourselves from, or "drop off" the body-mind, that is, as we let dissipate the clouds of our discriminatory, intentional thinking/feeling/willing, and as we thereby awaken to the open space of awareness that was always already there underneath the passing clouds, we realize that our true self, our original face, is the clear and open sky surrounding, and making room for, the passing clouds. Furthermore, we realize that since the clouds are in truth delimited forms of this unlimited openness, acts of thinking, feeling, and willing need not be delusive and egocentric restrictions, but can be creative and compassionate expressions of this open-minded and open-hearted freedom.

Along with the sky and the mirror, the third traditional metaphor that can be employed here is that of the ocean or, more specifically, that of the relation between water (formless nonthinking) and waves (forms of thinking). This metaphor too has a long pedigree in Mahāyāna Buddhism, appearing in the *Lankāvatāra Sūtra* as well as in *Awakening of Faith in Mahāyāna*, and we find Dōgen creatively employing it in such texts as the "Busshō [Buddha Nature]" and "Kai-in Zammai [Ocean Mūdra Samādhi]" fascicles of *Shōbōgenzō*. In "Busshō" he says "these mountains, rivers, and the great earth, all are the Ocean of the Buddha Nature [*busshōkai*]."[140] "Kai-in Zammai" begins: "The Buddhas' and the Patriarchs' manner of being is always that of the ocean mūdra *samādhi*," and their "virtuous acts on the surface" are at the same time their "penetration of the profound depths" of this ocean.[141]

The question is: How can we, who tend to restrictively identify ourselves solely with the waves of our mental and emotional discriminations, sink back into this ocean of nondiscriminatory awareness that nondually underlies and gives rise to these waves? How can we, as the perceiving/thinking/feeling/acting beings that we are, awaken to the nonthinking mirror-mind that freely "smashes itself into countless pieces"[142] in each moment of "being-time"[143] so as to express itself in every perspectivally delimited perception, thought, feeling, and action? How can we drop off our egocentric body-minds so as to attune ourselves to the "one mind" and "one body" of the universe,[144] that is, to the "empty space" in which every perspectival opening of a world takes place, be that world focused on a blooming flower or on a falling leaf, on a dusty tile or on a shiny pebble, on a donkey's jaw or on a horse's mouth, on a baby's infectious giggle or on a stranger's cry for help?[145]

Dōgen recommends zazen.

Notes

NOTES TO THE INTRODUCTION

1. Dogen, *Treasury of the True Dharma Eye: Zen Master Dogen's* Shobo Genzo, ed. Kazuaki TANAHASHI (Boston and London: Shambhala, 2010). Most paragraphs in *Shushōgi* are derived from the 12-fascicle *Shōbōgenzō*, although some are derived from the 75-fascicle version and a few from the 95-fascicle version. The first sentence in paragraph ten originates in the *Kegon Kyō* or *Avataṃsaka Sūtra*.

2. See Steven Heine, "Abbreviation or Aberration: The Role of the *Shushōgi* in Modern Sōtō Zen Buddhism," in *Buddhism in the Modern World: Adaptations of an Ancient Tradition*, eds. Steven Heine and Charles S. Prebish (Oxford: Oxford University Press, 2003), pp. 169–92. This invaluable essay has become perhaps the definitive historical and critical appraisal of *Shushōgi* in the English language. Heine also recounts that during this upheaval, not only were Buddhists persecuted in favor of the promotion of Shinto shrines in their new State-supported status, but the customary vocations of the priests themselves were radically altered: "After centuries of the valorizing of celibate, vegetarian monastic practice, they were encouraged or even required to marry and eat meat" (ibid., p. 174).

3. Heinrich Dumoulin, *Zen Buddhism: A History*, vol. 2: *Japan*, trans. James W. Heisig and Paul Knitter (New York: Macmillan, 1990), p. 414.

4. *shushō-ittō.*

5. Heine, p. 170. Nonetheless, the very title *Shushōgi* derives from Dōgen's phrase *shushō-ittō*, which he coined as early as 1231 CE in the fascicle "Bendōwa." That being said, *shushō-ittō* is not explicitly mentioned anywhere in *Shushōgi* (ibid., p. 180). Heine argues that *Shushōgi*, with its reliance on repentance (*sange*), causality (*inga*), and the precepts, is more indebted to the more controversial 12-fascicle *Shōbōgenzō* than the 75-fascicle version.

6. Ibid., p. 171.

7. Ibid., pp. 171–72.

8. Ibid., p. 180.

9. William M. Bodiford, "Zen in the Art of Funerals: Ritual Salvation in Japanese Buddhism," *History of Religions* 32, no. 2 (1992): 150.

10. Dogen, *Treasury of the True Dharma Eye*, p. 502.

11. Heine notes that this phrase appears nowhere in any version of *Shōbōgenzō* (p. 184).

12. Heine: "It seems clear that Ōuchi Seiran and other Meiji lay leaders created a view of repentance in *Shushōgi* based in large part on the challenge of Christianity during the Westernization process" (p. 186).

13. *busshō.*

14. The insistence on repentance as a way of eradicating sins and obtaining one's original purity implicates *Shushōgi* with the Critical Buddhists' accusation that "Buddhism fosters problems of social injustice, ethnic discrimination, and nationalism/militarism, in that the basic notion of original enlightenment proclaims a false sense of equality on the absolute level while allowing conflicts based on inequalities and hierarchical distinctions to be perpetuated on the everyday level" (Heine, p. 184).

15. Ibid., p. 185.

16. Ibid., p. 187.

17. Dogen, *Treasury of the True Dharma Eye*, p. 7.

18. Tendō Nyojō.

19. Sōtōshū.

20. *The True Dharma Eye: Zen Master Dōgen's Three Hundred Koans*, trans. Kazuaki TANAHASHI and John Daido Loori (Boston and London: Shambhala, 2009). See also *Sitting with Koans: Essential Writings on Zen Koan Introspection*, ed. John Daido Loori (Somerville, MA: Wisdom Publications, 2005). Although Sōtō practice, with some important and valuable exceptions, is no longer generally associated with *dokusan* and kōan training (that is more the provenance of the Rinzai school), this omission was not Dōgen's practice.

21. We have generally relied on both Heine's account (p. 182) as well as Matsubara's account for the sources of *Shushōgi* sentences and paragraphs in the various versions of *Shōbōgenzō*. See Matsubara Taidō, *Shushōgi ni Kiku: Dōgen Zen no Shinzui* (Tokyo: Chōbunsha, 1996).

22. Zen-en.

23. Quoted in Heinrich Dumoulin, *Zen Buddhism: A History*, vol. 1: *India and China*, trans. James W. Heisig and Paul Knitter (New York: Macmillan, 1988), p. 9.

24. *yuibutsu yobutsu.*

25. *shuryō.*

26. Davis writes: "While discursive thinking and the study of texts are not engaged in *during* the practice of 'just sitting' in the Monk's Hall (*sōdō*), Dōgen's conception of the monastery also includes an adjacent Study Hall (*shuryō*), wherein each monk is assigned a desk. In 'Shuryō Shingi [Regulations for the Study Hall],' Dōgen writes: 'In the study hall, read the Mahāyāna sutras and also the sayings of our ancestors, and naturally accord with the instructions of our tradition to illuminate the mind with the ancient teachings'" (the passage in "Shuryō Shingi" is quoted from *Dōgen's Pure Standards for the Zen Community: A Translation of Eihei Shingi*, trans. Taigen Daniel Leighten and Shohaku OKUMURA [Albany: SUNY Press, 1996], p. 109).

27. Dogen, *Treasury of the True Dharma Eye*, p. 8.

28. Ibid., p. 87.

29. Ibid.

30. Dogen, *Treasury of the True Dharma Eye*, "Gyōbutsu Igi [Awesome Presence of Active Buddhas]," p. 261.

31. *shushō-ittō.*

32. Dogen, *Treasury of the True Dharma Eye*, p. 182.

33. Ibid., p. 184.

34. Ibid., p. 192.

35. Ibid., p. 229.
36. Ibid., pp. 222–23.
37. Ibid., p. 222.

Notes to Chapter 1

1. Author's note: I would like to thank the translator, Dainen David Putney, for his hard work on my essay. As someone born and raised in Japan as well as someone whose training in Sōtō Zen was exclusively in Japan, it is easiest for me to express myself in my mother tongue. Zen in both the West and Japan is at a real crossroad, and I wanted to express my hopes for a better way forward for everyone in the subtle and nuanced fashion that this occasion merits. I am happy to see that my thoughts and dreams have made it to the other shore of the English-speaking world with their original subtlety intact. All the following notes in this essay are those of the translator, Dainen David Putney.

2. *sange metsuzai.*

3. *jukai nyūi.*

4. *hotsugan rishō.*

5. *gyōji hōʾon.*

6. The Sōtō sect has split into two branches: the original Eiheiji branch associated with Dōgen, and the Sōjiji branch associated with Keizan as well as Dōgen.

7. Following Steven Heine, I translate *kyōkai* as "fellowship," as opposed to "church," because this was a joint project of the Eiheiji and the Sōjiji branches.

8. Kōshō Itagaki explained in a note to me that, according to the Rev. Azuma Ryōshi, a specialist on Keizan Zenji, the Rev. Takiya Takasha, abbot of Eiheiji (though formerly a member of the Sōjiji branch), finalized the final version of *Shushōgi.* The head abbot of Sōjiji at that time was the Rev. Azegami Baisen. Although the two temples issued a joint edict promoting *Shushōgi* as a manual for lay devotion and monastic ritual, the abbot who finalized the present *Shushōgi* was primarily Takiya, with the Rev. Azegami putting in very little input. Takiya, as abbot of Eiheiji, kept the focus on Dōgen Zenji's magnum opus, *Shōbōgenzō.* Kikuchi Rōshi argues that *Shushōgi* should have had more content from Keizan's *Denkōroku.*

9. During this period, the government (*bakufu,* comprised of the Tokugawa shōguns and governmental officials) worked in part to limit the power of Buddhism, while at the same time using it to regulate the people of a village or district in a city. The Edo *bakufu* imposed what is called the *Danka* temple system. These regulations were meant for population control, both peasants and samurai, by minimizing their mobility by tying them to the village where they were born and to the temple where both their ancestors are buried and their family registries are kept. The government reduced the total number of local temples, making sure that each village had only one temple. Priests were ordered to marry, and the temple was passed down through the family so that it could continue to regulate the people from generation to generation. Many of these changes, though not in the repressive form of the Edo period, have continued up through the present.

10. For all practical purposes the Edo period, which lasted until the Meiji era in 1868, began in 1600, after the Battle of Sekigara, where Tokugawa Ieayasu defeated the primarily western *Daimyō* (feudal lords and absolute rulers of their fiefs). Ieyasu

officially took the title of Shōgun in 1603 and this became the official beginning of the Edo period, which lasted 265 years.

11. Christianity became illegal in Japan through the Expulsion Edict of 1614 and all Buddhist temples were required to issue a certificate confirming that no one in their village or precinct was Christian. Everyone in a village or rural area was also required to belong to a temple and temples were officially designated as the only approved operators of funerals. There was to be only one temple per village and everyone was required to belong to this temple, regardless of denomination.

12. *jizoku.*

13. Skt. *duḥkha.*

14. Tendō Nyojō.

15. Acts 9:18.

16. *Hannya Shingyō.*

17. *Kannon bosatsu.*

18. Skt. *śūnyatā;* Jp. *kū.*

19. *jiriki.*

20. *tariki.*

21. *furyū monji.*

22. *kyōge betsuden.*

23. *kenshō jōbutsu.*

24. *suimon.*

25. *honrai no menmoku.*

26. *shugyō.*

27. The *honzan* of the Japanese Tendai sect of Buddhism.

28. There is no evidence that Dōgen actually met Eisai. Records show that Eisai was in Kamakura in an effort to get the government to recognize his new temple. Older schools of Buddhism were trying to get his temple shut down. You needed government permission to establish a new type of temple.

29. Keitoku.

30. *shinjin datsuraku.*

31. *kūshu gennkyō.*

32. This is from Dōgen's "Buddha Nature" fascicle of *Shōbōgenzō* where he takes the phrase *"shitsu'u busshō"* from the *Great Nirvana Sutra.* Note: "All beings—Buddha Nature" is translated in Japanese as *shitsu'u busshō.*

33. *byōdō soku shabetsu. Shabetsu soku byōdō.*

34. Skt. *Pāramitāyana.*

35. Skt. *dāna, śīla, kṣānti, vīrya, dhyāna-samādhi, prajñā.*

36. Skt. *dharmas.*

Notes to Chapter 2

1. Dōgen, *Dōgen's Extensive Record: A Translation of the* Eihei Kōroku, trans. Taigen Dan Leighton and Shohaku Окимика, ed. with introduction Taigen Dan Leighton (Somerville, MA: Wisdom Publications, 2004).

Notes to Chapter 4

1. Skt. *upāya.*

2. *buppō.*

3. On this issue, see David Putney, "Some Problems in Interpretation: The Early and Late Writings of Dōgen," *Philosophy East and West* 46, no. 4 (October 1996): 497–531.

4. *busshō.*

5. Skt. *anātman*; Jp. *muga.*

6. Keiji Nishitani, *Religion and Nothingness*, trans. Jan Van Bragt (Berkeley and Los Angeles: University of California Press, 1982), p. 216.

7. *hongaku.*

8. *shikaku.*

9. The gerund form "awakening" is used here in order to highlight the aspect of process as opposed to the more static and thus potentially essentializing sense of the frequently used term "enlightenment."

10. It has been long debated in Buddhist scholarship whether the *tathāgatagarbha* tradition is genuinely Buddhist on the grounds that it is actually closer to a substantialist position. For recent considerations of this question in the context of "Critical Buddhism," see Matsumoto Shirō, "The Doctrine of *Tathāgata-garhba* Is Not Buddhist," trans. Jamie Hubbard, pp. 165–73; Sallie B. King, "The Doctrine of Buddha-Nature Is Impeccably Buddhist," pp. 174–92; Yamabe Nobuyoshi, "The Idea of *Dhātu-vāda* in Yogacara and *Tathāgata-garbha* Texts," pp. 193–204. These essays are found in Jamie Hubbard and Paul L. Swanson, eds., *Pruning the Bodhi Tree: The Storm Over Critical Buddhism* (Honolulu: University of Hawai'i Press, 1997).

11. The concept of *tathāgatagarbha* clearly invokes both feminine and masculine imagery, even if it refuses to situate Buddha Nature as being fundamentally one or the other. On the relation between the feminine and the masculine and between women and men in Buddhism, particularly with respect to Zen and Dōgen, see Erin McCarthy, "A Zen Master Meets Contemporary Feminism: Reading Dōgen as a Resource for Feminist Philosophy," in *Buddhist Responses to Globalization*, eds. Leah Kalmanson and James Mark Shields (Lanham, MD: Lexington Books, 2014), pp. 131–48.

12. Skt. *śūnyatā*; Jp. *kū.*

13. Skt. *tathatā.*

14. Nāgārjuna, *The Fundamental Wisdom of the Middle Way: Nāgārjuna's Mūlamadhyamakakārikā*, trans. with commentary Jay L. Garfield (Oxford and New York: Oxford University Press, 1995), XXV.19, p. 331. On the notion of emptiness in Nāgārjuna with reference to the *tathāgatagarbha* tradition, see Bret W. Davis, "Forms of Emptiness in Zen," in *A Companion to Buddhist Philosophy*, ed. Steven M. Emmanuel (Hoboken, NJ: Wiley-Blackwell, 2013), pp. 190–213.

15. Skt. *avidyā.*

16. Skt. *pratītyasamutpāda*; Jp. *engi.*

17. For other references to karma by Dōgen, see in *Shōbōgenzō*: "Keisei Sanshoku [Valley Sounds, Mountain Colors]," "Shoaku Makusa [Refrain from Unwholesome Action]," "Kesa Kudoku [Power of the Robe]," "Sansui Kyō [Mountains and Waters Sutra]," "Sanji no Gō [Karma in the Three Periods]," "Shizen Biku [Monk of the Fourth-Stage Meditation]."

   Also see in *Dōgen's Extensive Record: A Translation of the* Eihei Kōroku, trans. Taigen Dan Leighton and Shohaku Okumura, ed. with introduction Taigen Dan

Leighton (Somerville, MA: Wisdom Publications, 2004): volume 4, section 275 (references hereafter referred to as follows: 4:275), 5:383, 5:386, 6:437, 7:485, 7:517, 7:504, 7:510, 7:524.

18. *shushō-ittō.*

19. Daikan Enō.

20. *tongo.*

21. Dōgen, *Treasury of the True Dharma Eye: Zen Master Dogen's Shobo Genzo*, vol. 1, "Undivided Activity [Zenki]," ed. Kazuaki TANAHASHI (Boston and London: Shambhala, 2010), p. 451.

22. The principal text in English on this movement, which contains both supporting and critical essays on it, is Hubbard and Swanson, eds., *Pruning the Bodhi Tree: The Storm Over Critical Buddhism.*

23. Hee-Jin Kim, *Dōgen on Meditation and Thinking: A Reflection on His View of Zen* (Albany: SUNY Press, 2007), pp. 55–56. While there are numerous assessments both critical and supportive of Critical Buddhism, Kim offers one that is both, succinct, and balanced. See ibid., pp. 53–58. Also see his "Preface to the Wisdom Edition" of his masterful study *Eihei Dōgen: Mystical Realist* (Somerville, MA: Wisdom Publications, 2004), esp. pp. xix–xxii.

24. Kim, *Dōgen on Meditation and Thinking*, p. 55.

25. Dōgen, "*Universally Recommended Instructions for Zazen (Fukan zazengi)* [Fukanzazengi]," in *Soto School Scriptures for Daily Services and Practice*, ed. and trans. Carl Bielefeldt and T. Griffith Foulk, with Rev. Taigen Leighton and Rev. Shohaku OKUMURA (Tokyo: Sotoshu Shumucho and the Soto Zen Text Project, 2001). For a slightly different translation see Dogen, *Treasury of the True Dharma Eye*, p. 908.

26. In *Chants and Recitations* (Rochester, NY: Rochester Zen Center, 2005), p. 35.

27. Ibid.

28. *Shushōgi*, § 30.

29. Tendō Nyojō.

30. Sōtō Zen.

31. Rinzai.

32. "Zen is also deeply concerned with the question, 'What am I?' asking it in a way peculiar to Zen, that is: 'What is your original face before you were born?' Science seeks for the origins of our existence in a temporal and horizontal sense—a dimension which can be pushed back endlessly. To find a definite answer to the question of our origin we must go beyond the *horizontal* dimension and turn to the *vertical* dimension, i.e., the eternal and religious dimension" (Abe Masao, "God, Emptiness, and the True Self," in *The Buddha Eye: An Anthology of the Kyoto School and Its Contemporaries*, ed. Frederick Franck, with foreword by Joan Stambaugh [Bloomington, IN: World Wisdom, 2004], p. 65). This essay was previously published in *The Eastern Buddhist* 2, no. 2 (1969): 15–30.

33. See Masao ABE, "Kenotic God and Dynamic Śūnyatā" and "A Rejoinder," in *The Emptying God: A Buddhist-Jewish-Christian Conversation*, eds. John B. Cobb, Jr., and Christopher Ives (Maryknoll, NY: Orbis Books, 1990).

34. Dogen, *Treasury of the True Dharma Eye*, p. 12.

35. *myōshū.*

36. *hi-shiryō.*

37. Dogen, *Treasury of the True Dharma Eye*, p. 243.
38. Daii Dōshin.
39. Daimon Kōnin.
40. Dogen, *Treasury of the True Dharma Eye*, p. 241.

Notes to Chapter 5

1. All references to *Shōbōgenzō* are from *Master Dogen's Shobogenzo*, trans. Gudo Nishijima and Chodo Cross (Charleston: Book Surge Publishing, 2006).
2. Ibid., p. 5.
3. Ibid.
4. Maurice Merleau-Ponty, *The Visible and the Invisible*, trans. Alphonso Lingis and ed. Claude Lefort (Evanston: Northwestern University Press, 1968), p. 215.
5. *Master Dogen's Shobogenzo*, p. 27.
6. Ibid., p. 28.
7. Ibid.
8. Ibid., p. 27.
9. Ibid., p. 141.
10. Ibid., p. 142.
11. Merleau-Ponty, p. 134.
12. Ibid., pp. 137–38.
13. *Master Dogen's Shobogenzo*, p. 16.
14. Ibid., p. 26.
15. Ibid., p. 92.
16. Ibid., p. 141.
17. Ibid.

Notes to Chapter 6

1. Skt. *anātman*.
2. Robert Jay Lifton, *The Broken Connection: On Death and the Continuity of Life* (Washington, DC: American Psychiatric Press, 1979), p. 69.
3. Both are in the *Udāna*.
4. Dogen, *Treasury of the True Dharma Eye*, pp. 884–85.
5. Ibid., p. 429.
6. Ibid., pp. 30–31.

Notes to Chapter 7

1. Henry David Thoreau, *Walden*, chapter 2: "Where I Lived, and What I Lived For" (New Haven and London: Yale University Press, 1996), p. 96.
2. Thomas Merton, *New Seeds of Contemplation* (New York: New Directions, 2007), chapter 3 (opening paragraph).
3. *Shushōgi*, § 2.
4. Ibid., § 3.
5. Genesis 3:19.
6. Martin Buber, *The Way of Man: According to the Teaching of Hasidism* (New York: Citadel, 1996), p. 12.
7. *Shushōgi*, §§ 4–5.
8. Buber, p. 14.

NOTES TO CHAPTER 8

1. *gō.*
2. *sange.*
3. Shibayama Zenkei, *Zen Comments on the Mumonkan*, trans. Kudo Sumiko (New York: Harper & Row, 1974), p. 38.

NOTES TO CHAPTER 9

1. The *Daihōkō Butsu-kegon Kyō* (Skt. *Mahāvaipulya Buddhāvataṃsaka Sūtra*), or *The Great Vaipulya Sutra of the Buddha's Flower Garland*, is the central sutra for the Huayan (Jp. Kegon) school, which flourished in Tang Dynasty China and has been associated with Tōdaiji in Nara since the eighth century.
2. *mujō.*
3. *muga.*
4. For a summation of this debate, see Steven Heine, "Abbreviation or Aberration: The Role of the *Shushōgi* in Modern Sōtō Zen Buddhism," in *Buddhism in the Modern World: Adaptations of an Ancient Tradition,* eds. Steven Heine and Charles S. Prebish (Oxford: Oxford University Press, 2003), pp. 169–92.
5. For an alternative translation of this passage, see ibid., p. 169.
6. Ibid., p. 187.
7. Ibid., p. 170.
8. David Putney, "Dōgen: Enlightenment and Entanglement," *Buddhist-Christian Studies* 17 (1997): 25.
9. There is some debate among scholars as to whether or not Dōgen could have been motivated by such a question, or whether the question is in fact puerile. (Tiantong Rujing in Japanese is Tendō Nyojō.) See my *Purifying Zen: Watsuji Tetsurō's Shamon Dōgen* (Honolulu: University of Hawai'i Press, 2011), p. 12.
10. The most important of these has to do with Buddha Nature itself, and with the character of enlightenment itself. See Hee-Jin Kim, *Dōgen: Mystical Realist*, 3rd revised edition (Somerville, MA: Wisdom Publications, 2000); also see my *Purifying Zen.*
11. Dogen, *Master Dogen's Shobogenzo*, vol. 4, "Sanji no Gō," trans. Gudo NISHIJIMA and Chodo Cross (Charleston: Book Surge Publishing, 2006), pp. 118–19.
12. The passages in *Shushōgi* that also appear in "Sanji no Gō" about whether karma waits for continuance or skips continuance are excerpted from the *Abhidharma-mahāvibhāṣa-śāstra*, a Sarvāstivādin text.

NOTES TO CHAPTER 10

1. Skt. *anuttarā samyak-saṃbodhi.*

NOTES TO CHAPTER 11

1. Wilber thus speaks of three main axes of the psyche—states, stages, and shadow. The premodern religious traditions, according to Wilber, understood the first well but had much less to say on the second two, which descend from modern Western psychology: stages of development from James Mark Baldwin and Jean Piaget; and shadow as dissociation within the psychic system from Sigmund Freud and Carl Jung. Awakening in this view is to become one with the always already stateless state of nonduality (even as there are types of nonduality—that is, "type" in

the sense of style). Stage development and the integration of all forms of shadow do not necessarily or simply follow from awakening. Wilber here draws knowingly on large bodies of evidence in forwarding this conclusion.

NOTES TO CHAPTER 12

1. Dogen, *Treasury of the True Dharma Eye: Zen Master Dogen's* Shobo Genzo, ed. Kazuaki TANAHASHI (Boston and London: Shambhala, 2010).
2. Ibid., p. 656.
3. Ibid., p. 657.
4. Ibid.
5. Ibid., p. 658.
6. *bodai.*
7. *shin.*
8. *shinjin datsuraku.*
9. Dogen, *Treasury of the True Dharma Eye*, p. 662.
10. Ibid., p. 59.
11. Ibid., p. 60.
12. Ibid., p. 61.
13. Ibid., p. 51.
14. Ibid., p. 40.
15. Ibid., p. 41.
16. See "Keisei Sanshoku": "Although you may have wasted time so far, you should vow immediately, before this present life ends: Together will all sentient beings, may I hear the true dharma from this birth throughout future births. When I hear the true dharma, I will not doubt or distrust it. When I encounter the true dharma, I will relinquish ordinary affairs and uphold the buddha dharma. Thus, may I realize the way together with the great earth and all sentient beings" (Dogen, *Treasury of the True Dharma Eye*, p. 90).
17. Śāntideva, *The Way of the Bodhisattva*, revised edition, trans. the Padmakara Translation Group (Boston and London: Shambhala, 2008).
18. Ibid., p. 55, verse 17.
19. Ibid., verse 18.
20. Ibid., p. 56, verse 19.
21. Ibid., p. 82, verse 19.
22. This is from the opening paragraph of *Fukanzazengi* found in Part III of this book.
23. *shushō-ittō.*
24. Dogen, *Treasury of the True Dharma Eye*, p. 18.
25. Skt. *upāya.*
26. *Scripture of the Lotus Blossom of the Fine Dharma: The Lotus Sutra*, trans. Leon Hurvitz (New York: Columbia University Press, 1976), p. 199.
27. Ibid., pp. 200–201.
28. In putting Śāriputra's discrimination in its place, the dragon girl instantly turns into a man (ibid., p. 201). This, of course, has led some readers to conclude that the male form remains the requisite vehicle for awakening, although this fails to take into account that she was already fully awakened before she made sport of Śāriputra. In the seventh chapter of the *Vimalakīrti Sūtra*, Śāriputra the misogynist is even more thoroughly schooled. See *Vimalakīrti Sūtra*, trans. Burton

Watson (New York: Columba University Press, 1997), pp. 90–92. Śāriputra asks the goddess to change out of her form, but the goddess responds that a woman does not reduce to a mere form. "All things are just the same—they have no fixed form" (p. 91).

29. Dogen, *Treasury of the True Dharma Eye*, p. 16.
30. Ibid., p. 77.
31. Ibid., p. 80.
32. Ibid., p. 79.
33. Ibid., p. 81.
34. Ibid., p. 82.
35. Grace Shireson, *Zen Women: Beyond Tea Ladies, Iron Maidens, and Macho Masters* (Somerville, MA: Wisdom Publications, 1999), p. 83. See also the seminal discussion in Paula Kane Robinson Arai, *Women Living Zen: Japanese Sōtō Buddhist Nuns* (Oxford: Oxford University Press, 1999), esp. pp. 36–43.
36. Bernard Faure, *Visions of Power: Imagining Medieval Japanese Buddhism* (Princeton: Princeton University Press, 1996), p. 44.
37. Arai, p. 40.
38. Skt. *moha* and *avidyā*.
39. Skt. *rāga*; P. *lobha*.
40. Skt. *dveṣa*; P. *dosa*.
41. See especially Zenshin Florence Caplow and Reigetsu Susan Moon, eds., *The Hidden Lamp: Stories from Twenty-Five Centuries of Awakened Women* (Somerville, MA: Wisdom Publications, 2013); Eido Frances Carney, ed., *Receiving the Marrow: Teachings on Dōgen by Sōtō Zen Women Priests* (Olympia, WA: Temple Ground Press, 2012).
42. Shireson, p. 83.
43. Faure, p. 44.
44. William Bodiford, *Sōtō Zen in Medieval Japan* (Honolulu: University of Hawai'i Press, 1993), p. 204.
45. Ibid., p. 206.
46. Ibid.
47. Hakamaya Noriaki, "Thoughts on the Ideological Background of Social Discrimination," trans. Jamie Hubbard, in *Pruning the Bodhi Tree: The Storm over Critical Buddhism*, eds. Jamie Hubbard and Paul L. Swanson (Honolulu: University of Hawai'i Press, 1997), p. 344. See also Steven Heine, "Critical Buddhism and Dōgen's *Shōbōgenzō*: The Debate over the 75-Fascicle and 12-Fascicle Texts," in *Pruning the Bodhi Tree*, pp. 251–85. Heine articulates the nub of the problem: "Zen, in particular, has often hidden its support for the status quo behind what is, in effect, an elitist aestheticism based on the notion that everything reflects the Buddha Dharma (*zen'itsu-buppō*)" (p. 257).
48. Skt. Śrenika.
49. Hakamaya, p. 345.
50. Ibid., p. 347.
51. Ibid., p. 348.
52. *shushō-ittō*.
53. Dogen, *Treasury of the True Dharma Eye*, p. 30.

54. *Jōriki* means the power of *samādhi*, the concentrated power that arises from *dhyāna* (meditation).

55. Ruben L. F. Habito, *Zen and the Spiritual Exercises: Paths of Awakening and Transformation* (Maryknoll, NY: Orbis Books, 2013), p. xxiii.

56. Yasutani Hakuun, "The Three Aims of Zazen," in *The Three Pillars of Zen: Teaching, Practice, Enlightenment*, ed. Philip Kapleau, updated and revised edition (New York: Anchor Books, 2000), p. 55. *Saijōjō* Zen, Yasutani tells us, is the "last of the five types" and is "the highest vehicle, the culmination and crown of Buddhist Zen. This Zen was practiced by all the Buddhas of the past . . . and is the expression of Absolute Life, life in its purest form. It is the zazen that Dōgen Zenji chiefly advocated and it involves no struggle for *satori* or any other object" ("The Five Varieties of Zen," pp. 52–53). *Saijōjō* means the superior vehicle, the consummate teaching.

57. *kenchūtō.*

58. Yasutani, p. 56.

59. Dongshan Liangjie (Jp. Tōzan Ryōkai), a ninth-century monk and one of the founders of the Caodong (Sōtō) school, established in the *Song of Precious Mirror Samādhi* (*Hōkyō Zammaika*) the Five Ranks as one of this school's central teachings. The Five Ranks are, each corresponding to a stanza in Dongshan's poem: (1) *shōchūhen*: the relative within absolute emptiness (many within one, light within darkness, bent within straight); (2) *henchūshō*: absolute emptiness within the relative (one within many, darkness within light, straight within bent); (3) *shōchūrai*: awoken action that originates in absolute emptiness (the bent coming from the straight, light coming from darkness); (4) *kenchūshi*: arriving at the mutual integration and interpenetration of the opposites, and entering the marketplace as a bodhisattva; (5) *kenchūtō*: "attainment of unity" the practice of wakefulness in everyday life in everything that one does and thinks. See also Victor Sōgen Hori, *Zen Sand: The Book of Capping Phrases for Kōan Practice* (Honolulu: University of Hawaiʻi Press, 2003), pp. 24–25.

60. See Isshū Miura and Ruth Fuller Sasaki, *The Zen Koan: Its History and Use in Rinzai Zen* (New York: Harcourt, Brace & World, 1965), pp. 62–72.

61. Ibid., p. 63.

62. Ibid., p. 65.

63. Ibid., p. 70.

64. Ibid., pp. 71–72.

65. Ibid., p. 63.

66. Ibid., p. 72.

67. *busshō.*

68. *jinzū.*

69. Dogen, *Treasury of the True Dharma Eye*, p. 291.

70. See fascicle 38 of *Shōbōgenzō* ("Shinjin Gakudō [Body-and-Mind Study of the Way]"). "Without practice, the Buddha way cannot be attained. Without study, it remains remote" (Ibid., p. 422). "Sometimes you study the way by casting off the mind. Sometimes you study the way by taking up the mind. Either way, study the way with thinking and study the way not-thinking" (p. 423). "A moment or two of mind is a moment of mountains, rivers, and earth. . . . Just wholeheartedly accept

with trust that to study the way with mind is this mountains-rivers-and-earth mind itself thoroughly engaged in studying the way" (p. 424).

71. Ibid., p. 502.
72. Ibid., p. 507.
73. Ibid., p. 542.
74. Ibid., p. 543.
75. Ibid., p. 633.
76. Ibid., p. 635.
77. Hakamaya, p. 352.
78. Dogen, *Treasury of the True Dharma Eye*, p. 77.

NOTES TO CHAPTER 13

1. T. Griffith Foulk, "Ritual in Japanese Zen Buddhism," in *Zen Ritual: Studies of Zen Theory in Practice*, eds. Steve Heine and Dale S. Wright (Oxford: Oxford University Press, 2007), p. 71.
2. Philip Kapleau, ed., *Three Pillars of Zen: Teaching, Practice, and Enlightenment*, updated and revised edition (New York: Anchor Books, 2000), p. 236.
3. Ibid., p. 236.
4. Kazuaki TANAHASHI, ed., *Moon in a Dewdrop: Writings of Zen Master Dōgen* (San Francisco: North Point Press, 1985), pp. 44–45. Translations from *Shōbōgenzō* are based on the Tanahashi text, with my modifications.
5. Ibid., p. 44.
6. Ibid.
7. Ibid., p. 45.
8. Ibid., p. 44.
9. Kenneth Kraft, "The Greening of Buddhist Practice"; www.crosscurrents.org/greening.htm.
10. From the website of the Vermont Zen Center; www.vermontzen.org/ceremonies.html.

NOTES TO CHAPTER 14

1. My deep gratitude to Paul Forster and Timothy Engström for their careful readings and incisive comments on early drafts.
2. Compassion differs from empathy in that empathy involves feeling the pain of others but compassion adds the dimension of wanting to relieve the pain and suffering of others.
3. Thomas P. Kasulis, *Intimacy or Integrity: Philosophy and Cultural Difference* (Honolulu: University of Hawai'i Press, 2002), p. 118.
4. Dogen, *Master Dogen's Shobogenzo*, vol. 3, trans. Gudo Wafu NISHIJIMA and Chodo Cross (Berkeley: Bukkyō Dendō Kyōkai and Numata Center for Buddhist Translation and Research, 1998), pp. 41, 175a.
5. Ibid., p. 46n19.
6. Translated by Steve Bein as *Purifying Zen: Watsuji Tetsurō's Shamon Dōgen* (Honolulu: University of Hawai'i Press, 2011).
7. Ibid., p. 65.
8. Joan Tronto notes that one requirement of care, along with some kind of engagement, is the following: "First, care implies a reaching out to something other than

the self: it is neither self-referring nor self-absorbing" (*Moral Boundaries: A Political Argument for an Ethics of Care* [New York and London: Routledge, 1993], p. 102).

9. Watsuji Tetsurō, *Watsuji Tetsurō's Rinrigaku: Ethics in Japan*, trans. Seisaku YAMA-MOTO and Robert E. Carter (Albany: SUNY Press, 1996), p. 62.

10. Bein, p. 69.

11. Ibid., p. 78.

12. Dogen, *Treasury of the True Dharma Eye*, "Bodaisatta Shi Shōhō [The Bodhisat-tva's Four Methods of Guidance]," pp. 475–76.

13. See Thomas P. Kasulis, *Zen Action/Zen Person*, ch. 6: "Dōgen's Phenomenology of Zazen" (Honolulu: University of Hawai'i Press, 1985), for more on this.

14. *Master Dogen's Shobogenzo*, pp. 47n23, 222n172.

15. Ibid., pp. 47n23, 222n171.

NOTES TO CHAPTER 15

1. Skt. *bodhicitta*; Jp. *bodaishin*; may also be translated as the "thought of enlightenment."

2. Yokoi Yūhō, "Meaning of Practice and Enlightenment," *Zen Master Dōgen: An Introduction with Selected Writings* (New York: Weatherhill, 1976), p. 61.

3. Dogen, *Master Dogen's Shobogenzo*, vol. 3, trans. Gudo NISHIJIMA and Chodo Cross, Vol. 3, "Bodaisatta Shishōbō" (Berkeley: Bukkyō Dendō Kyōkai and Numata Center for Buddhist Translation and Research, 1998), p. 28.

4. My Japanese text for *Shushōgi* is taken from *Sanzen Yōten*, a manual of short Zen texts published by the Shūmuchō Kōhoshitsu (Tokyo: Sōtōshū Shūmuchō, 1956).

5. Skt. *anātman*; Jp. *muga*.

6. Skt. *śūnyatā*; Jp. *kū*.

7. Skt. *pratītyasamutpāda*; Jp. *engi*.

8. *Dharma* has many meanings in Buddhism. The two that most concern us here are (1) teachings, in general, or especially the Buddha's teachings (Buddha Dharma), and (2) phenomena (or phenomenon) that we sense and perceive with our six senses (as well as the karmic formations and consciousness in the five aggregates). Dharma is often translated in this sense as "thing," or dharmas as "things." The Japanese is *hō*. A phrase used in Japanese Buddhist writings is *shohō*, "all dharmas" or "all things," or "all phenomena."

9. *Tathāgata* could be interpreted in two ways. One is a combination between "*Tathā*" (suchness or reality), plus "*gata*" meaning "has gone," or "has attained": the One who has crossed to the other shore from suffering and ignorance. This meaning is often translated as the "Thus Gone One" (the One who has attained ultimate wisdom or *bodhi*). It is also translated as "Thus Come One" (The One who has come from ultimate wisdom, *bodhi*). *Tathāgata* is synonymous with Buddha. The pun, if it is one, cannot be translated into Chinese or Japanese. This gives *Tathāgata* the implication of Buddha as "savior" in East Asia.

10. The Japanese text is hard to translate. Where Nishijima and Cross translate "the task of cooperation," the Japanese text just says "*ji—*," the *ji* of *dōji*. Nishijima and Cross translate the sentence thus: "The task of cooperation means, for example, concrete behavior, a dignified attitude, and a real situation." Although Nishijima and Cross note the distinction between *dō* and *ji* in a footnote, I would alter-nately translate this passage as "task" (as in the "task of cooperation"), meaning

"appropriate form, solemnity, and bearing." The Japanese text I rely on is Dōgen, *Shōbōgenzō*, vol. 4, ed. with annotation Mizuno Yaoko (Tokyo: Iwanami, 1990); hereafter this four-volume edition will be cited by volume and page numbers. Translations are my own, but I will indicate the corresponding page numbers in the following English translation: Dogen, *Treasury of the True Dharma Eye: Zen Master Dogen's Shobo Genzo*, ed. Kazuaki TANAHASHI (Boston and London: Shambhala, 2010).

11. Dōgen, *Shōbōgenzō*, 4:426; *Treasury of the True Dharma Eye*, p. 476. Mizuno, in a note, translates the three into modern Japanese with terms that mean "dignity," "attitude," and "form."

12. This is a Chinese Daoist text in twenty-four volumes attributed to Guanzi Kanshi (Dōgen, *Shōbōgenzō*, 4:426; *Treasury of the True Dharma Eye*, p. 476). It is interesting to note that in the "Four Elements of a Bodhisattva's Social Relations," when the text discusses the relationship between the *Tathāgata* and humans, the text of this fascicle goes on to say: "Judging from this identification with the human world we can suppose that he might [also] identify himself with other worlds" (Ibid., 4:426; p. 476).

13. Ibid., 9:71–72; p. 274.

14. Ibid., 4:426; p. 476.

15. Ibid., 8:58; p. 303.

16. Ibid., 8:62–63; p. 308.

17. Ibid., 8:64ff; p. 310. For more on the question of women, see chapter 12.

NOTES TO CHAPTER 16

1. *hōon*.

2. *hōon kōshiki*.

3. Chuang Tzu, *Basic Writings*, trans. Burton Watson (New York: Columbia University Press, 1964), p. 109.

NOTES TO CHAPTER 17

1. Dogen, *Treasury of the True Dharma Eye: Zen Master Dogen's Shobo Genzo*, vol. 1, "Continuous Practice (2)," ed. Kazuaki TANAHASHI (Boston and London: Shambhala, 2010), p. 361. Unless noted otherwise, all subsequent quotations from Dōgen will be to this fascicle of *Shōbōgenzō* using this translation, referred to by the page number in the body of the text.

2. Friedrich Nietzsche, *Thus Spoke Zarathustra*, trans. Graham Parkes (Oxford: Oxford University Press, 2005), p. 173.

3. Dogen, *Treasury of the True Dharma Eye*, p. 365.

4. Unmon.

5. Master Yunmen, *From the Record of the Chan Teacher "Gate of the Clouds,"* ed. and trans. Urs App (Tokyo: Kodansha, 1994), pp. 104–5.

6. Dōgen, "Gakudō Yōjinshū [Points to Watch in Practicing the Way]," in *Dōgen Zen*, trans. Shohaku OKUMURA (Kyoto: Kyoto Sōtō Zen Center, 1988), p. 1.

7. Dōgen, *Shōbōgenzō*, "Senjō [Cleansing]" and "Senmen [Washing the Face]."

8. Dōgen, "Instructions for the Tenzo," trans. Arnold Kotler and Kazuaki TANAHASHI, in *Moon in a Dewdrop*, ed. Kazuaki TANAHASHI (San Francisco: North Point, 1985), p. 56.

9. Chōkei.

10. Dogen, *Treasury of the True Dharma Eye*, p. 369.

11. Ibid., p. 365.

12. Ibid., p. 362.

Notes to Chapter 18

1. *zammai-ō-zammai.*

2. *bonnō soku bodai.*

3. Dōgen, *Shōbōgenzō*, vol. 1, "Genjōkōan," ed. with annotation Mizuno Yaoko (Tokyo: Iwanami, 1990), pp. 53–54; Dōgen Kigen, "*Shōbōgenzō Genjōkōan,*" trans. Norman Waddell and Masao ABE, *The Eastern Buddhist* 5, no. 2 (1972): 134.

4. Skt. *upāya.*

5. Dōgen, *Shōbōgenzō*, vol. 4, "Shōji," ed. with annotation Mizuno Yaoko (Tokyo: Iwanami, 1993), p. 468; my translation.

Notes to Chapter 19

1. Nāgārjuna, *The Fundamental Wisdom of the Middle Way: Nāgārjuna's* Mūlamadhyamakakārikā, trans. with commentary Jay L. Garfield (Oxford and New York: Oxford University Press, 1995), XXV.19, p. 331.

2. *sokushin zebutsu.*

3. The dates for Bodhiruci vary. Traditional accounts hold he arrived in Luoyang, China, somewhere between 502–508 CE. More contemporary accounts situate his life two centuries later. Jinhua Chen states that Bodhiruci arrived in Luoyang sometime between 692–693 and during that time prepared a retranslation with an interpolation of the *Ratnamegha Sūtra* (*Philosopher, Practitioner, Politician: The Many Lives of Fazang (643–712)* [Leiden: Kloninklijke Brill, 2007], p. 232). Another account also places Bodhiruci in China during this time period. See Antonino Forte, "The Relativity of the Concept of Orthodoxy in Chinese Buddhism: Chih-sheng's Indictment of Shih-li and the Proscription of the *Dharma Mirror Sūtra,*" in *Chinese Buddhist Apocrypha*, ed. Robert E. Buswell, Jr. (Honolulu: University of Hawai'i Press, 1990), pp. 242–46.

4. Cited in William Theodore de Bary, *The Buddhist Tradition in India, China, and Japan* (New York: Random House, 1972), p. 100; translation modified to reflect gender-neutral language.

5. Skt. *upāya.*

6. Ch. *dao*; Jp. *dō.*

7. *mushin.*

8. Dogen, *Treasury of the True Dharma Eye: Zen Master Dogen's* Shobo Genzo, vol. 1, "Busshō [Buddha Nature]," ed. Kazuaki TANAHASHI (Boston and London: Shambhala, 2010), p. 243.

9. Ibid., p. 15.

10. *shinshō.*

11. Dogen, *Treasury of the True Dharma Eye*, "Genjōkōan [Actualizing the Fundamental Point]," p. 30.

12. Skt. *anātman.*

13. *bukkōjō ji.*

14. Skt. *tathatā.*

15. Skt. *śūnyatā*; Jp. *kū*.
16. Bodhidharma, "Wake-up Sermon," in *The Zen Teaching of Bodhidharma*, trans. Red Pine (New York: North Point Press, 1987), p. 41.
17. Bodhidharma, "Bloodstream Sermon," in *The Zen Teaching of Bodhidharma*, p. 9.
18. Huang Po, "The Chün Chou Record," in *The Zen Teaching of Huang Po: On the Transmission of Mind,* trans. John Blofield (New York: Grove Press, 1958), p. 29.
19. Rinzai Gigen.
20. Bodhidharma, "Bloodstream Sermon," pp. 18–19.
21. Huang Po, "The Chün Chou Record," p. 59.
22. Ibid., pp. 34–35.
23. Dogen, *Treasury of the True Dharma Eye*, p. 110.
24. *shushō-ittō*.
25. Bodhidharma, "Wake-up Sermon," p. 55.
26. *uji*.
27. *Shushōgi*, § 31.

Notes to Chapter 20

1. Dōgen, *Shōbōgenzō*, vol. 1, ed. with annotation Mizuno Yaoko (Tokyo: Iwanami, 1990), 30; hereafter this four-volume edition will be abbreviated as SBGZ followed by volume and page numbers. Although I will often use my own translations for this and other texts, I will also provide references to available English translations. In this case: *The Heart of Dōgen's Shōbōgenzō*, trans. Norman Waddell and Masao Abe (Albany: SUNY Press, 2002), p. 20, translation modified.

2. SBGZ 1:222; *Treasury of the True Dharma Eye: Zen Master Dogen's Shobo Genzo*, ed. Kazuaki Tanahashi (Boston and London: Shambhala, 2012), p. 579, translation modified.

3. My source for the original text of *Fukanzazengi* is *Dōgen Zenji goroku*, ed. Kagamishima Genryū (Tokyo: Kōdansha, 1990), pp. 170–85. In general I will adopt, with some modifications (such as "nonthinking" rather than "beyond thinking" for *hi-shiryō*), the translation by Taigen Dan Leighton and Shohaku Okumura published in *Dōgen's Extensive Record: A Translation of the* Eihei Kōroku (Somerville, MA: Wisdom Publications, 2004), pp. 532–35, and reprinted in the present volume. Given the brevity of this text, I will not cite page numbers for each quotation.

4. SBGZ 1:18; *The Heart of Dōgen's Shōbōgenzō*, p. 13.

5. Dōgen's earliest version of *Fukanzazengi*, which is no longer extant, probably dates from 1227 CE; the earliest surviving edition, "Tenpukubon," written in Dōgen's own hand, dates from 1233, and the "circulated text" or "Rufubon," Dōgen's final version and the one that has become the standard, was probably composed in 1242. The text that appears in the present book and the one commented on in the present essay is "Rufubon." For a detailed study of the two extant versions of *Fukanzazengi*, a study which compares them not only to each other but also to the previous manuals of meditation on which Dōgen critically draws, see Carl Beilefeldt, *Dōgen's Manuals of Zen Meditation* (Berkeley: University of California Press, 1988).

6. On the sociological factors and ideological problems involved in the composition of *Shushōgi*, see Steven Heine, "Abbreviation or Aberration: The Role of the

Shushōgi in Modern Sōtō Zen Buddhism," in *Buddhism in the Modern World: Adaptations of an Ancient Tradition,* eds. Steven Heine and Charles S. Prebish (Oxford: Oxford University Press, 2003), pp. 169–92.

7. A noteworthy exception is a contemporary Japanese group of scholars of "Critical Buddhism," who claim that nondiscursive practices of meditation play no essential role in Buddhism. They also claim that as Dōgen matured he came to wholly reject "original enlightenment thought" in his commitment to a "deep faith in karmic causality" and rational analysis thereof. See Jamie Hubbard and Paul Swanson, eds., *Pruning the Bodhi Tree: The Storm over Critical Buddhism* (Honolulu: University of Hawai'i Press, 1997), especially the chapter by Steven Heine. One of the main proponents of Critical Buddhism, Matsumoto Shirō, writes: "Simply put, I see zen [meditation] as synonymous with the cessation of conceptual thinking, its aim being to induce the suspension of thought. If this is true, and if we grant the obvious point that wisdom is the fruit of conceptual thought, then the only conclusion we are left with is that Zen thought is the negation or rejection of wisdom . . . if zen (Skt. *dhyāna*) means the cessation of conceptual thought, then Zen is a denial of Buddhism itself" ("The Meaning of 'Zen'"; ibid., pp. 243–44). It is true that Zen—along with most if not all schools of Buddhism—does deny the purportedly "obvious point" that "wisdom is the fruit of conceptual thought" alone. Indeed, insofar as one's fundamental attunement, that is to say, one's basic attitudinal awareness of and dispositional comportment toward the world, together with one's core intuitions about the nature of reality, contribute to the very formation and orientation of one's conceptual, discursive thought, then preconceptual and nondiscursive practices such as zazen can and do make a profound contribution to what most people, both within and beyond the Buddhist tradition, understand by the word "wisdom." Dōgen goes so far as to say: "The realm of Buddhas is utterly incomprehensible, not to be reached by the discriminative workings of the mind" ("Bendōwa," SBGZ 1:20–21; *The Heart of Dōgen's Shōbōgenzō,* p. 15; translation slightly modified). In *Fukanzazengi* he tells us that, in the practice of zazen, we must "give up the operations of mind, intellect, and consciousness; stop measuring with thoughts, ideas, and views." He instructs us rather to "think of not-thinking" and to do so ultimately by means of "nonthinking." This nonthinking "cannot be understood by discriminative thinking," it is "a standard prior to knowledge and views." And yet, as we shall see, this nonthinking by no means inhibits discursive thinking; it is rather the formless "ocean" or "empty space" of enlightening awareness that enables the functioning of wisdom, which includes the proper formulation and application of perspectivally delimited forms of knowledge by means of discursive intellection. Nonthinking is not antithetical to the faculty of reason; it is the prerequisite for the proper use of this faculty. While the Critical Buddhists' call for rational critique of past and present social injustices is surely commendable, a correct understanding of the practice of zazen in terms of what Dōgen means by nonthinking should see this practice as enabling, rather than impeding, such ethically motivated use of our human powers of discriminative intellection.

8. 1231 CE.

9. *jijuyū zammai.*

10. As Waddell and Abe point out, what Dōgen means by "the *samādhi* of self-enjoyment and employment" (*jijuyū zammai*) is not merely the counterpart of—much less is it opposed to—*tajuyū*, which refers to aiding others so that they too can experience the joy of awakening. "Here Dōgen uses the term *jijuyū* samādhi in an absolute sense, without distinguishing between it and *tajuyū*, with *jijuyū* being the basic source of *tajuyū* and including *tajuyū* in its own development. For Dōgen, the *jijuyū* samādhi is zazen, because zazen is a fundamental practice that includes both self-awakening and the awakening of all beings in the universe" (*The Heart of Dōgen's Shōbōgenzō*, p. 8; see also the translators' comments in *The Wholehearted Way: A Translation of Eihei Dōgen's* Bendōwa *with Commentary by Kōshō Uchiyama Rōshi*, trans. Shohaku OKUMURA and Taigen Dan Leighton [Rutland, Vermont: Tuttle, 1997], p. 43). As Dōgen goes on to say in "Bendōwa," *jijuyū* is a matter of "self-enlightenment qua enlightening others" (SBGZ 1:18; *The Heart of Dōgen's Shōbōgenzō*, p. 13; see also the final epigraph to the present essay).

11. 1234 CE.

12. 1235–37 CE.

13. *Shōbōgenzō Zuimonki*, compiled by Ejō, ed. Watsuji Tetsurō (Tokyo: Iwanami, 1982), pp. 30, 52, 65; *A Primer of Sōtō Zen: A Translation of Dōgen's* Shōbōgenzō Zuimonki, trans. Reihō MASUNAGA (Honolulu: University of Hawai'i Press, 1971), pp. 16, 34, 44; translation modified.

14. Steven Heine, *Did Dōgen Go to China? What He Wrote and When He Wrote It* (New York: Oxford University Press, 2006), p. 204.

15. 1242 CE.

16. 1243 CE.

17. 1243 CE.

18. 1244 CE.

19. Dōgen, *Dōgen's Extensive Record: A Translation of the* Eihei Kōroku, trans. Taigen Dan Leighton and Shohaku OKUMURA, ed. with introduction Taigen Dan Leighton (Somerville, MA: Wisdom Publications, 2004).

20. A handy collection of many of these texts in English translation can be found in *Zen Master Dogen, Beyond Thinking: A Guide to Zen Meditation*, ed. Kazuaki TANAHASHI (Boston and London: Shambhala, 2004).

21. *nembutsu.*

22. "Bendōwa," SBGZ 1:15; *The Heart of Dōgen's Shōbōgenzō*, p. 11; translation modified.

23. *Hōkyōki (Record from the Baoqing Era or Hōkyōki Period)*, in Takashi James Kodera, *Dogen's Formative Years in China: An Historical and Annotated Translation of the Hōkyō-ki* (Boulder: Prajna Press, 1980), p. 124, original on p. 236. Dōgen repeats Rujing's instructions to "just sit" without engaging in other Buddhist practices in "Zanmai-ō-zanmai," SBGZ 3:354; *Treasury of the True Dharma Eye*, p. 668.

24. See T. Griffith Foulk, "'Just Sitting'? Dōgen's Take on Zazen, Sutra Reading, and Other Conventional Buddhist Practices," in *Dōgen: Textual and Historical Studies*, ed. Steven Heine (New York: Oxford University Press, 2012), pp. 75–106.

25. Hee-Jin Kim, *Eihei Dōgen: Mystical Realist* (Somerville, MA: Wisdom Publications, 2004), p. 58.

26. Shohaku OKUMURA, "Introduction to *Bendōwa*," in *The Wholehearted Way*, p. 9.

27. *shushō ittō.*

28. *hi-shiryō.*

29. Quoted (in Japanese) from *Sansogyōgōki* [*The Record of the Deeds of the Three Ancestors*] and *Kenzeiki* [*The Record of Kenzei*] in Arifuku Kōgaku, *Dōgen no sekai* [*The World of Dōgen*] (Osaka: Ōsaka Shoseki, 1985), p. 20.

30. *dō.*

31. Okumura, "Introduction to *Bendōwa*," p. 12. Śākyamuni's "attainment of enlightenment" is thus referred to as *jōdō* or "fulfillment of the Way."

32. "Busshō," SBGZ 1:73; *The Heart of Dōgen's* Shōbōgenzō, p. 61; translation modified.

33. Kim, *Eihei Dōgen*, p. 23.

34. *Hōkyōki*, in Kodera, *Dogen's Formative Years in China*, p. 119, original on p. 228; translation modified. See also "Shinjingakudō," SBGZ 1:134–35; cf. *Treasury of the True Dharma Eye*, p. 427, where *jinen-gedō* is translated as "the view of spontaneous enlightenment."

35. *shō.*

36. "Bendōwa," SBGZ 1:11; my translation. Cf. *The Heart of Dōgen's* Shōbōgenzō, p. 9.

37. "Shinjingakudō," SBGZ 1:127; my translation. Cf. *Treasury of the True Dharma Eye*, p. 422.

38. *shikantaza.*

39. "Bendōwa," SBGZ 1:20; *The Heart of Dōgen's* Shōbōgenzō, p. 14.

40. Hakuin Ekaku, "Zazenwasan," in *Zenshū nikka seiten* [*Daily Scriptures for the Zen Sect*] (Kyoto: Baiyō Shoin, 1998), pp. 99–102.

41. *shinshōhonshōjō.*

42. "Bendōwa," SBGZ 1:34–36; *The Heart of Dōgen's* Shōbōgenzō, pp. 22–23. Here, "the oneness of body and mind" in Japanese is *shinjin-ichinyo.*

43. Akizuki Ryōmin Rōshi helpfully elucidates the deep affinities, as well as methodological differences, between Hakuin's Rinzai Zen and Dōgen's Sōtō Zen in his *Zen Bukkyō to wa nanika* [*What Is Zen Buddhism?*] (Tokyo: Hōzōkan, 1990), pp. 24, 35–39. See also Akizuki Ryōmin, *Dōgen nyūmon* [*Introduction to Dōgen*] (Tokyo: Kōdansha, 1970), pp. 164–82.

44. *mumonkan.*

45. *shokan.*

46. The term *kenshō*, "seeing [one's own] nature," is attributed to Bodhidharma; it appears in the *Platform Sutra of the Sixth Patriarch* (Huineng), and it is frequently used by Hakuin and others in the Rinzai Zen tradition. Dōgen, however, rejects the term (see "Sansuikyō [Mountains and Waters Sutra]," SBGZ 2:188; *Treasury of the True Dharma Eye*, p. 156; and "Shizen Biku [Monk at the Fourth Stage of Meditation]," SBGZ 4:355; *Treasury of the True Dharma Eye*, p. 864), presumably insofar as it can be misunderstood to imply a duality between the seer and the seen, and thus an objectification of the Buddha Nature. Curiously, he does not have the same qualms about the term "seeing Buddha" (see "Kenbutsu [Seeing Buddha]," SBGZ 3:217–39; *Treasury of the True Dharma Eye*, pp. 596–608). Dōgen even claims that the *Platform Sutra* is a spurious text (though it is not clear to which edition he is referring). "From Dōgen's standpoint," Kim writes, "the activity of seeing was itself one's own nature" (*Eihei Dōgen*, p. 57). Yet this sounds no different than the manner in which D. T. Suzuki explains the meaning of *kenshō* in the *Platform Sutra*: "the seeing with [Huineng] was self-nature itself," and so

"this seeing into self-nature is not an ordinary seeing, in which there is a duality of one who sees and that which is seen" (*The Zen Doctrine of No-Mind* [London: Rider and Company, 1958], pp. 42, 79; see also ibid., pp. 24–26, 45).

47. *shin.*

48. "Bendōwa," SBGZ 1:21; *The Heart of Dōgen's* Shōbōgenzō, p. 15.

49. *shōjō no shu.*

50. *honshō no myōshū.*

51. John Daido Loori, "Yaoshan's Non-Thinking," in *The Art of Just Sitting: Essential Writings on the Zen Practice of Shikantaza*, ed. John Daido Loori (Somerville, MA: Wisdom Publications, 2002), p. 136. See also Francis Dojun Cook's insightful essay "The Importance of Faith," in his *How to Raise an Ox: Zen Practice as Taught in Master Dogen's Shobogenzo* (Somerville, MA: Wisdom Publications, 2002). Along with D. T. Suzuki and others, Cook recognizes the profound resonances between the Zen experience of *satori* and Shin Buddhism's experience of utter reliance on the "other-power" of Amida Buddha; he even claims that "Dōgen's Zen is not really the Buddhism of self power (*jiriki*), it is the Buddhism of other power (*tariki*)" (p. 24). And yet, in conjunction with the nonduality of self and other in *jijuyū* samādhi, it would be better to say that Dōgen is calling on us to awaken to a nondual "power" that is beneath the very opposition of self- and other-power. See my "Naturalness in Zen and Shin Buddhism: Before and Beyond Self- and Other-Power," *Contemporary Buddhism* 15, no. 2 (July 2014): 433–47.

52. *Zengakudaijiten* (Tokyo: Daishūkan, 1985), p. 603.

53. *ekōhenshō.*

54. Jp. Rinzai.

55. *The Record of Linji*, trans. Ruth Fuller Sasaki, ed. Thomas Yūhō Kirchner (Honolulu: University of Hawai'i Press, 2009), p. 155. Note: "lack of faith in yourself" or "lack of self-confidence" (Ch. *zixin-buji*; Jp. *jishin-fukyū*).

56. Ch. *xinxin*; Jp. *shinjin.*

57. Ch. *dachengqixin*; Jp. *daijōkishin.*

58. See Yoshito S. Hakeda, *The Awakening of Faith* (New York: Columbia University Press, 1967), pp. 28–30.

59. *mokushō.*

60. *kanna.*

61. *shiryō-funbetsu.*

62. Nishimura Eshin, *Mumonkan* [*Wumenguan, The Gateless Barrier*] (Tokyo: Iwanami, 1994), pp. 21–23; Zenkei SHIBAYAMA, *The Gateless Barrier: Zen Comments on the Mumonkan* (Boston and London: Shambhala, 2000), pp. 19–20, translation modified. It is important to point out that, while such "initial barrier" (*shokan*) kōans are crucial, insofar as it is by breaking through them that one first attains *kenshō*, they are but the first step of the extensive kōan curriculum in Rinzai Zen, a curriculum that includes "investigation of words" (*gonsen*) and other types of kōan that focus more on cultivating an experiential understanding of the "Dharma reason" (*hōri*) of Zen. G. Victor Sōgen Hori points out that the "first half of kōan training puts major emphasis on *kyōgai* [existential state of being and behaving] and a lesser emphasis on *hōri*, whereas the second half reverses these emphases" ("Kōan and *Kenshō* in the Rinzai Zen Curriculum," in *The Kōan: Texts*

and Contexts in Zen Buddhism, eds. Steven Heine and Dale S. Wright [New York and Oxford: Oxford University Press, 2000], p. 286). See also Victor Sōgen Hori, "The Steps of Kōan Practice," in *Zen Sand* (Honolulu: University of Hawai'i Press, 2003), pp. 16–29.

63. Hakuin, *The Zen Master Hakuin: Selected Writings*, trans. Philip B. Yampolsky- (New York: Columbia University Press, 1971), p. 144.

64. *daigijō.*

65. *daifunshi.*

66. *daishinkon.*

67. *shinjin datsuraku.* There are, however, some modern scholars and Sōtō teachers who claim that the fourth Sōtō patriarch, Keizan, spuriously invented the story that Dōgen was "suddenly greatly awakened" upon hearing Rujing say "Studying Zen is the dropping off of body and mind" (*The Record of Transmitting the Light: Zen Master Keizan's Denkoroku*, trans. Francis Dojun Cook [Somerville, MA: Wisdom Publications, 2003], p. 254), and who argue that the reason why "Dōgen Zenji himself never wrote of a definitive enlightenment experience in any of his writings" is because he never had such an experience (Shohaku OKUMURA, *Realizing Genjokoan: The Key to Dogen's Shobogenzo* [Somerville, MA: Wisdom Publications, 2010], pp. 86–87). However, while it is indeed the case that, for Dōgen, "realization is a deep awareness of the fact that the existence of the self is not a personal possession of the self," it is also the case that there can be decisive moments when one comes to this realization, when one awakens this awareness. Such moments would not be properly characterized as "some sudden and special psychological satori experience" (ibid., quoting Suzuki Kakuzen Rōshi), but indeed may be described as a sudden experience of "dropping off the body and mind," or as "once, in sitting . . . immediately attaining an understanding of the Way" (*Gakudō Yōjin-shū* [*Guidelines for Studying the Way*]; see note 69 for full reference). Dōgen, after all, repeatedly affirms the traditional account of the Buddha attaining enlightenment upon seeing the morning star while sitting in zazen under the Bodhi Tree. "On this night the Tathāgata [Śākyamuni] completed true awakening. With effort and dropping away [body and mind], his eyes became clear." "Right now," Dōgen urges his disciples in another talk, "awaken the way and see the bright star" (*Dōgen's Extensive Record*, pp. 451, 165; see also ibid., pp. 318–19). Also note Dōgen's reference in *Fukanzazengi* to famous cases of "sudden enlightenment" when he speaks of "using the opportunity provided by a finger, a banner, a needle, or a mallet, and meeting realization with a whisk, a fist, a staff, or a shout."

68. Among other places, in *Hōkyōki* (*Record from the Baoqing Era*), "Zazengi [Instructions for Zazen]," and *Gakudō Yōjin-shū* (*Guidelines for Studying the Way*).

69. Dōgen, "*Gakudō Yōjin-shū* (*Guidelines for Studying the Way*)," trans. Ed Brown and Kazuaki TANAHASHI, in *Moon in a Dewdrop: Writings of Zen Master Dōgen*, ed. Kazuaki TANAHASHI (San Francisco: North Point Press, 1985), p. 42; translation slightly modified.

70. *busshōkai.*

71. Kajitani Sōnin, Yanagida Seizan, and Tsujimura Kōichi, eds., *Shinjinmei, Shōdōka, Jūgyūzu, Zazengi* (Tokyo: Chikuma, 1974), pp. 3–6.

72. See Case 33 of the *Wumenguan* (Jp. *Mumonkan*); *The Gateless Barrier*, p. 166.
73. *shiryō*.
74. *shikaku*.
75. *goshaku*.
76. "Genjōkōan," SBGZ 1:55; "The Presencing of Truth: Dōgen's *Genjōkōan*," trans. Bret W. Davis, in *Buddhist Philosophy: Essential Readings*, eds. Jay L. Garfield and William Edelglass (Oxford: Oxford University Press, 2009), p. 257.
77. *butsu-kōjō*.
78. *Moon in a Dewdrop*, p. 33.
79. *Dōgen's Extensive Record*, p. 165.
80. See Case 7 of the *Wumenguan* (Jp. *Mumonkan*); *The Gateless Barrier*, p. 67.
81. *tenzo*. See "Instructions for the Tenzo [Tenzokyōkun]," in *Dōgen's Pure Standards for the Zen Community: A Translation of* Eihei Shingi, trans. Taigen Daniel Leighten and Shohaku OKUMURA (Albany: SUNY Press, 1996), pp. 40–42.
82. *shushō-ittō* or *shushō-ichinyo*.
83. "Bendōwa," SBGZ 1:28–29; *The Heart of Dōgen's* Shōbōgenzō, pp. 19–20; translation modified.
84. *bonnō*, the Japanese word for *kleśa*.
85. *fuzenna no shushō*.
86. The phrases "the Dharma gate of peace and bliss" and "undefiled practice-enlightenment" are used in *Fukanzazengi* as well as in "Zazengi," SBGZ 1:225; cf. *Treasury of the True Dharma Eye*, p. 580, which, however, translates *fuzenna* loosely as "undivided" rather than as "undefiled." Dōgen adopts the phrase "undefiled practice-enlightenment" from a dialogue between Huineng and Huairang. See *Dōgen's Extensive Record*, pp. 328–29, 435–36, 575–76; and "Jishōzammai [Self-Enlightening Samādhi]," SBGZ 3:385; cf. *Treasury of the True Dharma Eye*, p. 695.
87. *taiho*.
88. *hō-i*.
89. "Genjōkōan," SBGZ 1:60; "The Presencing of Truth," p. 259.
90. Ch. *wuwei*; Jp. *mu-i*.
91. *The Record of Linji*, p. 143. According to Nishitani Keiji, "there is not the slightest difference between the fundamental spirit of this saying of Linji and that of Dōgen's 'oneness of practice and enlightenment.'" Nishitani Keiji, *Shōbōgenzō kōwa* [*Lectures on Shōbōgenzō*], vol. 1 (Tokyo: Chikuma Shobō, 1987), pp. 69–70.
92. *jinen-gedō*.
93. "Zazenshin," SBGZ 1:233; my translation. Cf. *Treasury of the True Dharma Eye*, p. 306.
94. "Kokyō," SBGZ 2:43; my translation. Cf. *Treasury of the True Dharma Eye*, pp. 220–21.
95. "Bendōwa," SBGZ 1:29; *The Heart of Dōgen's* Shōbōgenzō, p. 20; translation modified. The ontology (or kenology) implied in Dōgen's thought of the nonduality of practice and enlightenment should not be misunderstood either in terms of a metaphysical two-world theory or in terms of an anti-metaphysical doctrine of sheer immanence, be the latter a reductive positivism or a naturalistic pantheism. Abe endeavors to articulate this subtle yet crucial issue as follows: "Dōgen's view of the oneness of practice and attainment . . . indicates a reversible identity, in which an absolute irreversibility between attainment and practice, the Buddha

Nature and becoming a Buddha, can be reversed by virtue of the nonsubstantiality of attainment and the emptiness of the Buddha Nature. This point must not be overlooked. What is involved here is a reversible identity that is always inseparably connected with the aspect of irreversibility. . . . This means that Dōgen, and all of us, are always standing at the intersection of the temporal-spatial horizontal dimension and the transtemporal vertical dimension insofar as we awaken to the oneness of practice and attainment" (Masao ABE, *A Study of Dōgen: His Philosophy and Religion*, ed. Steven Heine (Albany: SUNY Press, 1992), p. 30.

96. *igi soku buppō, sahō kore shūshi*. See Ikkō Narasaki Rōshi's foreword to *Dōgen's Pure Standards for the Zen Community*, p. x.

97. Case 1 of *Biyanlu* (Jp. *Hekiganroku*); *The Blue Cliff Record*, trans. Thomas Cleary and J. C. Cleary (Boston and London: Shambhala, 1992), p. 1; translation modified.

98. Case 19 of *Wumenguan* (Jp. *Mumonkan*); *The Gateless Barrier*, p. 140; translation modified.

99. *chōshin*.

100. *chōsoku*.

101. *chōshin*.

102. Elsewhere Dōgen does relate the following: "My late teacher Tiantong [Rujing] said, 'Breath enters and reaches the *tanden*, and yet there is no place from which it comes. Therefore it is neither long nor short. Breath emerges from the *tanden*, and yet there is nowhere it goes. Therefore it is neither short nor long'" (*Dōgen's Extensive Record*, p. 349).

103. *susokukan*.

104. *zuisokukan*.

105. *shikantaza*.

106. *kanna*.

107. See Kim, *Eihei Dōgen*, esp. chapter 3; Hee-Jin Kim, *Dōgen on Meditation and Thinking: A Reflection on His View of Zen* (Albany: SUNY Press, 2007); and Steven Heine, *Dōgen and the Kōan Tradition* (Albany: SUNY Press, 1994).

108. *kattō*.

109. See especially the "Kattō [Entangling Vines]" and "Dōtoku [Expressive Attainment of the Way]" fascicles of *Shōbōgenzō*.

110. *watō*.

111. *Dōgen's Extensive Record*, pp. 327–28, 466–67.

112. "Zazenshin," SBGZ 1:226; translation adopted, with some slight modifications, from Carl Beilefeldt, *Dōgen's Manuals of Zen Meditation* (Berkeley: University of California Press, 1988), pp. 188–89.

113. Ch. *siliang*.

114. *susokukan*.

115. *zenjō*.

116. Shunryu SUZUKI, *Zen Mind, Beginners Mind* (New York: Weatherhill, 1970), p. 128; see also ibid., pp. 34–36; Loori, "Yaoshan's Non-Thinking," p. 138; Kosho Uchiyama, "The *Tenzo Kyokun* and *Shikantaza*," in Loori, *The Art of Just Sitting*, pp. 60–61; and Hakuyu Taizan MAEZUMI, "Commentary on *Fukanzazengi*," in ibid., pp. 82, 85.

117. Loori, "Yaoshan's Non-Thinking," p. 141.

118. *fushiryō*.

119. Shunryu SUZUKI instructs us: "do not try to stop your thinking. Let it stop by itself." Yet he also goes on to say that this "letting" requires a peculiar kind of "effort," an effort that ceases to be "my effort" and simply becomes a "pure effort" (*Zen Mind, Beginners Mind*, p. 34). This can be understood as describing the transition, or backward step, from the still dualistic effort of "thinking of not-thinking" to the "pure effort" of "nonthinking." The pure effort of nonthinking can then freely take this or that form of thinking or not-thinking, as the occasion demands.

120. *shōfunbetsu.*

121. Kim, *Dōgen on Meditation and Thinking*, p. 84.

122. *shōshiryō; shōshiyui.*

123. "Sanjūshichihon Bodaibunpō," SBGZ 3:294.

124. *The Platform Sutra of the Sixth Patriarch*, trans. Philip B. Yampolsky (New York: Columbia University Press, 1967), p. 135.

125. Case 19 of the *Wumenguan* (Jp. *Mumonkan*); *The Gateless Barrier*, p. 140.

126. "Genjōkōan," SBGZ 1:54; "The Presencing of Truth," p. 256.

127. Case 1 of *Biyanlu* (Jp. *Hekiganroku*); *The Blue Cliff Record*, p. 1.
Note: "I don't know" or "not knowing" (Ch. *bushi*; Jp. *fushiki*).

128. In Chinese and Japanese, "heart" and "mind" are written with the same character (Ch. *xin*; Jp. *shin* or *kokoro*). In other words, these languages do not dichotomize the seat of the intellect and the seat of the emotions, suggesting that a truly open mind entails an open heart, and vice versa.

129. Taigen Dan Leighton writes: "The Zen monastic community that Dōgen depicts and encourages in the *Eihei Shingi* cannot be understood except as the expression of a harmonious lifestyle based on and emerging from the experience of zazen. Throughout his career, Dōgen advocated this nondualistic, objectless meditation practice, known as 'just sitting,' which developed from the 'serene illumination' meditation elaborated by Hongzhi Zhengjue in China in the previous century" (Introduction to *Dōgen's Pure Standards for the Zen Community*, 16). While discursive thinking and the study of texts are not engaged in *during* the practice of "just sitting" in the Monk's Hall (*sōdō*), Dōgen's conception of the monastery also includes an adjacent Study Hall (*shuryō*), wherein each monk is assigned a desk. In "Shuryō Shingi [Regulations for the Study Hall]," Dōgen writes: "In the study hall, read the Mahāyāna sutras and also the sayings of our ancestors, and naturally accord with the instructions of our tradition to illuminate the mind with the ancient teachings" (ibid., p. 109). Dōgen's conception of Zen practice thus involves *commuting* between zazen and the study of texts (along with other activities). Such a practice of commuting between zazen on the one hand and textual study/discursive thinking on the other has been taken up in modern times by philosopher-practitioners such as Nishitani Keiji, who described his life as a back and forth movement of "sitting [in meditation], then thinking; thinking, then sitting" (see Horio Tsutomu, "Nishitani's Philosophy: The Later Period," *Zen Buddhism Today* 14 [1997]: 22).

130. *genjō kōan.*

131. For an in-depth study of Dōgen's use of these metaphors, see Arifuku Kōgaku, *"Shōbōgenzō" ni shitashimu: Dōgen no shizen shisō* [*Getting to Know* Shōbōgenzō: *Dōgen's Thought of Nature*] (Tokyo: Gakuseisha, 1991), chapters 4, 8, and 9.

132. On the various interrelated senses of "emptiness" in Zen, see Bret W. Davis, "Forms of Emptiness in Zen," in *A Companion to Buddhist Philosophy*, ed. Steven Emmanuel (Hoboken, NJ: Wiley-Blackwell, 2013), pp. 190–213.

133. Translated by Paul Swanson in "Original Enlightenment Debates," in *Japanese Philosophy: A Sourcebook*, eds. James W. Heisig, Thomas P. Kasulis, and John C. Maraldo (Honolulu: University of Hawai'i Press, 2011), p. 93. For how this idea gets taken up by other Zen figures, see section two of my "Forms of Emptiness in Zen."

134. "Kokū," SBGZ 3:413; cf. *The Treasury of the True Dharma Eye*, pp. 719–20.

135. "Kokyō," SBGZ 2:11; *The Treasury of the True Dharma Eye*, p. 204; translation modified.

136. Harada Sogaku, *Fukanzazengi kōwa* [*Lectures on Fukanzazengi*] (Tokyo: Daizō shuppan, 1982), pp. 91–92.

137. "Butsukōjōji [Going Beyond Buddha]," SBGZ 2:140; *Moon in a Dewdrop*, p. 208.

138. *zenki*.

139. *mufunbetsu no funbetsu*.

140. "Busshō," SBGZ 1:80; *The Heart of Dōgen's* Shōbōgenzō, p. 67; translation modified.

141. "Kai-in Zammai," SBGZ 1:253; my translation; *The Treasury of the True Dharma Eye*, p. 380.

142. See "Kokyō," SBGZ 2:21–30; *The Treasury of the True Dharma Eye*, pp. 209–14.

143. *uji*.

144. Dōgen is a nondualist, rather than either an idealist or a materialist. Thus, on the one hand, he says that "the mind-nature . . . embraces the entire universe. . . . All dharmas . . . are alike in being this one Mind"; "Bendōwa," SBGZ 1:35; *The Heart of Dōgen's* Shōbōgenzō, pp. 22–23; see also "Sangai-yuishin [The Three Worlds Are Only Mind]," SBGZ 2:406–16; *The Treasury of the True Dharma Eye*, pp. 487–92. On the other hand, he affirms that "the entire earth [*jindaichi*] is the true human body [*shinjitsu-nintai*]" ("Yuibutsu-yobutsu [Only Buddha and Buddha]," SBGZ 4:455; *The Treasury of the True Dharma Eye*, p. 878). The "Shinjin Gakudō [Study of the Way with the Body and Mind]" fascicle of *Shōbōgenzō* begins by saying: "The Study of the Buddha Way can be provisionally approached in two manners: what is called study with the mind and what is called study with the body." Yet these two paths converge insofar as, on the one hand, one discovers that "mountains and rivers, the great earth, the sun, moon and stars are the mind . . . walls, tiles, and pebbles are the mind"; and, on the other hand, one realizes that "the whole world in all ten directions is this true human body" (SBGZ 1:127–34; my translation; cf. *The Treasury of the True Dharma Eye*, pp. 423–26).

145. See Bret W. Davis, "The Philosophy of Zen Master Dōgen: Egoless Perspectivism," in *The Oxford Handbook of World Philosophy*, eds. Jay L. Garfield and William Edelglass (New York: Oxford University Press, 2011), pp. 348–60.

Contributors

STEVE BEIN is assistant professor of philosophy at the University of Dayton. He received MA and PhD degrees in philosophy from the University of Hawai'i and did graduate work at two Japanese universities, Nanzan University and Ōbirin University. He is the author of *Compassion and Moral Guidance* (Hawai'i 2012), a comparative study of compassion in ethics East and West, and the first English translator of the landmark study on Dōgen, *Purifying Zen: Watsuji Tetsurō's Shamon Dōgen* (Hawai'i 2011).

KANPŪ BRET W. DAVIS is professor of philosophy at Loyola University Maryland. His publications include several books and dozens of articles, written in English and in Japanese, on such topics as Heidegger, the Kyoto school, and Zen. He received a PhD in philosophy from Vanderbilt University and spent thirteen years studying and teaching in Japan, during which time he studied Buddhist thought at Otani University, completed the doctoral program (with thesis in progress) in Japanese philosophy at Kyoto University, and undertook formal practice of Rinzai Zen as a member of *Chishōkai*, a group of lay practitioners at Shōkokuji (one of the main Zen training monasteries in Kyoto), whose members have included Kyoto school philosophers Nishitani Keiji and Ueda Shizuteru. Since 2005 he has served as leader of the Heart of Zen Meditation Group at Loyola University Maryland, and he is a founding member of CoZen. In 2010 he received formal recognition as a teacher (*sensei*) and director of a Zen center (*dōchō*) from Kobayashi Gentoku Rōshi, abbot of Shōkokuji.

STEVEN DECAROLI is associate professor of philosophy at Goucher College. He holds both an MA and PhD in philosophy from Binghamton

University, and an MA in comparative literature from the University of Wisconsin. He has published numerous articles and book chapters on political philosophy and philosophical aesthetics, and he has presented extensively at national and international conferences. He is the coeditor of *Giorgio Agamben: Sovereignty and Life* (Stanford 2007).

TENSHIN CHARLES FLETCHER RŌSHI was born in Manchester, England, and came to the United States in 1979 to study at the Zen Center of Los Angeles with founder Taizan Maezumi Rōshi, from whom he received dharma transmission in the White Plum lineage in 1994. He received *inka* from Genpo Merzel Rōshi in 2006. He acted as administrator for many years at ZCLA and is now the primary teacher and abbot at Yokoji Zen Mountain Center. He is one of a few North American teachers officially certified as a *Kokusaifukyōshi* (Official Foreign Representative), a title appointed in 2009 by the Sōtō Zen headquarters in Japan. Tenshin Rōshi also has over twenty years of voice dialogue experience, a psychological technique described by its founders as an "empowering psycho-spiritual approach to relationship, personal growth, and communication." He is coauthor with David Keizan Scott Sensei of *The Way of Zen* (St. Martin's 2001).

STEVEN HEINE is professor of religious studies and history and director of Asian studies at Florida International University. A recipient of the Order of the Rising Sun Award in 2007, Heine has for many years conducted research at Komazawa University in Tokyo, and he has published more than two dozen books on Zen Buddhism and Japanese religions in the medieval and modern periods. These publications include several volumes dealing with the life and teachings of Dōgen, such as *Dōgen and the Kōan Tradition* (SUNY 1993), *The Zen Poetry of Dōgen* (Dharma Communications 2004), *Did Dōgen Go to China?* (Oxford 2006), *Dōgen: Textual and Historical Studies* (Oxford 2012), and *Dōgen and Sōtō Zen: New Perspectives* (Oxford 2015). In addition, he wrote an in-depth study of *Shushōgi* in an article that was contained in his coedited volume with Charles S. Prebish, *Buddhism and the Modern World* (Oxford 2003). Heine has also published numerous books on Zen kōans, including works dealing extensively with the "fox kōan" and "mu kōan."

KŌSHŌ ITAGAKI is a Sōtō Zen priest. He is the abbot of Eishōji, a Sōtō Zen training facility located in the southern part of the city of Seattle and also operating director of the Northwest Zen Community. After training at Saijōji Sōtō Zen monastery under the Rev. Suigan Yogo (located in Minami Ashigara, in the Kanagawa Prefecture) and Hōʻonji Sōtō Zen monastery under the Rev. Amafuji Tenkō (located in Morioka, in the Iwate Prefecture), he received Dharma transmission from the Rev. Saikawa Dōshō. After working for seven years as the resident priest at Zenshūji, the Sōtō Zen temple on the Hawaiʻian island of Kauai, he moved to Seattle in 2006 and founded the various facilities and programs that comprise the Northwest Zen Community. Eishōji received its name from the Rev. Dōnin MINIMIZAWA, vice-abbot of Daihonzan Eiheiji, in 2010 and moved into its present location in 2012. For more information, see: http://nwzencommunity.org/about.html.

LEAH KALMANSON is associate professor of philosophy and religion at Drake University. She received a PhD in philosophy from the University of Hawaiʻi at Mānoa in 2010. Her articles in Asian and comparative philosophy appear in the journals *Continental Philosophy Review*, *Hypatia*, *Shofar*, and *Comparative and Continental Philosophy*. She is the coeditor of collections *Buddhist Responses to Globalization* (Lexington 2014), *Levinas and Asian Thought* (Duquesne 2013), and *Confucianism in Context* (SUNY 2010). She serves as an assistant editor at the *Journal of Japanese Philosophy* and as a member of the American Philosophical Association's Committee on Asian and Asian-American Philosophers and Philosophies. Her current research focuses on connections between postcolonial theory and comparative philosophy.

DREW LEDER, MD, PhD, is professor of philosophy at Loyola University Maryland where he teaches both Western and Eastern philosophy. Trained in phenomenology, he is the author of many articles and books on embodiment and the mind-body relationship, the philosophy of medicine, and cross-cultural spirituality. These works have spanned the more scholarly, such as *The Absent Body* (Chicago 1990) and *The Distressed Body* (Chicago 2016), to trade books such as *Spiritual Passages* (Penguin Putnam 1997) and *Sparks of the Divine* (Sorin 2004). His book *The Soul Knows No Bars* (Rowman & Littlefield 2000) recounts work done over the years teaching philosophy to inmates, another passion of his.

TAIGEN DAN LEIGHTON, a Dharma heir and priest in the Suzuki Rōshi lineage, leads the Ancient Dragon Zen Gate in Chicago. He is author of several books including *Faces of Compassion: Classic Bodhisattva Archetypes and Their Modern Expression* (Wisdom 2012), *Zen Questions: Zazen, Dōgen, and the Spirit of Creative Inquiry* (Wisdom 2011), and *Visions of Awakening Space and Time: Dōgen and the Lotus Sutra* (Oxford 2007), and he has cotranslated a number of Zen texts, including *Dōgen's Extensive Record* (Wisdom 2004), *Dōgen's Pure Standards for the Zen Community* (SUNY 1995), and *Cultivating the Empty Field* (Tuttle 2000). Leighton teaches online at the Berkeley Graduate Theological Union, where he also received a PhD.

TETSU'UN DAVID ROBERT LOY is a writer and Zen teacher in the Sanbō Kyōdan tradition of Japanese Zen Buddhism. His many essays and books have been translated into numerous languages. Many of his writings, as well as audio and video talks and interviews, are available on the web (http://www.davidloy.org/articles.html). He lectures nationally and internationally on various topics, focusing primarily on the encounter between Buddhism and modernity: what each can learn from the other. He is especially concerned about social and ecological issues. His most recent books are *The World Is Made of Stories* (Wisdom 2010) and *A New Buddhist Path: Enlightenment, Evolution, and Ethics in the Modern World* (Wisdom 2015). He also leads meditation retreats (www.davidloy.org).

JOHN C. MARALDO received a DPhil in German philosophy at the University of Munich in 1970, and while there began reading about Zen. He went to Tokyo in the early 1970s, taught at Sophia University, worked for the historian of Zen Heinrich Dumoulin, SJ, and began serious zazen with some itinerant monks. He then taught at Naropa, went back to Japan, and then later studied under Maezumi Taizan Rōshi at the Los Angeles Zen Center. He taught philosophy at the University of North Florida from 1980–2008, except for a few more years in Japan and Europe, and now is Distinguished Professor of Philosophy Emeritus at the University of North Florida. He has been a sporadic student of Sasaki Jōshu Rōshi and he taught at the 1989 and 2011 Summer Seminars in New Mexico and attended many others. He publishes on Heidegger as well as the Kyoto school and its intersections with phenomenology and contemporary philosophy. His most recent work is *Japanese Philosophy: A Sourcebook*, coedited with James W. Heisig and Thomas P. Kasulis.

GLEN A. MAZIS is professor of philosophy and humanities at Penn State Harrisburg, where he has been coordinator of their interdisciplinary master's program and honors program. He is the author of *Emotion and Embodiment: Fragile Ontology* (Peter Lang 1993), *The Trickster, Magician and Grieving Man: Returning Men to Earth* (Inner Traditions 1994), *Earthbodies: Rediscovering Our Planetary Senses* (SUNY 2002), *Humans, Animals and Machines: Blurring Boundaries* (SUNY 2008), and *Merleau-Ponty and the Face of the World: Silence, Ethics, Imagination, and Poetic Ontology* (SUNY 2016). He has published more than two dozen essays on aspects of Merleau-Ponty's philosophy in journals and collections, as well as numerous essays on emotion, imagination, art, film, dreams, embodiment, animality, archetypal psychology, gender issues, ethics, ecology, technology, etc. He is also a poet who gives readings and performances, and has published about seventy-five poems in leading literary reviews and a recent collection, *The River Bends in Time* (Anaphora Literary Press 2012). He discovered zazen and the Buddha Way as a college student and his teacher was Philip Kapleau.

JIEN ERIN MCCARTHY is professor of philosophy and Asian studies at St. Lawrence University. In her work she compares Japanese philosophy, ethics, and feminist and continental philosophy. She is the author of *Ethics Embodied: Rethinking Selfhood through Continental, Japanese and*

Feminist Philosophies (Lexington 2010), as well as several comparative philosophy articles that have appeared in both French and English in journals and anthologies. She has served as chair of the board of directors of ASIANetwork and is currently coeditor of the *ASIANetwork Exchange: A Journal for Asian Studies in the Liberal Arts*. She is a founding member of CoZen, a group dedicated to the cooperative integration of contemplative practice and academic study. Currently, she is looking at the ways in which Contemplative Education can be enriched by incorporating feminist philosophies, as well as pursuing her work on Dōgen and feminist philosophy.

GRAHAM PARKES, born and raised in Glasgow, taught Asian and comparative philosophy for thirty years at the University of Hawai'i at Manoa before taking up his present position as professor of philosophy at University College Cork, in Ireland, where he is also the founding director of the Irish Institute for Japanese Studies. He is the author of *Composing the Soul: Reaches of Nietzsche's Psychology* (Chicago 1994) and the editor of *Heidegger and Asian Thought* (Hawai'i 1987) and *Nietzsche and Asian Thought* (Chicago 1991). He has also translated (with commentaries) Detlet Lauf's *Secret Doctrines of the Tibetan Books of the Dead* (Shambhala 1974), Nishitani Keiji's *The Self-Overcoming of Nihilism* (SUNY 1990), Reinhard May's *Heidegger's Hidden Sources: East-Asian Influences on His Work* (Routledge 1996), François Berthier's *Reading Zen in the Rocks: The Japanese Dry Landscape Garden* (Chicago 2000), and Friedrich Nietzsche's *Thus Spoke Zarathustra* (Oxford 2005). He is currently writing a book with the working title *Climate Change and China*.

DAINEN DAVID PUTNEY is associate professor emeritus of philosophy at Old Dominion University. He received a BA in Japanese language and literature at the University of Washington and an MA and PhD in philosophy at the University of Hawai'i. He then spent roughly ten years in Japan at different periods, where he also practiced Zen, especially Dōgen's *shikantaza*. His publications include the essays "Shen-hsiu, the *Platform Sutra*, and Dōgen: Issues of Mind and Buddha Nature" (1990),

"Identity and the Unity of Experience: A Critique of Nishida's Theory of Self" (1991), "Some Problems of Interpretation: The Early and Late Writings of Dōgen" (1996), and "Dōgen: Enlightenment and Entanglement" (1997).

SHŪDŌ BRIAN SCHROEDER is a priest in the Sōtō Zen lineage of Yashiki Chijō, abbot of Yōkōji (established in 1317 by Keizan Jōkin Zenji), and professor of philosophy and director of religious studies at the Rochester Institute of Technology (RIT). He has published numerous books and articles on European philosophy, Buddhist philosophy, the history of philosophy, environmental philosophy, and philosophical theology. He founded and guides the Idunno Zen Community at RIT, is a founding member of CoZen, and is an active member of the Rochester Zen Center. He has served as codirector of the Society for Phenomenology and Existential Philosophy, codirector of the International Association for Enviromental Philosophy, director of the Collegium Phaenomenologicum, executive officer of the Comparative and Continental Philosophy Circle, and executive committee member of the Nietzsche Society. He holds an MA and a PhD in philosophy from Stony Brook University and an MDiv from the Princeton Theological Seminary.

MICHAEL SCHWARTZ is professor of the history and philosophy of art at Augusta University. He has published and lectured widely in the United States, Europe, and Asia in fields such as art history, comparative and continental philosophy, integral theory and meta-theorization, art criticism, quantum social theory, and contemplative studies. He is cofounder of the international Comparative and Continental Philosophy Circle as well as founding associate editor of that organization's book series and its peer-reviewed journal. His two most recent books are the coedited and coauthored *On the True Sense of Art: A Critical Companion to the Transfigurements of John Sallis* (Northwestern 2016) and *Dancing with Sophia: Integral Philosophy on the Verge* (SUNY 2017). He is a long-time spiritual practitioner, his commitments centered in the Vajrayāna and Dzogchen ways of Tibetan Buddhism.

Mark Unno is associate professor of Japanese Buddhism and the head of the Department of Religious Studies at the University of Oregon. His research is in Classical Japanese Buddhism, in particular key practices in Shin Buddhism, Shingon, and Zen. He also works in the areas of comparative religious thought, Buddhism and psychotherapy, and interreligious dialogue. He is the author of *Shingon Refractions: Myōe and the Mantra of Light* (Wisdom 2004) and the editor of *Buddhism and Psychotherapy Across Cultures* (Wisdom 2006), as well as a wide range of articles and translations.

Tetsuzen Jason M. Wirth is professor of philosophy at Seattle University, a Sōtō Zen priest, a founding member of CoZen, and founder and codirector of the Seattle University EcoSangha. His recent books include *Commiserating with Devastated Things: Milan Kundera and the Entitlements of Thinking* (Fordham 2015), *Schelling's Practice of the Wild* (SUNY 2015), *The Conspiracy of Life: Meditations on Schelling and His Time* (SUNY 2003), a translation of the third draft of *The Ages of the World* (SUNY 2000), the edited volume *Schelling Now* (Indiana 2004), and the coedited volume (with Bret W. Davis and Brian Schroeder) *Japanese and Continental Philosophy: Conversations with the Kyoto School* (Indiana 2011). He is the associate editor and book review editor of the journal *Comparative and Continental Philosophy*. He is currently at work on a book titled *Zen and Zarathustra*.

Index

Page numbers in bold type indicate text from *Shushōgi* or *Fukanzazengi*. Page numbers followed by "n" or "nn" plus one or more numbers as in "226n20" and "229nn10,11" indicate numbered endnotes. Page numbers followed by "q" or "+q" indicate quotations or discussions plus quotations.

What to Read Next from Wisdom Publications

DŌGEN'S EXTENSIVE RECORD
A Translation of the Eihei Kōroku
Translated by Taigen Dan Leighton and Shohaku Okumura
Edited and Introduced by Taigen Dan Leighton
Foreword by Tenshin Reb Anderson

"Taigen and Shohaku are national treasures."
—Norman Fischer, author of *Sailing Home*

EIHEI DŌGEN
Mystical Realist
Hee-Jin Kim
Foreword by Taigen Dan Leighton

"A beacon of scholarship."
—John Daido Loori, editor of *The Art of Just Sitting*

REALIZING GENJŌKŌAN
The Key to Dōgen's Shōbōgenzō
Shohaku Okumura
Foreword by Taigen Dan Leighton

"A stunning commentary. Like all masterful commentaries,
this one finds in the few short lines of the text the entire span
of the Buddhist teachings."
—*Buddhadharma: The Buddhist Review*

How to Raise an Ox
Zen Practice as Taught in Zen Master Dōgen's Shōbōgenzō
Eihei Dōgen
Francis Dojun Cook
Foreword by Taizan Maezumi Roshi

"Simply the best introduction to Dōgen's Zen."
—Barry Magid, author of *Ordinary Mind*

Zen
The Authentic Gate
Kōun Yamada
Foreword by David R. Loy

"Yamada's introduction to Zen is a welcome and dense
primer that has much to offer novices as well as experienced
practitioners."
—*Publishers Weekly*

Living by Vow
A Practical Introduction to Eight Essential Zen Chants and Texts
Shohaku Okumura

"An essential resource for students and teachers alike."
—Dosho Port, author of *Keep Me in Your Heart a While*

A New Buddhist Path
Enlightenment, Evolution, and Ethics in the Modern World
David R. Loy

"This gripping, important, and ultimately heartening book by David
Loy is a wake-up call for Buddhists and everyone else on how to
respond to the current multiple crises."
—Lila Kate Wheeler, author of *When Mountains Walked*

About Wisdom Publications

Wisdom Publications is the leading publisher of classic and contemporary Buddhist books and practical works on mindfulness. To learn more about us or to explore our other books, please visit our website at wisdompubs.org or contact us at the address below.

Wisdom Publications
199 Elm Street
Somerville, MA 02144 USA

We are a 501(c)(3) organization, and donations in support of our mission are tax deductible.

Wisdom Publications is affiliated with the Foundation for the Preservation of the Mahayana Tradition (FPMT).